THE WORRY CLOCK

D1560373

THE WORRY CLOCK

CLOCK

A PARENT'S GUIDE TO WORRYING SMARTER ABOUT
THE <u>REAL</u> DANGERS TO YOUR CHILD

By Natalia E. Pane, M.A., M.B.A.

Published by Natalia Pane through CreateSpace
Copyright © 2013 by Natalia E. Pane
All rights reserved,
including the right of reproduction
in whole or in part in any form.
ISBN-13: 978-1492774785
ISBN-10: 1492774782

Pane, Natalia.
The Worry Clock: A Parent's Guide to Worrying Smarter about
the <u>Real</u> Dangers to Your Child / Natalia Pane.
p. cm.
1. Parenting. 2. Children's health. 3. Pregnancy and childbirth.

To Douglas, Abhaya, and Anastasia for their patience, support, love and encouragement! You are my endless joy.

To the mothers, fathers, and loved ones of those whose stories, lessons, and pain fill this book. May we make together some small bit of good.

To the unsung heroes of the federal statistical agencies, and the politicians who have the chutzpah to support them.

Finally, to the neoempiricists, the datumists, who question everything and use science and its data to answer questions and restore our sanity.

CONTENTS

When I had my first child, I had already spent more than ten years helping federal agencies, foundations, and programs use data to help them do what they do even better. It never occurred to me that I might apply this approach to parenting. And then I got pregnant, we moved into a new house, and there I was walking around the house cutting the cords for the blinds when my husband asked skeptically, "How many kids really die from that anyway?" That was all I needed. It was an empirical question, and I knew where to get the answer.

It probably is not a stretch to see how it expanded from there. Once I learned that strangulation was a small number (and percentage) of deaths, I wanted then to know, "what *do* children die from?" At that time, I was interested in infants, but then that baby started to walk. My journey began.

This book was written on nights and weekends over two years, fit in when I wasn't working my fulltime job or enjoying time with my family. In other words, it is a data geek's side project meant for other data geeks (even if you are not a data geek, you have to be geeky enough to want to be a research-based parent!).

I approached this as a mom, not as a statistician. I make assumptions that may make statisticians queasy. For example, a major assumption is that how kids died from 1999-2007 is a reasonable reflection of how kids are dying now. Clearly, it cannot be exactly the same (things change, thank goodness!), but as a parent, I'd rather have a rough idea than no idea at all.

The recommendations for action in this book are primarily based on our government's reading of the research, which is generally really good. However, if I had another two years, I might go through those recommendations more closely and really unpack which ones have good data supporting them and which do not.

I wrote this book not because I thought I had all the answers but because I thought I had the beginnings of answers—ones that could *start* a conversation. If you have better ideas, better questions, better recommendations, speak up; join me in the conversation.

This book never would have been more than a few data tables on scratch paper if it were not for the support of some incredible people. Thank you to my husband whose amazing fathering made it possible for me to *lean in* and who tirelessly supported me, spent long hours debating and discussing big and little points, and quietly showed day after day his patience and love. Drs. Kyle Potter and Andrea Berger were enormously helpful for their reviews and excellent suggestions. Thank you to Drs. Becky Smerdon, Stephanie Cronen, Laura Desimone, and Michelle Divito for their ongoing encouragement, advice, and overall support. Thank you to Dean Michael Feuer for his guidance and endless ability to inspire. Thank you also to Deborah Ingram and TJ Matthews at the Centers for Disease Control for their pointers. And to my former colleagues including Dahlia Shaewitz, Larry Condelli, Mark Schneider, and so many other wonderful people at AIR, thank you for encouraging me to take the leap. Coach Ilona Birenbaum was instrumental in getting me to stop, reflect, and begin writing. Finally, thank you to Carol Emig, President; Frank Walter, VP for Communications; August Aldebot-Green, Communications Manager and cover designer for this book; and all of the incredible researchers and data gurus working within Child Trends whose daily endeavors entail using research and data to improve the lives of children.

Cut the cord on the baby recently? Before that, you may have also cut the cord on all the blinds in the house, covered the outlets, made the drawers and toilet lid impassable, and bought a crib mattress that had many similarities to that rock of a futon you had in college. The baby-safety checklist is long and getting longer, and it is driven by fear.

With all the scary anecdotes and attention-grabbing advice and advertisements related to caring for a baby, it's no wonder that new parents feel overwhelmed. Every product seems a must-buy to keep your baby safe, leaving many parents to default to purchasing all of it so as to avoid the dreaded "what if." For every other worrisome possibility (heart disease, car accidents), we tend to think things won't happen to us, but with babies, bring on the fear.

No one is immune; in fact, there appears to be an inverse relationship with education. The more you know, it seems, the more susceptible you are to losing rationality. I have seen plenty of previously logical individuals buy a few parenting books and turn into irrational, neurotic parents obsessing over their untouchable—at least in the first three months— infant. New parents seem to spin out of control and lose any and all preexisting ability to apply what previously seemed entirely rational rules to their decision making. I know—I was one of them.

This book is about the facts behind the fear. What are the most likely dangers? What are the things that children *really* die from? And how and why? How do those dangers change as your child grows? This book and the statistics within offer some fuel for regaining rationality—what to worry about, why, and how to reduce the danger—while providing the opportunity to regain sanity by not sweating the unlikely, truly bizarre, or, dare I say it, unpreventable.

This book addresses our ultimate fear: the death of a child. Injury matters, of course, but injuries, most of which your child can recover from, are not the focus of this book.

Warning! This book is about data, data, and more data. If data do not interest you, this book is not for you. You do not need to have taken a class in statistics or even have to like math, but you do need to want to know about the numbers behind the hype.

Point #1: The death of a child is rare.

Take a look at the pie (circle) graph that shows the percentage of children from birth to age nineteen who die in the United States.[1] *Burn this image into your mind.* The percentage of children who die is so small that it is almost not visible. That tiny sliver shows that .07 percent of children died, which is about one-fifteenth of 1 percent. Another way to say it is that seven children out of every ten thousand children, who were under twenty years old at any point in the eight years, died. Chances are excellent that your baby will grow up just fine.

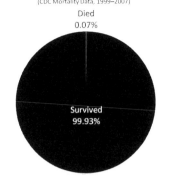

Percentage of Children Who Died Ages 0–19
(CDC Mortality Data, 1999–2007)
Died
0.07%
Survived
99.93%

For those parents whose children fit into that sliver, this statistic is meaningless. For those of us who worry that we may end up in that tiny sliver, it is small consolation. For me, even knowing the odds well, I nonetheless felt like I was destined to be one of the unlucky few. Worse yet, I felt there might be something I could do to prevent disaster from happening. I wrote this book for parents like me.

But can parents really do anything?

> **Point #2:** A significant number of deaths are preventable.

At least one-third of these childhood deaths are from what most would agree are preventable incidents, such as drowning or hyperthermia.[2] That's right, one out of every three is an accident—a preventable event.

This book *only* addresses those preventable events or accidents; I don't talk about genetic disorders, cancer, or other types of medical conditions over which most would agree we have less control.

The nature of these accidents may surprise you, especially if you thought the most likely causes of death are associated with baby safety products. Consider outlet covers. There are about four deaths per year from children sticking things into outlets,[3] a number so small that the government reports it as unreliable. This number of deaths is about the same as the number who die from falling down steps. Both of these accidents—dying from electrical currents and falling down stairs—are only *half* the number of those children being killed by a dog. Yes, that's right: **two and a half times as many children age one to four were**

killed by dogs as died by falling down steps or sticking something in an outlet.

As the title suggests, this book gives you the data to worry smarter. I am going to worry; it is a part of who I am. I have come to accept this about myself. I can, however, help myself—and my children—by focusing my worry and my actions where they might matter most.

This book is a journey for me, to help me prepare myself to be a better parent and a smarter worrier for my children. Take the data and apply as you see fit, for what makes the most sense for you and your children. I wish I could say that if you read this book you will worry less, but I suspect anxiety is more of a trait (who you are) than a state (the situation you are in). You will, however, have more information that may help you direct that worry to be a force for good, as it is intended to be.

> **Point #3:** There are no guarantees. This book provides data for thought; the data cannot tell you what will happen to your child.

Data inform us. Data should begin, not end, discussion. My hope is that this book provides and fosters many discussions about the data and their important place in the discourse of our children's lives and well-being.

There are no guarantees in this book. Its contents are not advice but food for thought. Eat at your own risk. Cut it up into small pieces to avoid choking.

The Worry Clock Concept

We hear horror stories all the time of how children die. My mother called recently to tell me that the grandson of an old neighbor had choked to death on a latex balloon he was chewing. A friend of a friend had a son die from choking on a hot dog. And just yesterday I read about a freak gun accident. What does it all mean for my child?

This book puts all the anecdotes in context; it stacks them up and compares them. The book tells you which are the most likely dangers and by how much.

How does the book compare the stories? It uses years and years of data on all the childhood deaths in the United States from 1999 to 2007. Using data on all the deaths over that time, I am able to list the most common causes of death and compare those numbers to other causes. But I said you didn't have to know statistics for this book. Instead of data tables, the book uses "Worry Clocks" to present the information in each chapter.

The Worry Clocks are sixty-minute clocks that present the most common causes of death and their relative importance, based on frequency of death. The idea is that if you are going to worry for one hour, the clock presents the amount of time you might spend on each cause of death, if you were to follow the actual data. For example, if car accidents account for half of all possible ways children die, then the Worry Clock would suggest spending half of the hour—thirty minutes—worrying about car accidents.

The Worry Clock: One Hour of Worry

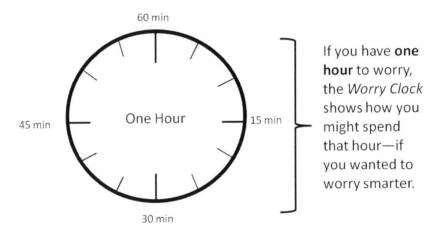

If you have **one hour** to worry, the *Worry Clock* shows how you might spend that hour—if you wanted to worry smarter.

Here is an exercise to help explain the Worry Clock idea. If you think you get the idea, skip ahead to the "important caveats" section.

Let's take a highly unlikely event that has nothing to do with children so we can focus on getting the Worry Clock idea. Let's look at an imaginary Worry Clock for death after being marooned alone on a deserted island. What do people die from? Lack of water (dehydration), lack of food (starvation), other causes? Here is one list of possible causes, ordered by frequency, with the more common causes first.

Sample of guesses for causes of death for people marooned on a deserted island:
Dehydration
Starvation
Drowning
Poisoning

Infection
Suicide

Now let's put a percentage on those categories. What percent of deaths fall into each of these causes? Let's say that dehydration far outweighs any other cause and makes up 40 percent, not quite half. Then starvation and drowning tie for second, about even with 20 percent each. For those who failed to follow the *US Army Survival Manual*'s thirteen-step Universal Edibility Test[4], poisoning has to be up there—say at 10 percent. The last two categories make up the last 10 percent. Look at the table below.

Estimated Percentages Based on Above Guesses

	Percent of deaths	Minutes that the percent translates to in one hour
Dehydration	40%	24 minutes
Starvation	20%	12 minutes
Drowning	20%	12 minutes
Poisoning	10%	6 minutes
Infection	5%	3 minutes
Suicide	5%	3 minutes

The table shows those percentages along with "worry minutes": the number of minutes you should spend worrying about the category, assuming the percentages are right and you want to use the data to guide you. The number is just the percentage multiplied by sixty to get the number of minutes for each over a sixty-minute (one-hour) period.

Why one hour? It seemed a discrete enough amount of time that people can wrap their heads around it easily. Is this an hour a day, week, month, or year? That's up to you. If you're like me, worry tends to be constant rather than discrete, which is actually another good reason to time-bound the worry. One of the strategies to worry less is to set aside a special time to worry and don't do it outside that time.

Continuing the above example, the Worry Clock below shows the minutes as a clock dial and leaves out the percentages entirely to keep things simple.

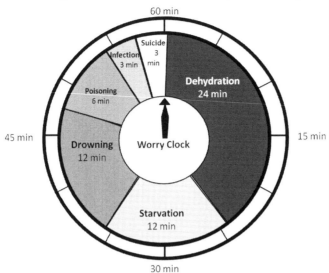

Worry Clock Example
for Being Marooned on a Deserted Island (Data Not Real)

60 min

Suicide
3 min

Infection
3 min

Poisoning
6 min

Dehydration
24 min

45 min

Drowning
12 min

Worry Clock

15 min

Starvation
12 min

30 min

This is what a Worry Clock might look like based on the made-up data above.

Nearly half of your hour of "worry time" would be spent on dehydration.

Reading the Worry Clock

The Worry Clock, like any clock, represents sixty minutes, one hour of worry. In each clock, I include the major causes of death and the number of minutes associated with each. I always put the number of deaths on average per Worry-Clock minute at the beginning of the chapters in case the data geeks among you want to translate the minutes back into the average annual deaths for the given age group.

If you were focused on worrying about being marooned on a deserted island and were using the above Worry Clock, you would spend twenty-four minutes worrying about dehydration, twelve minutes on starvation and drowning, six minutes on poisoning, and three each on infection and suicide. Worry time may be used for prevention activities, further research, or unabated worry, all of which is up to you.

Please note that the data above are completely fictional, but all the rest of the data in this book are *actual* data. The degree to which those data apply to the specific case of your child is impossible to predict, and you are the best one to determine how useful those data are.

Important Caveats

The Worry Clock will be used throughout the rest of this book to help give you a sense for how to translate the numbers and rates presented. The clock is only a guide, based on the available data. The data have limitations, and averages describe groups of people. All the data are based on the past, and things change. The fact that so many parents, for example, cover electrical outlets may explain why electrocution is nearly nonexistent in children, but then again it may not. The point is that we cannot tell. I present existing data about the past, hoping that in some way it will inform our collective future.

Nothing in this book should be used to come to any conclusions about what will or will not happen to your child. Statistics cannot—repeat, *cannot*—be applied to the individual. I can talk about what happens most often, but just because an outcome is unlikely based on past data, this does not mean it will not happen to your child. We learn and we try, but life offers no guarantees, even to those who are the most prepared.

Organization of This Book

The book is organized by age groups. The first chapter covers infants (birth to age one). The rest of the chapters are grouped as follows: age one to four (toddlers), five to nine (young children), ten to fourteen (preteens and early teens), and fifteen to nineteen (teenagers). The final chapter puts all the data together and asks the question: Across your child's life, what are the biggest areas for worry? We also take a look at the data related to parents' reported worst fear: child abduction. If abduction is not on your list of big fears, skip the final chapter. If you were really going by the data, you would not read it. The goal of this book is to make you a more informed, smarter worrier, not more paranoid.

Each chapter is organized in this sequence: introduction, Worry Clock categories, descriptions of categories and related recommendations, what is NOT on the clock, a quiz, and a top ten summary.

Story boxes also appear throughout the book. The stories are real and recent news stories about children in the United States who died in various ways. These stories are intended to help readers understand each category better. I debated whether or not to include the story boxes. Ultimately I felt the stories made the statistics both more understandable and more memorable. To be consistent with the data, the number of stories directly relate to the number of minutes on the Worry Clock. There is approximately one story for each three minutes on the Worry Clock.

A word about the data. Except where noted, the data in this book come from the Centers for Disease Control and Prevention mortality database. I used a data set that combined data from 1999 to 2007, the most recent data available at the time of writing. A big assumption here, although a reasonable one, is that past data will predict future data. Of course, things are changing. For example, we know that the numbers of children with severe disabilities is on a steep rise. My assumption is that although we may miss some of the current trends, the majority of the data will be similar. Again, these data should not be used to draw any conclusions about what will or will not happen to your child. For those who cannot get enough, or who want updated numbers on a more regular basis, go to my website, www.worryclock.com.

Anyone who has heard the words "just hold her for a minute" before receiving a friend's unfamiliar baby, or "you may take your baby home now" for the first time, knows that feeling of being overwhelmed by the fragility—and the responsibility—of a baby. Babies are scary. And it turns out they should be.

The data, perhaps not surprisingly, support the notion of fragility during this first year. A huge number of infants—more than all the other age groups combined—die from *any* cause in this first year. This number is approaching one out of every one hundred infants (see pie chart). For the one time in this book, the pie slice that represents the number of deaths is large enough to be clearly visible.

Percent of Children Less Than 1 Year Old Who Died
(CDC Mortality Rates, 1999–2007)

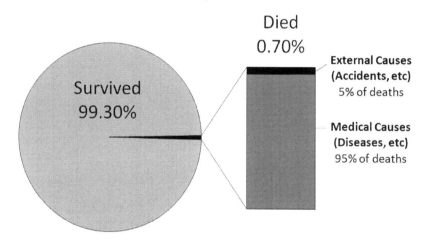

What may be comforting (or not) is that almost all of the deaths that occur in this first year are largely out of parental control. In other age groups, such as toddlers, half of the deaths are from accidents, but for infants, **only 5 percent** of deaths are accident related (see black portion of the bar that shows the types of death that compose the slice of pie).

Ninety-five percent of infant deaths are due to things it's too late or unlikely[5] for you to do anything about. For example, for mothers with more than college education, a quarter of infant deaths are from chromosomal abnormalities, and half are from disorders originating in the perinatal period.

This book is about the accidents only,[6] and the rest of this chapter looks deep into that small—in this case, 5 percent—piece of the visible slice in the pie.

Though it is true that many more infants die of medical and similar causes than from accidents, the accident rate for infants is very high relative to all other ages except teenagers. Infants are second only to teenagers in their accident rate. About one-third of all accidental deaths from birth through age nineteen occur in this first year (see Chapter 6 for more age comparions).

Lessons from the infant year include:

- Sleeping safety, sleeping safety, sleeping safety. If you forget everything else from this chapter, remember that your baby's safety during sleep is a huge concern, deserving of half of your worry time. In particular, babies' wedging themselves in tight spaces while sleeping causes three times more deaths than auto accidents.
- In case you aren't already painfully aware, inconsolable crying is a normal part of many infants' development. It is also an identified trigger for shaken baby syndrome, which can kill within seconds of shaking. Men (fathers and boyfriends) are the majority of perpetrators (63 percent), and baby-sitters accounted for an additional 18 percent.
- Falls and poisoning are far less common than one might expect, occupying only one minute of the clock each.
- Drowning is three times more likely than fatal falls, and over half (60 percent) of drowning deaths occurred in bathtubs.

First I review the Worry Clock for Infants, which presents the main causes of death, and then I go into each category in more detail and pass along recommendations, primarily from the government, on how to prevent these accidents.

The Worry Clock for Infants
The Infant Worry Clock (see below) points to a clear culprit: suffocation (including strangulation), almost all of which occurs in bed, accounts for nearly half of the hour. Homicide (e.g., shaking to death) is number two, with fourteen minutes. The last quarter comprises motor vehicle accidents (six minutes), drowning (three minutes), choking (three minutes), fire-related deaths (two minutes), and falls, poisoning, and medical complications (one minute each).

Worry Clock for Infants

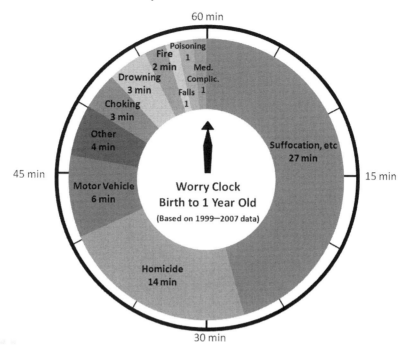

Each of these areas is reviewed in more depth below, followed by examples of incidents that did not make the Worry Clock. The explanations of these categories and examples of deaths are difficult to read. If you need to skip through the chapter, just read the boxed points and definitely skip the story boxes.

Suffocation & Strangulation: 27 Minutes

Suffocation and strangulation is the single largest Worry Clock category of *any* age group, and it accounts for twenty-seven minutes in this first year. Suffocation is when an external object, such as a blanket or plastic bag, blocks the nose and mouth. Strangulation is an external compression of the airway from an object, such as a string that becomes caught around the neck. Choking—an internal blockage of the airway—is covered in a separate section.

> **Suffocation Point #1:** Protecting your infant's breathing while in bed is the most important thing to do; infant suffocation is one of the largest single categories in any age group and accounts for a significant proportion of total deaths in children up to age nineteen—and this is probably a conservative estimate.

Most infant suffocation and strangulation take place in and around beds. Given the amount of time infants spend in bed, this shouldn't be surprising. As we will see later when we look across ages, suffocation in bed has the second highest rate of death, surpassed only by teenage car accidents. Yet this estimate is likely far too conservative. These data do not include sudden infant death syndrome (SIDS) cases, a significant cause of infant death.[7] SIDS is "the sudden death of an infant less than one year of age that cannot be explained after a thorough investigation is conducted, including a complete autopsy, examination of the death scene, and review of the clinical history."[8] That's right: if we cannot call it anything else, we call it SIDS. Technically, according to the CDC, that makes SIDS a *medical* condition and not an external cause of death (i.e., an accident). However, the American Academy of Pediatrics's recently released guidelines for safe sleeping noted that the recommendations for SIDS are basically the same as those for avoiding accidental suffocation in bed.[9]

What happens in beds? It seems there are five major[10] types of incidents: wedging, mouth/nose obstruction, overlay, entrapment, and hanging (see table). Let's go through each.

Suffocation and Strangulation's 27 Minutes

	Minutes
Accidental suffocation and strangulation in bed	**19**
Wedging (e.g., between bed and wall)	8*
Mouth/nose obstruction (e.g., plastic bag on head)	4*
Overlain obstruction (e.g., person rolls on top of baby)	2*
Entrapment with suspension (e.g., fall through broken crib, head stuck)	1*
Hanging (e.g., caught clothing)	1*
Other causes in bed	3*
Other (likely mix of above)[11]	**8**

* Estimates not based on CDC data but on separate data set in Drago & Dannenberg (1999).

Suffocation Point #2: Infant wedging—when infants are trapped between mattresses and walls, for example—is the most frequent cause of bed suffocation and accounts for more deaths than auto accidents.

Wedging—when an infant gets stuck or wedged between two objects and suffocates—accounts for about 40 percent[12] of suffocations/strangulations in bed, and eight minutes on the infant Worry Clock. One-third of wedging cases are wedging between the mattress and the wall. An infant gets stuck between the bed and the wall because she has the mobility to reach the edges of an adult bed but not the control to pull her head out of the gap.

But do not conclude that wedging only happens in adult beds; one in five incidents occurs in a crib. A Consumer Product Safety Commission analysis of these cases showed that this was likely due to people using cribs that did not meet current standards (e.g., hand-me-down cribs), or, in a few cases, cribs that were damaged or put together improperly.[13]

Prevention of wedging is fairly simple: put the infant in a crib (not a bed) that meets current safety standards for the crib, its mattress, and their fit together. And don't forget to buy something safe for frequent travel or for a regular sleepover location.

Objects covering the nose and mouth (mouth/nose obstruction) accounted for a quarter of infant suffocation/strangulation, four minutes of the infant Worry Clock. Pillows, bedding, and plastic bags were the main culprits, with the first two primarily affecting babies less than three months old. Our cozy beds and blankets can endanger infants by allowing for small spaces where the infants rebreathe—breathe in previously exhaled air. Adults can just pick up their heads and move them instead of continuing to rebreathe, but as with wedging, infants lack that control. A dimple in the bed, a snug spot under the blanket, or mom's pillow can allow rebreathing, which leads to suffocation.

> **Suffocation Point #3:** Putting infants to bed or down for a nap in adult beds, including while visiting family who don't have cribs, is a *bad* idea, and not just because of wedging. Infants may begin rebreathing under blanket or in tiny mattress divots or find other hazards difficult for adults to anticipate (e.g., bags lining trash cans that are set next to the bed).

Plastic dry-cleaning bags gained their infamy from their quick adherence to objects (due in part to static electricity) and their strength, making tearing by infant hands difficult. One researcher claimed that if a plastic film of this kind was not removed from an infant's face within one minute, the infant would ultimately die of suffocation.[14] Although it generally takes longer than a minute to suffocate, the danger is real and can occur within very short periods of time.

You might wonder who does not know the dangers of plastic bags. Yet these bags are ubiquitous. When I read about an infant who rolled off the bed and onto a trash can lined with a plastic bag, and then read of another who rolled onto a plastic bag full of clothes, I suddenly remembered the bag of old maternity clothes that I had had next to my bed...for ages.

Suffocation Point #4: The incidence of infants being suffocated by someone with whom they are sleeping has risen steeply in recent years, and the American Academy of Pediatrics concludes that choosing room sharing (instead of bed sharing) may reduce the risk of death by as much as 50 percent.

Then there are the cases that are the horror among horrors: when a loved one rolls over onto the infant and smothers the child. What are called "overlain obstructions" account for another two minutes on the clock. Rates of death due to overlying are increasing (although this may be due to classification changes). The estimated mortality rate tripled in the second half of the '80s over the first half, and then nearly doubled again for the first half of the '90s.[15]

Most incidents occurred in beds (nearly 60 percent), but couches are notably high and fill in the remaining 40 percent. I doubt that people sleep on couches 40 percent of the time, which suggests there are more deaths on couches per sleep hour—i.e., couches may be more dangerous.

It pains me to write this, because a favorite image of mine is my first daughter sleeping soundly on my husband's chest as the two took a nap on the living room couch. In researching this chapter, I uncovered similar stories of dads napping with infants that ended tragically.

The American Academy of Pediatrics has recently summarized some research, mostly on SIDS but likely related to suffocations, that identifies risk factors in the infant's sleeping environment. These factors include having more than three people in the bed, having lots of soft materials on the bed, or having someone in the bed who is not the child's parent (including siblings). In addition, having anyone in the bed who is a current smoker, is using medications (e.g., some antidepressants and pain medications) or substances (e.g., alcohol) that could impair his or her alertness, or is excessively tired (is there someone with an infant who is not?) is also a risk factor. Because of the myriad risk factors and the difficulty of controlling some of them, the AAP made the somewhat unpopular statement that they do "not recommend any specific bed-sharing situations as safe."[16] Even "devices promoted to make bed-sharing 'safe' (eg, inbed co-sleepers) are not recommended." Instead, room sharing without bed sharing is recommended: "There is evidence that this arrangement decreases the risk…by as much as 50 percent." Cribs, play yards, bassinettes meeting safety standards are the only sleepers that get the seal of approval.

You will have to decide what benefits balance this equation to decide whether cosleeping is right for you. Even if you do not share many of the risk factors, there is clearly still risk. The question you have to answer is whether the benefits are worth it. And if you are pregnant, you may want to choose your course now, before you enter a sleep-deprived haze.

Research has identified two potential protective factors. Breast-feeding is a protective factor for suffocation and SIDS deaths. *Any* breast-feeding was associated with a reduced risk, but the AAP recommends that, if possible, "mothers should exclusively breast-feed or feed with expressed human milk for six months since the protective effect of breast-feeding increases with exclusivity." Interestingly, pacifiers also appear to be protective. The AAP suggests, "Consider offering a pacifier at nap time and bedtime [after breast-feeding is established]. Although the mechanism is yet unclear, studies have reported a protective effect of pacifiers on the incidence of SIDS. The protective effect persists throughout the sleep period, even if the pacifier falls out of the infant's mouth."

Suffocation Point #5: Infants in later months can be surprisingly dexterous in getting to places and things you forget are nearby. Regularly scan the sleeping environment (look up, too) for hazards, and do the same at Grandma's house.

The last two gruesome categories, entrapment from suspension and hanging, each contribute one minute to the Worry Clock. Deaths due to entrapment from suspension are similar to the wedging issues, except for the mechanism of death; I don't think I need to go into it. The same action step applies: put your infant to sleep in an approved crib in good condition with an approved mattress and nothing else. Remember that your baby may stand for the first time in the crib. For the hanging deaths, entangled clothing and blind cords topped the list of culprits. Anything around the neck that could potentially get caught on a protruding piece of a crib or crib hardware, for example, can be a hazard. Even the cord to the baby monitor is a hazard and one that has caused so many strangulations that the Consumer Product Safety Commission recently put out a warning to parents.[17]

And in case it ran through your head that these types of things don't happen to well-educated[18] moms, they do. I ran a separate analysis linking this data set to another and found that nearly one in ten of the moms whose babies died from these accidents was college-educated (sixteen or more years of education).[19]

Warning! The stories below are real and are intended to give you a sense for the lives behind the statistics. The number of stories is directly related to the number of minutes on the Worry Clock, which is why there are so many infant suffocation stories. Too much? Just skip the story boxes.

Story Box: Suffocation in Bed, Ages Birth to One

Infant Suffocates under Couch Cushions
In Hastings, Michigan, on July 25, 2012, a child was put down on a couch for a nap. The seven-month-old pushed her way under the edge of the couch cushion and was later found dead.[20]

Bassinet in Reach, Baby Dies next to Mom
In Anderson, South Carolina, on August 11, 2012, an infant girl was found by her father, dead in the bed next to her mother. Mom "knew the danger of sleeping with an infant…Heartbreaking…"[21]

Infant Dies between Bed and Wall
In New Lenox Township Illinois, on February 27, 2012, a mom put her five-month-old down for a nap and lay down for a nap herself in a separate room. When she awoke later, she didn't find him on the bed or with his dad. She then found him trapped between the bed and the wall, and unsuccessfully performed CPR.[22]

Sleeping Away from Home, Infant Pulls Plastic off Window and Suffocates in Crib
In Macon, Georgia, at midday on May 4, 2012, an eight-month-old in a crib reached up and pulled some plastic off a window. The infant was found later having suffocated.[23]

Suffocated on Grandma's Chest
In Indianapolis, on August 16, 2012, an infant boy took a nap with his grandmother on the couch. When his mother checked on them, she found the infant was no longer breathing.[24]

Mom Rolls Over and Suffocates Child
In Waterford, California, on June 26, 2012, a mother and baby went to sleep together, but only the mom woke up. The likely cause of death was the mother rolling over onto the child.[25]

The Consumer Product Safety Commission keeps a database of consumer products related to deaths. The database includes doctors' accounts of incidents where infants died in bed-related accidents; here are just a few:[26]

"[Infant was] **playing in bed with parents** when they [parents] awoke in the a.m. and noticed baby not breathing or moving…"

"**Sleeping in bed w/Dad.** Mom left room, returned & didn't see [infant], found scooted to head of bed w/head in/on bag filled with clothing."

"Mom found…**baby-sitter [had] placed [infant] on thick comforter** and [infant was] unresponsive…multiple attempts to resuscitate infant unsuccessful."

Suffocation Point #6: Consider following the American Academy of Pediatrics and Consumer Product Safety Commission recommendations for improving safe sleeping.

In 2011, the American Academy of Pediatrics produced recommendations for a safe sleep environment that can reduce the risk of all sleep-related infant deaths. Many branches of the US government expressed support for the new recommendations.[27] Below are a few of the AAP recommendations,[28] plus some from the federal agencies that I found most helpful.

For those who want more detail and references, particularly those considering cosleeping, I strongly recommend reading the full AAP policy statement and recommendations as part of your research: http://pediatrics.aappublications.org/content/early/2011/10/12/peds.2011-2284.

1. Always put infants to sleep on their backs. Even an infant with acid reflux will be better in this position.
2. Don't put an infant to sleep on a bed or couch, with or without an adult.
3. Don't use car seats, strollers, swings, or slings for routine sleep, especially if child is less than four months old.
4. Use only a crib, bassinet, or portable crib/play yard that conforms to CPSC and ASTM international standards and remains in excellent condition.

5. Use a firm infant mattress made to fit your specific crib (no more than one-inch gap). If you use a waterproof mattress cover, the cover should be tightly fitting and thin.

6. Do room sharing but not bed sharing (including avoiding the cosleeper units that extend the bed).

7. Avoid feeding your infant where you are likely to fall asleep beside her.

8. Do not use portable bed rails. Check and remove from the sleeping area any dangling cords or wires.

9. When using a sling or cloth carrier, make sure that the infant's head is up and above the fabric, the face is visible, and the nose and mouth are clear of obstructions.

10. Use no soft bedding, pillows, pillow-like bumpers, stuffed animals, or products claiming to prevent SIDS in the child's sleeping area or attached to the pacifier.

11. Use sleep clothing designed to keep the infant warm without the possible hazard of head covering or entrapment.

12. Breast-feed (any length of time, but ideally for six months) or feed with expressed human milk.

13. Consider offering a pacifier (without any strings or attachments) before naps.

14. Avoid overheating, with no more than one layer more than an adult would wear to be comfortable in that environment. Signs of overheating include sweating or the infant's chest feeling hot to the touch.

Homicide: 14 Minutes

In the United States, you are more likely to be murdered on the day you are born than at any other time during your life.[29] This sad reality falls mostly outside the scope of this book because most of those cases involve births outside hospitals to teen mothers with a history of mental illness.[30]

Despite the high rate of death on the day a child is born, 90 percent of the infant-year homicides actually occur in later weeks,[31] with a peak during the eighth week of life. Why then? Because that is also the peak of inconsolable infant crying, and researchers have demonstrated a link, citing the increased homicide rate as reflecting caregivers' out-of-control reactions to infants' persistent crying.[32] Many of these incidents occur without the intent to kill.[33]

Ask someone who has cared for an infant with colic if they remember this period of inconsolable crying. It is simply counterintuitive to think of this unrelenting, ear-shattering crying as "normal."[34] I remember being utterly unable to stop my daughter from crying—or even understand why she was crying. It was a horrible and helpless feeling. I tried changing breast-feeding patterns, changing my diet, increasing swaddling, and just about any solution I came across that seemed plausible. I felt desperate. And it seems I wasn't alone:

> Dr. Ian St. James-Roberts, of the University of London, U.K., explains that while excessive crying, or colic, was once attributed to gastrointestinal disturbance, more recent research has begun to nuance this view. In fact, organic disturbances are rare; proper diagnosis is therefore important. Dietary treatments (such as eliminating cow's milk from the mother's diet) lack evidence of practical effectiveness and may cause women to abandon breast-feeding...[35]

In fact, researchers at the Centre of Excellence for Early Childhood Development have concluded that "it seems regardless of the strategies used to sooth the infant, prolonged unsoothable bouts of crying are likely to occur regardless."[36]

Homicide Point #1: Inconsolable crying is **normal**, peaks around six to eight weeks of age, and coincides with a peak in homicides for infants.

But what happens when the desire to care for and console a crying infant turns destructive?

Remember the name Louise Woodward? This au pair's case in Massachusetts back in 1997 brought shaken baby syndrome into our collective consciousness. Shaken baby syndrome and similar forms of abuse may be responsible for up to 75 percent of the infant homicides.[37]

Shaken baby syndrome (SBS)[38] is a form of abusive head trauma (AHT) and inflicted traumatic brain injury (ITBI). It results from violently shaking an infant by the shoulders, arms, or legs. The whiplash causes the bridging veins running on surface of the brain to rupture and bleed. "Direct traumatic damage occurs to the brain; hypoxia during and after the assault causes further irreversible damage to brain tissue."[39] And "the most common trigger for shaking a baby is inconsolable or excessive crying—a normal phase in infant development."[40,41]

Biological fathers, stepfathers, and boyfriends are responsible for nearly two-thirds of deaths from shaken baby syndrome (see pie graph).[42,43] Baby-sitters and boyfriends were responsible for nearly one in five cases each. If we factor in how much more time mothers (or baby-sitters) spend with babies than fathers (nearly twice as much time for coupled mothers as coupled fathers),[44] this makes fathers (and boyfriends) far more likely to be the perpetrators.

Victims are also more likely to be boys,[45] and while there is a peak at just under two months old, the incidents may occur throughout the child's first year (and up to age five).[46] Minority children and children of those in active military service have been found to be at increased risk.[47] Although minority children are at higher risk for all traumatic brain injury, what this may actually suggest is that that race/ethnicity "is a marker for other social factors that put children at risk for injury."[48]

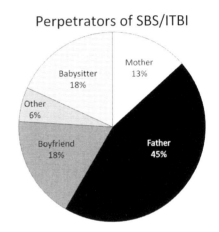

Perpetrators of SBS/ITBI

Mother 13%
Babysitter 18%
Other 6%
Boyfriend 18%
Father 45%

In most cases, the period of shaking is five to ten seconds long,[49] and researchers note that death may result from as few as five seconds of shaking.[50]

And in case you were wondering, no, it does not seem that bouncing a baby as some people do playfully has the same effect. According to the CDC, "While jogging an infant on your knee or tossing him or her in the air can be very risky, the injuries that result from SBS are not caused by these types of activities."[52] For a good summary in answer to this frequently asked question, see the National Center on Shaken Baby Syndrome, http://dontshake.org/sbs.php?topNavID=3&subNavID=24.

> **Homicide Point #5:** Relax; playful bouncing does not cause shaken baby syndrome.

Deaths from shaken baby syndrome and related abuse are significantly higher for infants of only high school–educated mothers (mother's education is tracked because it has been found to be consistently a good predictor of child outcomes). Although lower, the rates of infant death by homicide for college-educated mothers remain significant.[53]

Also be aware that there is evidence that shaken baby syndrome incidents have increased with the recession.[54] Any additional stress, in this case economic, may lower one's tolerance threshold. Being aware of stress in your and your caregivers' lives may be helpful.

> **Homicide Point #6:** Homicide occurred more frequently in families with mothers who achieved only a high school education; economic stress may be a factor.

How will you know if your baby has been shaken? The most common initial symptoms, which are reported to occur immediately, were limpness, seizures (convulsions), vomiting, lethargy, and apnea (breathing interruptions). [55] The government[56] describes a longer list of symptoms, adding to those above: extreme irritability or other changes in behavior, sleepiness, not smiling, loss of consciousness, loss of vision, breathing problems, pale or bluish skin, and lack of appetite.

Note that there may not be any physical signs of injury, such as bruising, bleeding, or swelling. Rib fractures are common but may only be seen on X-ray. Also know that when the baby-sitter was the perpetrator, the sitter was far less likely than others to have admitted any abuse when asked.[57]

> **Homicide Point #7:** Symptoms of SBS include limpness, sleepiness, lethargy, convulsions, vomiting, blindness, and breathing difficulty. There may be no signs of bruising, bleeding, or swelling.

The recommendations below are based primarily on advice from the CDC[58] for caregivers and community members. Following these recommendations won't guarantee your child's safety and may not be right for your child. As with all recommendations in this book, they are food for thought. Please develop your own recommendations based on your review of the data and consultation with your health care professionals.

1. **Know that babies can cry a lot** in the first few months of life. This can be frustrating, but it will get better. Remember, you are not a bad parent or caregiver if your baby continues to cry after you have done all you can to calm her. Understand that you may not be able to calm your baby and that it is not your fault, nor your baby's. It is normal for healthy babies to cry frequently in the first four months of life.

2. **You can try to calm your crying baby** by rubbing his back, gently rocking him, offering a pacifier, singing or talking, or taking him for a walk or a drive. There are many products and services available that teach strategies for calming a baby; you can find the one that works best for your family.

3. **If you have tried various ways to calm your baby and she won't stop crying, check for signs** of illness or discomfort like diaper rash, teething, or tight clothing. Assess whether she is hungry or needs to be burped. Call the doctor if you suspect your child is injured or ill.

4. **If you find yourself pushed to the limit by a crying baby, you may need to focus on calming yourself first**. Treat it like an airplane's emergency oxygen mask: take care of yourself first so that you can then help your baby. Put your baby in a crib on his back, make sure he is safe, and then walk away for a bit and call a friend, relative, neighbor, or parent helpline for support. Check on your baby every five to ten minutes.

5. **Tell everyone who cares for your baby about the dangers of shaking a baby and what to do if they become angry**, frustrated, or upset when your baby has an episode of inconsolable crying or does other things that caregivers may find annoying, such as interrupting television, video games, sleep time, etc.

6. **Be aware of signs of frustration and anger among others** caring for your baby. Let them know that crying is normal and that it will get better.

7. **See a health care professional if you have anger management** or other behavioral concerns.

8. **Assess people who are around your infant for their ability to remain calm and not lose their temper.** Try to choose caregivers who remain calm under any circumstance.

For all those who know new parents, particularly those with infants in the peak crying period, offering your support may be helpful. If you are planning to provide support to new parents, consider skipping the birth and coming to help out around weeks six, seven, or eight.

Story Box: Homicide, Ages Birth to One

Father Booked for Infant Shaking Death
In Draper, Utah, on August 27, 2012, a father reported the drowning of his one-month-old baby. He later admitted to shaking the baby, who died after cardiac arrest.[59]

Mother's Boyfriend Accused in Infant Death
In Ansonia, Connecticut, on June 16, 2011, a five-month-old baby died of blunt-force trauma. The baby was in the care of the mother's boyfriend at the time.[60]

Baby-Sitter Charged Because of Inaction after Infant Shaken, Thrown by Nine-Year-Old
In Franklin County, Pennsylvania, on April 18, 2012, a fifty-seven-year-old caregiver was sentenced to jail for failing to call 911 after seeing that the infant in his care was behaving strangely in his crib and not breathing well. Two visiting older children had taken the baby out of his crib, violently shaken him, and thrown him back into the crib.[61]

Motor Vehicles: 6 Minutes

When I began this book, I thought motor vehicle accidents would have topped the list of dangers to infants—babies seem so fragile! But as you can see, these deaths account for only six minutes on the infant Worry Clock, which is one-fifth of the breathing-related deaths and less than half of homicides.

Per the CDC guidelines, infants should be in a rear-facing car seat in the middle of the back seat, the safest seat in the car. Child safety seats reduce the risk of death in passenger cars by 71 percent for infants.[62] Yet estimates are that over 80 percent of rear-facing seats are installed with critical misuses.[63]

In the next chapter on toddlers, I spend a lot of time reviewing the different causes of motor vehicles accidents that apply well for infants, too.

Motor Vehicle Point #1: Although infant car seats reduce the risk of death by over 70 percent, more than 80 percent of installed car seats demonstrate critical misuses.

The recommendations below are primarily from the CDC[64] and are straightforward ones you have likely heard before:

1. Make sure children are properly buckled up in a rear-facing car seat.
2. Never place a rear-facing car seat in the front seat or in front of an air bag. Airbags can kill young children riding in the front seat.
3. Strive to place children in the middle of the back seat, because "it is the safest spot in the vehicle."[65]
4. Of course, don't consume alcohol and drive. **More than two-thirds of fatally injured children were killed while riding with a drinking driver, and most of those kids were not restrained.**[66]

All Ages Car Safety Restraint Recommendations from the CDC:[67]

Birth through Age 2 – Rear-facing child safety seat. For the best possible protection, infants and children should sit in the back seat in a rear-facing child safety seat, buckled with the seat's harness, until they reach the upper weight or height limits of their particular seat. The weight and height limits on rear-facing child safety seats can accommodate most children through age two; check the seat's owner's manual for details.

Between Ages 2 and 4/Until 40 lbs. – Forward-facing child safety seat. When children outgrow their rear-facing seats (the weight and height limits on rear-facing car seats can accommodate most children through age two), they should ride in the back seat in forward-facing child safety seats, buckled with the seat's harness, until they reach the upper weight or height limit of their particular seat (usually around age four and forty pounds, though many newer seats have higher weight limits; check the seat's owner's manual for details).

Between Ages 4 and 8 OR until 4" 9" Tall – Booster seat. Once children outgrow their forward-facing seats (by reaching the upper height and weight limits of their seat), they should ride in belt-positioning booster seats. Remember to keep children in the back seat for the best possible protection.

After Age 8 AND/OR 4' 9" Tall – Seat belts. Children should use booster seats until adult seat belts fit them properly. Seat belts fit properly when the lap belt lies across the upper thighs (not the stomach) and the shoulder belt fits across the chest (not the neck). When adult seat belts fit children properly, they can use the adult seat belts without booster seats. For the best possible protection, keep children in the back seat and use lap-and-shoulder belts.

Choking: 3 Minutes

Infants may choke on food, of course, but they are just as likely to choke on their own vomit or nonfood objects such as toys.

Choking	3 minutes
Choking on food	1 minute
Choking on nonfood objects	1 minute
Choking on gastric contents (vomit)	1 minute

Food. Although it is possible for infants to choke even on liquids such as milk, the major food worries for this age group are the same as they are for older children, and are the ones about which most parents are well informed. As a rule of thumb, be careful of round foods, like grapes and carrots. If the child is well into solid food, then beware of hot dogs and nuts, too.

Other objects. Other objects, too, tend to be the same old players: latex balloons, balls, and toy parts.[68] Children can choke on uninflated balloons or the remnants of a popped balloon, such as are found on the floor at many kids' parties. Children suck the balloon into their throats when they attempt to chew on, blow up, or otherwise play with the balloon pieces near their mouths.

Balloons are so dangerous in mouths that even older children and teenagers have died from inhaling deflated balloons.[69] The Consumer Product Safety Commission describes a case in which "a child was chewing on an uninflated balloon when she fell from a swing. The child hit the ground and, in a reflex action, inhaled sharply. She suffocated on the balloon."[70]

The toys other than balloons that cause issues are primarily small, round objects, similar to those in the food category. Small balls, marbles, magnets (see also the section on poisoning), and toys such as the heads from little figurines or dolls.[71] Button batteries are also becoming an issue (see Chapter 2 for more). Anything with a diameter less than 3.2 cm (1.25 inches) is a potential danger.

Gastric contents. Babies can and do throw up. Most of the time, infants do just fine getting it out. I can remember thinking that it looked like a throw-up bomb had gone off in my back seat after just a five-minute ride to the doctor to get a rotavirus confirmation.

In fact, infants—including healthy infants—throw up a lot; it is a part of what they do. There is even a name for it: gastroesophageal reflux. Reflux is a condition in which stomach contents go back up into the esophagus (the tube from the mouth to the stomach) after eating—i.e., the infant throws up. And most infants will have reflux to some degree: the National Institutes of Health note that "more than half of babies will have reflux during their first three months."[72]

However, infants are still developing the ability to manage swallowing, and sometimes things go wrong. Reflux, for example, has been noted to be potentially fatal.[73] Reflux associated with weight loss or that causes breathing difficulty is considered abnormal.[74]

Choking Point #1: Choking risks, equally common, are food, nonfood objects, and vomit. Round foods and objects and clinging plastics are some of the most common items in these rare events.

Story Box: Choking, Ages Birth to One

One-Year-Old Chokes to Death on a Penny While Mom Thinks He Is Napping
In Las Cruces, New Mexico, on October 4, 2011, a one-year-old boy was found unconscious on the sofa, where his mother thought he was taking a nap. A preliminary autopsy report found a penny lodged in his throat.[75]

The recommendations below are primarily based on recommendations from Washington and New York states.[76] As always, decide what is right for your child based on your review of the data and consultations with your health care professionals.

Recommendations for Preventing Choking and Suffocation
1. Remember that the size of a young child's trachea (windpipe) or breathing tube is approximately the same diameter as a drinking straw. Cut foods into small pieces. Cut hot dogs lengthwise and widthwise.

2. If balloons are present, make sure children do not play with the leftover uninflated balloons and discard all balloon pieces as soon as possible (this includes those tiny water balloons).

3. Warn baby-sitters and older siblings about choking hazards and ask them not to share certain foods (e.g., hard foods that infants cannot chew, round foods) with the baby. I'll never forget seeing one of our baby-sitters show us with pride the bubbles she could blow in a piece of balloon she carried in her pocket!

4. Avoid toys with detachable parts (heed the warnings on the labels) and be mindful of older children's toys in the hands of an infant.

5. Periodically check your child's environment for small objects and ask older children to protect younger siblings by checking the carpet for small pieces from toys or games. Pay extra attention to cleaning up after parties. "An especially dangerous time is the morning after parties, when a toddler may find dangerous foods on the floor."[77]

6. Keep magnets and button batteries away from infants and off floors.

7. Never leave a small child unattended while he is eating. Direct supervision is necessary.

8. When eating, children should be calm and unhurried. They should sit up straight and not eat while walking, riding in a car, or playing.

9. Children should have sufficient number of teeth, and the muscular and developmental ability needed to chew and swallow, for the foods chosen. Remember, not all children will be at the same developmental level. Children with special health care needs are especially vulnerable to choking risks.

10. Model safe eating habits and chew food thoroughly.

11. Offer plenty of liquids to children when eating, but solids and liquids should not be swallowed at the same time. Offer liquids between mouthfuls.

12. Peanut butter can stick to the roof of a child's mouth and form a glob, so only use a little.

13. Get trained in first aid and CPR for an infant, and get retrained with each new child. The methods are different than those for adults and are constantly being updated based on new research.

Drowning: 3 Minutes

Sixty percent of infant drowning deaths occurred in bathtubs and only about 8 percent in swimming pools, a pattern that reverses for toddlers. Another 7 percent drown in other ways, such as in the five-gallon buckets discussed in the next chapter.

The next chapter discusses different types of drowning to worry about as your child becomes more mobile. For the infant year, you should know not to leave an infant unattended in a bathtub, *ever*, even one that is barely filled. Infants can drown in very small amounts of water.

Story Box: Drowning, Ages Birth to One

Four-Month-Old Girl Dies in Bathtub When Father Briefly Attends to Another Child

In San Tan Valley, Arizona, on December 20, 2013, a four-month-old girl drowned when her father left her alone for about ninety seconds to attend to another child.[78]

Fire: 2 Minutes

Almost all infant fire deaths occur at home. The next chapter addresses home fire prevention in detail.

Falls: 1 Minute

While short falls, such as falling from a bed or off a dresser, may cause injury, they are not likely to be the causes of death. Short falls are very common. Several studies that asked parents retrospectively about falls found that *one-half* of infants fell from an elevated surface before their first birthday.[79] Further, no deaths resulting from short falls were reported at large, licensed daycare centers in any peer-reviewed articles indexed in the National Library of Medicine.[80] And in a large study of infant falls within hospitals, no deaths were found to result from falls (e.g., rolling out of mom's bed onto the floor).[81] Falling just doesn't seem to result in infant death.

Having said that, half of the deaths that did occur were actually classified as short falls. So what's going on? An in-depth study on the misclassification of deaths as due to short falls noted that "generally, when a child between the ages of birth and five years is brought for medical care (or otherwise presented) with an injury that is fatal and a history of a short fall, abuse is suspected and an investigation ensues."[82] So it may be that falls are overestimated here and that half of the worry minute should be reclassified under homicide.

For the longer falls that do appear to matter, the summary is that "the risk of a fatal outcome is related to fall height and the nature of the impacting surface."[83] There are not many studies describing how high is too high,

28

for example, but two studies found no deaths in children who fell from less than three stories.[84]

Common recommendations for preventing fatal falls include moving furniture away from windows (to avoid the child crawling up and out) and installing window guards (screens don't stop children).

Poisoning: 1 Minute

The majority of all poisoning cases in the US (as determined by calls to poison control centers) are for children up to age five, but these are for accidents, not deaths. Turns out, these poisonings rarely end up being fatal.[85] Although they account for about 55 percent of the poisoning incidents, the up-to-age-five group accounts for only about 3 percent of the all the poisoning fatalities.

When poisonings is fatal for infants, three-quarters of these deaths are from drugs, both prescription and illegal. Infants may find pills or other substances dropped on the floor or left on tables. There is no one drug or substance that stands out. In one analysis of pediatric fatal poisonings from poison control centers, no single poison accounted for more than three deaths, and the majority of cases were caused by a substance that did not cause any other deaths.[86] Nonetheless, here are a few examples of the few substances that had repeat offenses: carbon monoxide, aluminum phosphide (a pesticide), hydrofluoric acid (a highly corrosive acid that melts glass found in, e.g., metal cleaning fluids), lamp oil, smoke, diphenhydramine (an antihistamine with sedative properties used to treat allergies and found in some "PM" pain medications, and sold by itself under the brand name Benadryl), and flecainide (a heart medication).

The remaining quarter of deaths is from exposure to gases and vapors (e.g., carbon monoxide), which is a theme discussed in later chapters.

To prevent poisoning, the American Association of Poison Control Centers[87] recommends constant supervision of children and the storage of all medicines and household cleaning products in locked cabinets (not in purses, remember). Remember the Before, While, and After Rule:

BEFORE using a cleaning product, read the instructions on the bottle. WHILE using a cleaning product, never leave it alone. A child may find it. AFTER using a product, put it back in a locked cabinet. Make sure the container is closed tightly.

The rule seems to apply equally to medicines, even the child's medicines.

Medical Complications: 1 Minute

These deaths occur when something goes wrong during medical treatment. They generally do not arise during routine care; about 60 percent relate directly to surgery. Other authors have addressed the mistakes that happen in medicine (see Dr. Atul Gawande's *Complications: A Surgeon's Notes on an Imperfect Science* for an excellent and eye-opening account, for example). There is enough evidence out there that, if my child were in need of medical care, I would strongly consider hiring a patient advocate, one of those individuals who makes it their job to know everything about your case and the related research and to serve as a constant check on the doctors and hospital.

What Doesn't Appear on the Clock

Below are a few causes of death that I have singled out for a special look, either because they had no findings or because of how they compared to other findings (but didn't rate enough to talk about in the main section of the chapter).

Although the incidence of many incidents on this table is very low, their appearance does not necessarily mean that your child is safe from these causes of death. Your child may have a particular susceptibility—to bee stings, for example—that is not taken into account here. What this table does show is that across the country and over many years, these incidents were relatively rare. Similarly, although some numbers may be low, it is important to remember that we are only covering deaths; injuries are not a part of this measure.

Miscellaneous Causes of Death for Infants	Worry Clock
Exposure to excessive natural heat	*27 seconds*
Exposure to excessive natural cold	**
Contact with hot tap water, hot drinks, oils, etc.	**
Contact with other hot fluids	**
Victim of cataclysmic storm	**
Victim of flood	**
Struck by thrown, projected, or falling object	*9 seconds*
Caught, crushed, or jammed between objects	*12 seconds*
Lack of food	**

Lack of water	**
Contact with sharp glass	**
Handgun discharge or other firearm discharge	**
Bitten or struck by dog or other mammal	**
Contact with hornets, bees, or other venomous animals	**
Exposure to electric transmission lines	**
Exposure to other electric current	**

*** The government says this number is too small to estimate accurately.*

There were only three "miscellaneous" categories that even mapped onto the Worry Clock. "Excessive natural heat" deaths are likely those that happen from infants being left in cars. I discuss this at length in the next chapter. The struck/caught deaths are consistent with furniture (such as bookshelf falling on the child).

All the rest of the incidents, including dog and other animal bites, electric current (outlets), contact with hot fluids, and exposure to cold did not happen frequently enough that the government could even put a reliable number to them.

Quiz Time for Infants!
Here's a chance to test your ability to keep all these statistics in your head. After the quiz, I propose a top ten list of action steps to give you some idea of where to start.

1. What is the number-one cause (major category) of death for infants?

2. If we included SIDS deaths in the Worry Clock, the numbers of deaths that the Worry Clock represents would:
    ☐ Increase by 50 percent.
    ☐ Increase by 100 percent.
    ☐ Increase by 200 percent.
    ☐ Stay about the same.

3. Which is more likely: "wedging" (e.g., where a child gets a head stuck between the bed and the wall) or mouth/nose obstructions (e.g., blanket covers face) and by how much—2, 4, 6, or 8 times?

4. True or false: Choking on vomit is the most common form of choking.

5. Which is more common, drowning in a pool or dying in a fire?

6. Name the percentage of time shaken baby syndrome was found to be perpetrated by the baby-sitter.
   - ☐ 0–10 percent
   - ☐ 11–20 percent
   - ☐ 21–30 percent
   - ☐ 31–40 percent
   - ☐ More than 41 percent

7. Which is more common cause of death: dying from choking on objects, poisoning, or falling?

8. Which is more common, dying in a car accident or dying from "wedging"?

9. True or false: Bouncing and tossing a baby have been found to produce shaken baby syndrome.

10. Which is more common: dying from electrocution from an outlet, or dying from bees and other animals?

Answers to Quiz

1. Threats to breathing. Extra points if you got more specific and said suffocation in bed.

2. Increase by 200 percent.

3. Wedging, by two times.

4. False. Choking on vomit was as likely as choking on food or choking on other objects.

5. Fire.

6. Eleven to twenty percent.

7. All three are the same frequency (one Worry Clock minute).

8. Wedging, by nearly 50 percent more.

9. False.

10. Neither; both are so uncommon that the statistics are unreliable.

Top Ten for Infants

You made it through all the data; now where to begin? If you feel overwhelmed and don't know where to start, here are some suggestions based on the most frequent causes of death in the past data. As you are keenly aware, doing these things doesn't guarantee a safe child, and you have to decide if these are even appropriate for your child. But these suggestions give you a place to start.

Top ten suggestions for increasing safety for infants:

1. Always put infants to sleep on their backs in a crib, bassinet, or portable crib/play yard that conforms to CPSC and ASTM international standards. No pillows, no blankets—nothing except the baby and crib.
2. Use room sharing without bed sharing (at a minimum, pull the bed away from walls to avoid wedging and do not use blankets or pillows).
3. Avoid the possibility of the infant's falling asleep, with or without an adult, on a couch, armchair, or adult bed.
4. Check for and remove from the sleeping area any dangling cords or wires, including infant monitor wires.
5. Consider breast-feeding, a protective factor for your baby.
6. Know that inconsolable crying is normal. Go through your checklist of needs and then take care of yourself. Teach anyone who is in contact with your child how to deal with inconsolable crying.
7. Know how your baby's caretakers (including those you love) deal with frustration, and choose ones for individual care who remain calm.
8. Ensure that your child is in a rear-facing car seat in the middle of the back seat in any caregiver's car.
9. Never leave an infant unattended in the bathtub.
10. Always scan the environment for any hazards, from cords to plastic bags to little circle batteries or untaken pills on counters.

Conclusion

The big worry in the infant years is breathing trouble, particularly in bed. Half, if not significantly more, of your worry (i.e., more than half if we included SIDS), would go into this category. The other big worry is homicide. All caregivers should be trained in how to deal with the frustrations of inconsolable crying.

Congratulations, you made it through infancy! In the toddler stage, the rate of death now halves. It's not the golden ages of five to nine, but you should be resting easier (mentally, if not physically!). As a visual reminder of just how few deaths we are talking about, check out the barely visible slice in the pie graph that represents all the children who died in this age group.

Less than half of that slice (44 percent) comprises those who died from accidents—things over which we arguably have some control—rather than cancer, diseases, genetic disorders, and other similar causes over which we are likely to have significantly less control. This chapter, like all of the others, focuses solely on the portion of that slice due to accidents.

Percent of Children Ages 1–4 Who Died
(CDC Mortality Rates, 1999–2007)

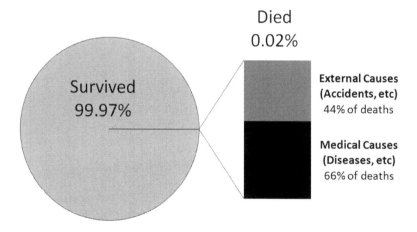

Lessons from the toddler years include:

1. Drowning is the number one cause of death, and it isn't a stranger's or public pool—it's yours or your friends'. Most of the toddlers who drowned were last seen in the home, had been out of sight less than five minutes, and were in the care of one or both parents at the time.[88]

2. Bathtub drowning is *half* the threat of ponds, streams, and other natural water. Again, a common scenario is that children last seen in the house are later found outside in a nearby pond.

3. Homicide linked to crying is again the second largest cause of death in this age group, continuing from the infant years.

4. Fire-related deaths are a significant percentage of deaths, equal to pedestrian deaths, and seven times more likely than falls. Why? Toddlers are mobile but don't know how to get out of a pitch-dark house. When was the last time you really checked all your fire alarms? Did a household fire drill? In the dark, with the usual proportion (i.e., nearly all) of the non–night lights in the house off?

5. Falls, often cited as a top killer in the home, are mostly fatal for *older* adults, and represent a very small, although still significant, portion of the fatal accidents at this age.

Let's look at the Worry Clock.

The Worry Clock for Ages One to Four

Let's look at the Worry Clock for Children Ages One to Four. The largest category is drowning, worth thirteen minutes of your time. Drowning is followed by homicide, an additional eleven minutes. Motor vehicle accidents (child in the car) total only 17 percent of accidents, and add ten minutes. So more than half of your worry (thirty-four minutes), by the data, would be for drowning, homicide, and motor vehicle accidents.

The other half of the worry comprises pedestrian accidents and fire accidents, each adding seven minutes (about half the remaining worry). Choking (three minutes), suffocation (one), and poisonings (one) add another five minutes. Falls, a category that is probably high on most people's lists for causes of death for this age group, comes in again at just one minute (and includes far more than falling down stairs).

Reminder: The number of children who die is small. The entire Worry Clock for Ages One to Four is based on half of that tiny slice of the pie at the beginning of the chapter and is an average of about 2,150 children per year, which means each minute represents about thirty-six deaths.

As in all chapters, these data and recommendations do <u>not</u> tell you what will definitely happen or how to protect your child perfectly, but are here to help you think through the issues. Consult your health care professionals.

Worry Clock for Ages One to Four

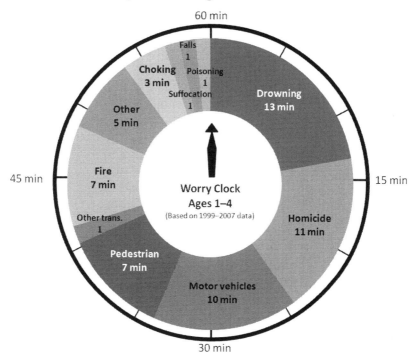

The following sections provide more detail on the causes within each of the major components of the Worry Clock and provide recommendations for what to do about them.

Drowning: 13 Minutes

Drowning caused the most deaths of children ages one to four. Swimming pools are the most likely place for drowning to occur. And if all US states were as warm as Florida and swimming pools were open all year, these deaths would be significantly higher. In California, Arizona, and Florida, drowning in pools is the leading cause of accidental death for toddlers.

Here is how the thirteen minutes break out:

Swimming pool	6 minutes
Natural water (streams, etc.)	2 minutes
Bathtub	1 minute
Other, unspecified	4 minutes

The image of a public pool swarming with children may be what comes to mind, but most drowning occur in residential (home) swimming pools, and most of the children who drowned were children who lived in that house (65 percent). Fewer than 2 percent of the pool accidents were a result of children trespassing on property where they didn't live or belong.[89]

Most of these children were last seen in the home, had been out of sight less than five minutes, and were in the care of one or both parents at the time.[90] More than two-thirds (69 percent) were not expected to be in or at the pool. Nearly half of the child victims were last seen in the house before the pool accident occurred.[91]

Nearly 80 percent of people of any age who die from drowning are male,[92] and for one- to four-year-olds, boys are almost twice as likely to drown in a pool.[93]

Drowning Point #1: Most drowning occurred in home swimming pools. Most of those who died lived in the house with the pool, were under parent supervision at the time, and were not near the pool when last seen.

Toddlers were next most likely to have trouble in natural water, such as rivers, oceans, and lakes. Boys were twice as likely as girls to drown in natural water.[94] It was challenging to find reliable data for these incidents. Some reported that the chance of drowning at a beach with trained lifeguards is less than one in eighteen million.[95] These incidents then may be occurring in rivers or unguarded areas. For example, there were just three deaths in Virginia last month (at the time of this writing) from people getting swept away from flooding. In one case, a twelve-year-old boy went into *his own backyard* to check out the swollen stream and was swept away by flood waters.

Less than one in ten deaths occurs in a bathtub. My readers are undoubtedly familiar with the dangers of leaving children in bathtubs, so I'm not going to spend time going into greater detail here.

The 30 percent "unspecified" is a collection of undocumented causes likely to fall into the above categories, and miscellaneous other incidents. Drowning in toilets leapt to mind as I remembered fighting the oh-so-wrongly-challenging potty blockers, but this accounts for a minuscule number (about four deaths a year), so low that the data probably aren't reliable.[96]

In one study, the Consumer Product Safety Commission reported that for product-related drowning, children younger than five (including infants) drowned in bathtubs (62 percent), baby seats or "bathinettes" (15 percent), buckets and pails (11 percent), landscaping or yard products (6 percent), and other products (4 percent). Interestingly, the CPSC also reported that children drowned in five-gallon buckets (think bright orange or white painters' buckets) three and a half times more often than in toilets. They concluded, "Of all buckets, the five-gallon size presents the greatest hazard to young children because of its tall, straight sides. That, combined with the stability of these buckets, makes it nearly impossible for top-heavy infants and toddlers to free themselves when they fall into the bucket headfirst."[97] The majority of drowning involved children younger than two years old. This shouldn't surprise you; the whole idea is that when children have a Sputnik-size head, their relatively tiny bodies cannot get it out of the water.

One of the repeated cautions to parents across websites is that they should *not* expect to hear a child drowning. Many sites point out that the drowning shown in movies is far from what actually happens; when someone is drowning, even an adult, they are *silent*. No arms flapping, no splashing, no screaming. The Coast Guard's guide "It Doesn't Look Like They're Drowning"[98] notes that when people, including toddlers, are drowning, they 1) are not able to call for help (the ability to talk shuts down until breathing is restored); 2) bob in and out of the water but don't stay out long enough to breathe; 3) cannot *voluntarily* control their arm movements, so they cannot wave for help, move toward a rescuer, or reach out for a piece of rescue equipment; 4) remain upright in the water, with no evidence of a supporting kick; and 5) unless rescued by a trained lifeguard, can only struggle on the surface of the water from twenty to sixty seconds before submersion occurs.

Drowning Point #2: Drowning is silent! You will not hear splashing or commotion! Victims cannot call for help and will not wave their arms or look like they are in trouble. The drowning response is silent and may be over within twenty seconds.

Parents might assume that there would be enough commotion to alert them or other bystanders, but this is probably not the case.

Story Box: Drowning, Ages One to Four

Multiple Swimming Pool Drowning Incidents in Massachusetts
In Attleboro, Massachusetts, July 4–7, 2011, three four-year-old children died falling into swimming pools in separate events. Two were visiting other families' homes, including a Fourth of July party.[99]

Missing Nephew Found in Nearby Lake
In Monroe Township, New Jersey, on August 2, 2011, a woman caring for her two-year-old nephew called police immediately upon noticing that the boy was missing. The toddler was found in a lake about one hundred yards from his home.[100]

Backyard Hot Tub Claims Toddler
In Fontana, California, on July 17, 2011, a father was getting ready for work while the mother got their two older children ready for school when they noticed their twenty-month-old daughter was missing. The father quickly found her in the back yard hot tub, but it was too late. The parents each thought the other had the child. "It only took fifteen minutes."[101]

Toddler Drowns in Plastic Tank after Mom Distracted
In Kailau-Kona, Hawaii, on February 22, 2013, a mother was with her eighteen-month-old son, who was playing outside. She reported that she looked away for a few seconds and he disappeared. After ten to fifteen minutes of searching, she found him unresponsive in a plastic tank filled with water. [102]

What to do about drowning? Some seemingly research-based advice that was shared that I found useful included:[103]

- *Secure home pools:* Ensure either a locked fence around any pool your child has access to or an alarm on the house door that leads to it.
- *Swim classes:* Participation in formal swimming lessons can reduce the risk of drowning by 88 percent among children ages one to four. Learning about the strategies related to various kinds of water may be helpful, too. For example, children near the beach should know that if they are caught in a rip current (a strong current that can pull the child away from shore), they should swim parallel or at an angle to the shore to break free from the current, rather than try to swim against it.
- *Touch supervision:* Adults should provide "touch supervision," meaning they are close enough to reach the child at all times. Adults should not be involved in any other distracting activity (such as reading, playing cards, talking on the phone, or mowing the lawn) while supervising children.
- *Look for the lifeguard:* Select swimming sites that have lifeguards whenever possible. Always swim with a buddy.
- *Avoid alcohol:* Alcohol is involved in many water and boating accidents (most on this later in the teen section). Avoid drinking

alcohol before or during swimming, boating, or water-skiing. Do not drink alcohol while supervising children.

- *Use US Coast Guard–approved life jackets when boating,* regardless of distance to be traveled, the size of the boat, or the swimming ability of the boaters.

I have a pool, and since I only have a three-sided fence (the house is the fourth side), I bought a door alarm for about twenty dollars. It worked great and chimed whenever someone went outside. When my friends come to visit with their son, whom they've nicknamed "Destructo," I change the alarm from "chime" to "siren" mode.

Remember that following these steps is no guarantee that your child will be protected, and these recommendations may not be right for your child. Talk to your health care provider about what is best.

Drowning Point #3: Think about swim lessons as soon as possible. Make sure the houses you visit have the pools locked up or alarmed (or bring your own alarm, which isn't that expensive or difficult). Use "touch" supervision, and don't drink alcohol while minding young children. Keep unsupervised children away from natural water, especially after a storm.

Homicide: 11 Minutes

After drowning, death by homicide (e.g., shaking child to death)[104] is the second leading cause of death for one- to four-year-olds, continuing a trend from the infant year (see the infant homicide section in Chapter 1 for a more detailed discussion).

As a reminder, these cases include deaths due to the momentary insanity of a caregiver who is unable to get a small child to stop crying. If you are a mother and think this doesn't apply to you, you are probably right. But you are not the only person who cares for your child, and whoever has contact with a young child should know how to deal with crying.

Based on the available data,[105] homicide by the child's own parents accounts for about seven of the eleven minutes on the clock. Acquaintances (such as sitters or their boyfriends) account for three minutes, and other family members and strangers account for less than one minute each. Of children under age five killed by someone other than their parent, 80 percent were killed by males.[106]

Homicide Point #1: The majority of children less than two years old who die in homicides are killed by a parent. Of those killed by someone else, 80% were killed by males.[107]

The means of the homicide are a laundry list of the horrible, from intentional poisoning to drowning. Intentional use of a firearm accounted for about 11 percent (not including children who died by accidental firearm discharge).

For most of the homicide category, the lessons are an extension of those from the infant chapter. The parental homicide numbers are highest for infants—50 percent higher than for one-year-olds and three times those for two-year-olds. Three- and four-year-olds have the lowest rate of homicide during any time in childhood.

The main avenues for prevention are extensions of those presented in the infant chapter: teaching parents and caretakers what to do when a baby or young child cries or seems inconsolable.

Story Box: Homicide, Ages One to Four

Mother Charged in Murder of Child; No Previous Abuse
In Affton, Missouri, on November 16, 2011, a mother repeatedly struck her toddler because he would not stop crying. There was no evidence of previous abuse. The mother was charged with murder.[108]

Potential Baby-Sitter Homicide
In Philadelphia, on December 31, 2011, a baby-sitter called 911 after a two-year-old child became nonresponsive. The sitter told authorities that she tried to revive the child after he swallowed a bottle cap, but this explanation was reportedly inconsistent with his injuries. The child died from head and brain injuries.[109]

Motor Vehicle Accidents: 10 Minutes

Ten minutes of the Worry Clock hour go to motor vehicle accidents. This includes incidents in which a vehicle (car, minivan, or light truck) hits another vehicle or an object like a tree, falls into a ditch, or is struck by another object. Accidents in which children who are walking (i.e., pedestrians) are struck by a vehicle, including in their own driveways, are discussed next in the pedestrian section.[110]

I make a distinction here between traffic and nontraffic motor vehicle accidents. Traffic accidents are just what they sound like: accidents that happen in traffic, such as head-on collisions between cars. Nontraffic accidents are those incidents that involve cars but not in traffic, such as children dying from hyperthermia after being left in cars.

By far, the biggest danger is traffic accidents. Based on my data set,[111] you should spend nine minutes and fifty-eight seconds of worry on traffic accidents and only two seconds on nontraffic accidents. That is likely an underestimate of the nontraffic accidents, in part because I am separating out pedestrian accidents, many of which are classified as traffic accidents in the government data because they happen on city sidewalks, for example, but it is consistent with the US Department of Transportation summarization that "traffic fatalities accounted for nearly 95 percent of transportation-related fatalities."[112] Striking a balanced estimate, we'll give nine of the ten minutes to traffic accidents.

Traffic accidents: 9 minutes
Nontraffic accidents: 1 minute

We'll look at traffic first, but the lesson here is simple, and all my readers know it: *buckle up*.

Traffic Accidents: 9 Minutes

To get more detail on the types of traffic accidents, I turned to the US Department of Transportation's Fatality Analysis Reporting System (FARS). In 2010, there were 1,298 crashes involving children ages one to four, resulting in 338 fatalities. Many types of accidents contributed.

Based on the 2010 deaths for ages one to four, the breakout of the nine minutes to traffic accidents is:

Collision with another motor vehicle: 4 minutes *40 seconds*
Hit tree, ditch, guardrail, etc.:   3 minutes
Rollover: 1 minute
Falling/jumping out of car: *15 seconds*
Hitting an animal: *5 seconds*

Studies looking at all fatalities, not just incidents involving the deaths of one- to four-year-olds, have found fairly similar results, but reverse the top two categories, putting run-off-the-road crashes at the top of the list and collisions next.[113] Single-vehicle drunk-driving incidents could explain this difference.

Of these children who died, only about 18 percent were using a front-facing car seat correctly (22 percent were using the front-facing seat, but 4 percent were noted by police as using those seats incorrectly).[114] So **82 percent were not restrained properly**. In fact, about half of these children were wearing no restraint at all—no seat belt, no nothing. Neither taxis nor buses had any fatalities linked to them in this year, so the lack of restraints was not due to these forms of transportation.

The government estimates that 82 percent of us regularly wear seat belts.[115] Assuming the same percentage holds for ages one to four,[116] then those who were not wearing seat belts are significantly overrepresented in the fatal accidents. Usually only 18 percent are unbelted, but unrestrained children accounted for 50 percent of the fatalities. Sure, the driver may have some characteristic that makes them more likely to get into accidents as well as to have their children unbuckled, but they were not, for example, more likely to be under the influence of drugs or alcohol, at least in this sample.

In fact, the government goes so far as to estimate that seat belts saved 13,250 lives in just one year,[117] and that child safety seats reduce deaths by 71 percent for infants and 54 percent for toddlers (children one to four years old).[118] The Insurance Institute for Highway Safety (IIHS) summarized, "By far the biggest problem contributing to child injury and death in motor vehicle crashes is nonuse of restraints."

Part of the reason *any* restraint is good is because getting ejected from the car is so bad. Ejection from a vehicle accounts for one-fifth to one-third of these fatalities.[119]

A small number of children (accounting for fifteen seconds on the Worry Clock) also fell or jumped out of cars. See the story box for examples. I include this statistic because it highlights the restraint issue with an important note: if the car is in motion, restraints count. Some of these children fall out of the vehicle in the driveway, when the driver may be expecting the children to be in the process of getting seat belts on. Children mess around before belts are on, a door opens, and someone falls out, all too quickly for the driver to stop.

> **Motor Vehicle Point #1:** Children without seat belts or other restraints are disproportionately represented in those killed in car accidents. And the seat belts need to be on before the car starts moving.

I found three no-no's consistently cited by those reviewing the fatality data: alcohol, speeding, and distraction.

It's no great surprise that drinking alcohol is also a major factor in about one-third of all traffic deaths.[120] While the rates in my sample were low, the government estimates that of traffic deaths among children up to age fourteen in 2009, 14 percent involved an alcohol-impaired driver—and about half of the alcohol-impaired drivers were in the car with the child![121] There is a much higher proportion of alcohol-related deaths at night (duh), which may, in part, explain this finding. The youngest children are at home in bed, but as children get older, they may be out later with Mom and Dad at a neighborhood party.

Speeding is estimated to be a factor in about one-third of fatal crashes for all ages.[122] I know some of you are thinking about the study that showed it was differential speed—being significantly faster or slower than other cars in the vicinity—that was problematic, not high speed per se. Not so, says the IIHS: "Although research conducted in the 1950s on two-lane rural roads indicated that vehicles traveling much faster or much slower than average were more likely to be involved in crashes, severe crash involvement increased with speed. The risk of death and severe injury is a direct exponential function of speed, not speed differences.[123]

Coming in at an estimated 16 percent of fatal crashes is distracted driving, the number-three cause of accidents.[124] The AAA Foundation reports that using a cell phone while driving almost quadruples the risk of crashing. As we all now know, hands-free phones are not any better. In Washington, DC where I live, I'm often able to see directly into cars around me, and I see no less than half of drivers engaged with their cell phones. But here's something I did not consider that AAA also reported: passengers are one of the most frequently reported causes of distraction, with young children being four times more distracting than adults and infants being eight times more distracting. And although I suspect my readers are in a certain elite (in education of dangers) class, I do not think that we can all claim to belong to one of the less than 3 percent of those who are able to successfully multitask behind the wheel.[125]

I did not see anything else that leapt out as trends in my analysis. Regular cars (two- and four-door sedans, for example) accounted for about 56 percent of the accidents, sport-utility vehicles were another 25 percent, and light trucks accounted for most of the remaining quarter. This is very close to the percentages of registered vehicles (55 percent cars and 45 percent SUVs and light trucks). So the type of car does not seem to make much difference, unlike with many of the pedestrian accidents presented later.

Motor Vehicle Point #2: You don't drink, you follow the speed limit…now try not to look at your children, and keep your eyes on the road. In the car, young children are reportedly four to eight times more distracting than adults.

The Centers for Disease Control considers motor vehicle injuries and deaths "a winnable battle," and they are targeting four key areas:

> Improving child passenger safety
> Improving teen driver safety
> Reducing alcohol-impaired driving
> Increasing safety belt use

Child passenger safety means putting every child in an age-appropriate seat. Safety belt use cuts across all our age groups. Teen driving related to alcohol impairment features prominently in the teen chapter. So, in case this is not yet clear, if you do *nothing else*, make sure to:

Buckle up from start-up. Before you start the car, have everyone including you[126] put on seat belts. Get children used to the rule that the car doesn't move until everyone is belted. Similarly, no one unbelts until the car is off—when the driver removes her seat belt, that's the sign that the child can unbuckle. If you are driving in a state with low seat belt usage, start a new trend. (In some states seat belt use exceeds 90 percent, while in others more than 30 percent of drivers fail to buckle up.[127]) You are reading this book, so you have it in you. If anyone says anything, show them the data (or give them a copy of this book!).

Some other recommendations from government sources and the AAA Foundation [128] include:

Stow electronic devices. AAA recommends, "Turn off your phone before you drive so you won't be tempted to use it while on the road. Pull over to a safe place to talk on the phone or to send and receive text messages or emails."[129] Of course, only do this if you are confident that you will not then try to reach for these devices while you are driving. I roared through comedienne Elayne Boosler's routine in which (at least in my memory) she described a chocolate craving that led her to the store in the middle of the night. Having put the cookies in the back seat, she concluded that her ride back home was worse than driving drunk, because "the difference between drunk drivers and people who eat and drive is that drunk drivers are actually trying to drive!" If you're addicted, put the electronics somewhere you cannot reach them.

Prepare children and pets for the trip. "Get the children safely buckled in and situated with snacks and entertainment before you start driving," says AAA. "If they need additional attention during the trip, pull off the road safely to care for them. Similarly, prepare and secure pets appropriately in your vehicle before getting underway."[130] I'll add that if having the children watch a movie keeps the driver's eyes on the road, then let go of the guilt over putting them in front of a screen. The driver is the important one for the car ride, period. Finally, know that air bags are meant to work *with* seat belts, not instead of them.

Practice zero tolerance for seat belt removal while car is in on. If children take seat belts off, pull over and stop the car until they are rebelted. If a child takes off his belt before the driver turns off the car and takes her own seat belt off, make that child get out last, or implement some other consequence that will have the opposite effect of getting the child out of the car sooner.

Nontraffic Accidents: 1 Minute

Nontraffic accidents that happen in cars include hyperthermia, power window accidents, vehicle roll-aways, seat belt entanglements, and trunk entrapments. Back-overs and front-overs, when a driver accidentally drives over a child in a front or back blind spot, are often grouped with these accidents, but I cover these in the next section on pedestrians. I wanted to focus this section on what happens when children are *in cars* and the pedestrian section on when they are *outside but around cars.*

Remember, nontraffic motor vehicle accidents only account for one minute on our Worry Clock, so compared to everything that we have discussed so far, these accidents are far less prevalent. However, they differ from car accidents in a big way: they seem much more controllable. There is no one outside the family coming in to wreak havoc; these are just terrible, meaningless accidents that happen at home.

Hyperthermia (heatstroke) is much more common than the other accidents here[131] and is worth forty-five seconds on the Worry Clock out of the sixty seconds for nontraffic accidents. Hyperthermia happens when a child is accidentally left in the car, left in the car while someone runs an errand, or gets into the car by herself and cannot get out.

The problem is that cars heat up really fast, even on mild days, and children are way more sensitive to the temperature than adults. The younger they are, the more sensitive they are. The National Highway Traffic Safety Administration (NHTSA) points out that: [132]

- *Vehicles heat up quickly,* even with a window rolled down two inches. If the outside temperature is in the low eighties, the temperature inside a vehicle can reach deadly levels in only ten minutes.
- *Children's bodies overheat easily,* and infants and children under four years of age are among those at greatest risk for heat-related illness.
- *Children's bodies absorb more heat on a hot day than an adult's.* Also, children are less able to lower their body heat by sweating. When a body cannot sweat enough, the body temperature rises rapidly.
- *A young child's body temperature may increase three to five times as fast as an adult's.*

The NHTSA notes that even a quick stop at the store may be enough. "You leave your child unattended, thinking, 'I'll just run into the store for a minute,' which is illegal in many states," says the NHTSA. "It is in the sixties outside, so [you think] the children should be fine. In the first ten minutes, the temperature inside the car has gone up twenty degrees, and rises to a deadly 110 degrees Fahrenheit long before the parent returns."[133]

KidsandCars.org, an organization with a lot of good information on its website about all the above issues, says that the majority of cases of vehicular heatstroke death are similar: they involve a loving, busy parent who is rushing off to work, happens to have a change in routine, and forgets that the child is in the car. Even on a relatively mild day, the temperature in a vehicle can prove deadly (see story box example).[134]

This increasing problem may stem in part from parents not seeing Junior in the back seat. With rear-facing seats, there is nothing to remind the parent that the child is still there. In fact, heatstroke deaths have increased tenfold since car seats were moved to the backseat.[135] With recommendations for rear-facing seats extending to two years old, heatstroke deaths are likely to increase further.

Horrified? Think it could never happen to you? Read the 2010 Pulitzer Prize–winning *Washington Post* piece by Gene Weingarten, "Fatal Distraction: Forgetting a Child in the Backseat of a Car Is a Horrifying Mistake. Is It a Crime?" (March 8, 2009; see http://www.washingtonpost.com/wp-dyn/content/article/2009/02/27/AR2009022701549.html). Weingarten covers many stories of accomplished moms and highly organized and thoughtful dads doing the unthinkable. The parents manage everything beautifully, and then one day there is a change in the routine, and their brain says that they dropped off the baby when they did not—until that horrible moment when they realize what happened. Read just the first page, if you can. Even after writing this book, I still have not been able to read the full article.

Children playing in cars is a no-no, too. KidsandCars.org says that 30 percent of child vehicular heatstroke deaths involve children who have been playing in or around cars or trucks and either become trapped in the trunk or get disoriented enough that they are unable to use the lock system or door releases to open the doors.[136]

All the rest of the in-car, nontraffic accidents combined compose the remaining fifteen seconds on the Worry Clock. I will go through these quickly.

Worth fifteen seconds *combined* are these accidents, roughly in order of frequency based on the very limited data available:

Falling object: Something such as a tree, rock, tire, or cargo from another vehicle hits the car and kills a child inside.

Power window accident: Aka "vehicle window asphyxia," when children's necks are caught in power windows or sunroofs or in regular, stationary windows. Children may step on the armrests and accidentally close the windows, get their heads stuck in a gap of a fixed window,[137] or play with the sunroof, closing it on another child. Many of these are probably preventable by using the window lock function found in virtually all power window–equipped cars and/or simply having a rule that the children are not allowed to roll down or play with the windows.

Trunk entrapment: Children playing (e.g., hide-and-seek) get trapped or overheat in the trunk. Remember, overheating can happen in *just ten minutes.*

Roll-away car: A car is left with keys in the ignition and gets shifted into gear. The car starts rolling and hits a child.

Seat-belt entanglement: A child within reach of a seat belt may become entangled if he or she pulls the belt all the way out and wraps it around his or her head, neck, or waist.

Drowning: This occurs when the driver thinks the vehicle can handle crossing a road flooded by the local stream, but then the vehicle stalls, the water level rises, and the vehicle is swept away before help comes. The driver and child drown in the vehicle.

Hypothermia: A child is trapped in the vehicle (e.g., locked in the trunk) and freezes to death.

Safe Kids USA[138] says that these accidents happen in three ways:

1. Children are left in vehicles unknowingly when the driver becomes distracted at the destination and forgets the child in the vehicle.

2. The driver knowingly leaves the child in the vehicle while they run an errand.

3. The driver leaves a vehicle unlocked or the key fob in reach and an unattended child or children gain access to the car.

Thus, many of the recommendations in this section focus on limiting these factors. The below recommendations for avoiding these accidents come from the NHTSA and KidsandCars.org, and, again, are no guarantee of safety.

- Teach children not to play in or around cars. Teach them that vehicle trunks are for cargo, not for playing. Teach them that seat belts are not toys.
- Lock your car doors and trunk, and be sure keys and remote-entry devices are out of sight and reach of your children.
- Never leave children alone in or around cars, not even for a minute— even if the air conditioning is on or a window is cracked.
- Engage your emergency brake every time you park.
- Keep the rear fold-down seats closed/locked to keep your children from climbing into the trunk from inside your car.
- Check the trunk right away if your child is missing (OK, right after you check a pool).
- Always ensure children are properly restrained, even when you get out for gas (and pay at the pump).
- Buckle unused seat belts. Pull the seat belt out all the way to the end without yanking. Then feed the excess webbing back into the retractor. (Do this before car seat installation and as directed.)
- Keep a visual cue in the car seat when the seat is empty, but place the cue up front when your child is riding with you. For example, you

might put a small teddy bear in the car seat and then move it to the front when you put your child in the car.

- Make it routine to put your handbag, wallet, cell phone, or laptop on the floor of the *back seat*.
- Make it a habit to look in the back seat by opening the back door of your vehicle before locking the car and walking away.
- Arrange to have your daycare provider call you if your child has not been dropped off within thirty minutes of your usual routine.
- If you normally bring your child to daycare, and your partner or someone else happens to take the child instead, make a (prearranged) call to that person to verify that the child arrived safely.
- If you see a child alone inside a vehicle, call 911 immediately! Do not wait. A few minutes can be the difference between life and death inside a vehicle.
- Be especially careful about keeping children safe in and around cars during busy times, schedule changes, and periods of crisis or holidays.
- Use drive-thru services when available at restaurants, banks, pharmacies, drycleaners, etc. (i.e., don't leave children in cars).
- Retrofit your car:
  - Trunk release: As of September 1, 2001, auto manufacturers were required to equip all new vehicle trunks with a glow-in-the-dark trunk release inside the trunk compartment. Show your children how to use the release in case of an emergency. If your car is older and does not have the trunk release, ask your automobile dealership about getting your vehicle retrofitted with a trunk-release mechanism.
  - Brake Transmission Safety Interlock (BTSI): This safety technology is intended to prevent vehicles from accidentally being put into gear. All new vehicles with automatic transmission with a "park" position must have BTSI.
  - See about getting "pull to close" switches on windows, also required in new cars, that prevent windows from being triggered by a child's foot.
  - Get a sensor to remind you that child is in the back seat.

"Our cars tell us if the key is left in the ignition, if gas is getting low, or if the headlights are on; somehow we've decided it's more important to not have a dead car battery than a dead baby," says Janette Fennell, president and founder of KidsandCars.org. Technological solutions are coming, but you can get some now. To check your vehicles safety ratings or get more information on car safety from the government, go to the vehicle rating pages on www.safercar.gov.

> **Motor Vehicle Point #3:** Hyperthermia, or heatstroke, is the biggest nontraffic danger and can happen in as little as ten minutes even on a relatively mild day with windows cracked. Build in strategies like the front-seat teddy bear or a briefcase in the back seat, or retrofit the car with a back-seat sensor.

Story Box: Motor Vehicle Accidents, Ages One to Four

Collision on Ramp to Beltway
In Baltimore, Maryland, on December 28, 2011, a five-year-old boy died after an accident on I-83 at the ramp to the Beltway. A Jeep Cherokee failed to slow and hit the boy's car. The mother and father were in stable condition; the Jeep driver walked away. Speed was believed to be a factor in the crash.[139]

Car Spins and Jumps Curb; Child Ejected
In Oak Lawn, Texas, on March 23, 2011, a three-year-old toddler died when he and his mother were ejected from their car after their vehicle hit another car, spun, and the jumped a curb. The child was not properly secured in a child seat.[140]

Toddler, Playing Outside, Gets into Car, Dies from Hyperthermia
In Northern Virginia, on June 17, 2011, a two-year-old boy died after being found unresponsive in the family minivan. The mother's screams attracted the attention of a neighbor. "She loved that boy. It's horrible," said the neighbor. The cause of death might have been heat related on the partly cloudy, low-eighties day. [141]

Pedestrian Accidents: 7 Minutes

Pedestrian accidents, worth seven minutes on the Worry Clock, are a big concern during toddler years. Like motor vehicle accidents, there are traffic accidents (e.g., child crossing a busy street) and nontraffic accidents (child hit in a private driveway), but traffic accidents account for only just over half here. Pedestrian danger is a theme throughout this book. Moving cars pose almost twice the danger to nearby children as all that food you spent hours chopping up into tiny little pieces.

Pedestrians in Traffic: 4 Minutes

Four minutes on the Worry Clock are for traffic accidents, such as crossing streets. Most of these children (94 percent) were on foot rather than on, for example, a tricycle. The children were disproportionately two-year-olds and boys.

Three-quarters of the accidents took place on streets away from intersections. The causes varied, but here are the top types of accidents and their respective allocations on the Worry Clock for Ages One to Four according to my (limited) analysis of the 2010 fatality data:[142]

Child dashes or darts out into road	1.5 minutes
Child not yielding (walking when he shouldn't)	1 minute
Child playing in the street	*35 seconds*
Cars backing over child in traffic	*20 seconds*
Other and unknown causes	1 minute

Children darting or dashing out into roads was the most common incident. One could argue that a child not yielding, worth another minute, is basically the same thing. Children who were playing in the street prior to being hit accounted for another half of a minute.

Cars backing up into children added twenty seconds, and driver failure to yield to the child pedestrian added five more (not shown). Frankly, I was expecting these numbers to be higher. Things like drivers hitting children getting in and out of cars did not even register one fatality for this age group in 2010.

The other causes varied widely. For example, ice cream trucks (yes, the government has a code specific to ice cream trucks) accounted for the same (albeit very small) number of deaths, worth six seconds.

Many incidents that the government tracks showed no occurrences in 2010. This may be a fluke, or it may suggest that these incidents are in fact rare. Crossing expressways, something I have witnessed with jaw dropped, showed no incidents in 2010.

Pedestrian Point #1: Children (unpredictably) darting or dashing out into the road accounted for the majority of traffic incidents.

Pedestrians in Nontraffic Accidents: 4 Minutes

The other four minutes on the Worry Clock for pedestrians is for the nontraffic incidents. These are primarily "back-overs" and "front-overs," where drivers accidentally drive over a child positioned in a front or back blind spot. Here's what might happen. Dad is running out for an errand, walks around his SUV, jumps in, looks down to plug in his cell charger, and doesn't realize in that time that his toddler has run out to pick up a ball behind the car. The child sees the car moving but just stares at it. Although the child is standing now, the blind zone is higher than the child's head. Dad checks his mirrors, looks behind him, sees nothing, and backs up on his way to the store. See the story box if you want to (can stand to) read some other examples.

Here is a summary of the data:

- One-year-olds were at greatest risk (55 percent of the fatalities), but ages two (25 percent), three (10 percent), and four (10 percent) were still at risk.[143]
- Girls and boys were equally likely to be victims.[144]
- Most of the accidents (70 percent) happened in driveways or residential lots, while the rest (30 percent) happened in commercial (e.g., shopping center) parking lots.[145]
- At least 70 percent of the children were struck by a driver related to them, often a parent.
- Men were more likely (67 percent) to be the drivers[146] (perhaps more likely to drive bigger cars).

Shocking as it may be (not), larger cars, which have larger blind zones, are significantly overrepresented in fatalities, accounting for over 60 percent, about double the percentage one would expect.[147]

All vehicles have blind spots, now called blind zones to more accurately reflect their magnitude. We are used to thinking about the corner blind spots when changing lanes, but we do not seem to talk as much about the blind zones in the front and back of the vehicle. Every car has them. Consumer Reports measured the back blind zones[148] by testing how far behind the vehicle a twenty-eight-inch traffic cone had to be before a person in the driver's seat could see its top through the rear window.

Height of the driver makes a big difference. For the ten types of vehicles they measured, Consumer Reports found that, on average, a five-foot-eight driver has about a fifteen-foot blind zone behind the car. A five-foot-one person averages a whopping twenty-five feet.

Consumer Reports found that the type of car made a big difference, too. Average blind zones for wagons (fifteen feet), midsize sedans (twenty-two), midsize SUVs (twenty-eight), minivans (twenty-six), and pickups (thirty-five) varied more than twenty feet (the numbers in parentheses are the blind zones for a five-foot-one driver). If you look at the specific make and model of vehicles, the numbers are all over the place. The award for the worst blind zone goes to the 2007 Chevy Avalanche, which measured fifty feet, about the size of a school bus. Add an incline and all those numbers get bigger.[149]

To see how Consumer Reports did these tests and to look up your car, go to http://www.consumerreports.org/cro/cars/car-safety/car-safety-reviews/mind-that-blind-spot-1005/overview/index.htm.

KidsandCars.org cites the "bye-bye syndrome" when children who don't want to be separated from a parent "impulsively follow them out and put themselves in a dangerous position near the vehicle where they can't be seen."[150]

> **Pedestrian Point #2:** Children (unpredictably) darting or dashing out into the road accounted for the majority of traffic incidents.

Story Box: Pedestrian Accidents, Ages One to Four

Child Killed after Darting into Street; Horrified Driver Gave CPR
On September 13, 2011, in Westfield, Indiana, as the family was outside talking, two-year-old Alex Ekstedt darted into the street and was hit by a truck that had no time to swerve. The distraught driver got out of his car and tried to perform CPR, but the child was dead. The family is building a fence around the yard to protect the other children and has posted a sign, "Children Dart, Drive Smart," a slogan that was part of a discontinued safe-driving campaign.[151]

Teen Kills Toddler in Accidental Back-Over
On March 22, 2011, in Kent, Washington, a fourteen-month-old snuck out of his house, wandered to a neighbor's house, and was struck when the eighteen-year-old living next store backed out in her car and didn't see him. It was said to be "a true accident."[152]

Father Backs Over Child
This story is about Cameron Gulbransen, the child for whom the legislation to require backup cameras on vehicles is named, and is told by his father:

"October 19, 2002 at 9:30pm Leslie and I had returned from dinner with friends. Cameron and Scott were put to bed earlier but upon returning Cameron heard our voices and called out for us. While Leslie went to pay the babysitter, I could not resist the temptation to go and get the little guy. When I peeked into this room there he was sitting up with a great big smile. I quickly took him out of his crib and brought him downstairs to be with Leslie and myself. After a short while I announced I needed to move the SUV into the driveway for the evening..."

Recommendations to keep pedestrian children safe come from
KidsandCars.org and government sources and include:

- Distinguish the driveway as a place for cars, not children. No children
  should be permitted in the driveway unless allowed by an adult. Keep
  toys out of the driveway. If you need the driveway for a play area,
  have a way to designate when the area is safe for play, such as a cone
  behind the car.
- Fence off play areas from the driveway or other roadways.
- Walk around and behind a vehicle prior to moving it.
- Teach children that drivers cannot see behind cars, so children need
  to stay away from cars.
- Measure the size of the blind zone behind the vehicles you drive. A
  five-foot-one-inch driver in a pickup truck can have a rear blind spot
  of fifty feet. Keep in mind that inclines increase the zone.
- Retrofit the car. Consider installing cross-view mirrors, audible
  collision detectors, a rear-view video camera, and/or some type of
  backup detection device.
- Make sure you have good visibility of sidewalk traffic that may cross
  the driveway. Trim shrubs, put in mirrors, or try other strategies to
  get good visibility of sidewalks.

I read once that the big problem with smart children is that parents
overestimate the child's abilities. As brilliant as your child is, do not
assume that he or she will always be rational and won't just dart into the
street if there is a clear path. Those brief lapses in perfect judgment
happen and may have horrible consequences. Hold hands tightly, take a
longer route farther from traffic, or maybe put even a decorative fence to
slow kids down.

Other Transportation Accidents: 1 Minute

This is a special message for all-terrain-vehicle lovers; others can skip this
section and just know that bicycle riding didn't make the list.

ATV lovers: really, letting your four-year-old *drive* the ATV? Children are
listed as dying from riding and driving them. We'll see that number go up

as children get older. Call me crazy (and I know some of you will!), but my guess is that many, many more children probably ride bicycles than ATVs, which means that ATVs are especially dangerous for children! Perhaps it is also because fewer children wear helmets? Plus, since the death rate only increases, consider getting children into helmet-wearing habits when young.

Know also that small bumps on an ATV can have big consequences. I read one story about a child who died when he and his father were done with their ride and simply pulling the ATV back into the garage. The little hump entry into the garage was enough to shoot the child off.

Heads up to West Virginians: you have two times the rate of fatalities compared to any other state, factoring in population. Next in line are North Dakota, Alaska, Wyoming, Kentucky, Idaho, Montana, Vermont, Mississippi, and South Dakota.

ATVs are dangerous enough that the federal government even has a special site discussing ATV accidents, recognizing how deadly these vehicles can be if not used properly: www.atvsafety.gov.

Fire: 7 Minutes

Almost every incident here in this category took place in a house or building. Although the relative risk of children under age fifteen dying in a fire is lower than for the general population, half (52 percent) of all child fire deaths occurred in those four and younger.[153] Here's the breakout of causes in cases of child fatalities:[154]

Incendiary/Suspicious (yes, arson)	2 minutes
Open-flame fires (candles mostly)	2 minutes
Heating fires and other heat sources	2 minutes
Smoking	*30 seconds*
Children playing with fire	*20 seconds*
Electrical	*10 seconds*

Arson, open flames, and heat-related fires are the most common. Arson includes fires set by teenagers living in the home (see Chapter 5).

Open-flame fires are primarily due to candles in the home. December is the peak month for candle fires; Christmas is the peak day. The top five days for home candle fires are Christmas, Christmas Eve, New Year's Day, Halloween, and December 23. Over half (55 percent) of home candle fires start because the candle is or comes too close to some combustible material (e.g., curtains, Christmas tree, mattress). Bedrooms are likely candidates for sources (38 percent), and half of all household-candle fire deaths occur between midnight and six a.m.[155]

Electrical fires are due mostly to distribution or lighting equipment (41 percent), followed by ranges, washer/dryers (but usually dryers that people didn't clean), and fans.[156]

Although children playing with fire is low in this data set, other sources reported significantly higher incidence. However, I was unable to find a linked citation, which is why I do not report those data (see http://www.usfa.fema.gov/citizens/parents/curious.shtm). Many of those sites cited children's bedrooms as being the main place children started fires.

Notice also that cooking fires are not listed. Although kitchen fires are common and the most likely to produce injury, they do not (at least based on these available data) account for the fatal fires.[157]

It should be noted that fire alarms are reportedly frequently absent or not working. In fact, from 2006 to 2008, smoke alarms were reported as not present in 23 percent of residential fatal fires, and in another 40 percent of these fires, firefighters were unable to determine if a smoke alarm was present. Consider that, nationally, only 3 percent of homes do not have a smoke alarm installed.[158]

One-third of American households who made an estimate thought they would have at least six minutes before a fire in their home would become life threatening. The time available is often less. And only 8 percent said their first thought on hearing a smoke alarm would be to get out![159] This summary from FEMA may bring that idea a bit closer to home:

> **Fire is FAST!** There is little time! In less than thirty seconds, a small flame can get completely out of control and turn into a major fire. It only takes minutes for thick black smoke to fill a house or for it to be engulfed in flames. Most deadly fires occur in the home when people are asleep. If you wake up to a fire, you won't have time to grab valuables because fire spreads too quickly and the smoke is too thick. There is only time to escape.
>
> **Fire is HOT!** Heat is more threatening than flames. A fire's heat alone can kill. Room temperatures in a fire can be one hundred degrees at floor level and rise to six hundred degrees at eye level. Inhaling this super-hot air will scorch your lungs. This heat can

melt clothes to your skin. In five minutes, a room can get so hot that everything in it ignites at once. This is called flashover.

Fire is DARK! Fire isn't bright, it's pitch black. Fire starts bright, but quickly produces black smoke and complete darkness. If you wake up to a fire you may be blinded, disoriented, and unable to find your way around the home you've lived in for years.

Fire is DEADLY! Smoke and toxic gases kill more people than flames do. Fire uses up the oxygen you need and produces smoke and poisonous gases that kill. Breathing even small amounts of smoke and toxic gases can make you drowsy, disoriented, and short of breath.[160]

This is why younger children are likely at greater risk; the situation is very disorienting, and younger children especially may not fully understand the situation, how to exit the building, or the importance of doing so as quickly as possible. One of the stories I read from 2011 was how the whole family got out of a house on fire except the toddler boy. He had an escape route, and everyone just wondered why he didn't come out.

Story Box: Fire, Ages One to Four

Fireplace Embers Moved by Visitors Cause Fire
In Stamford, Connecticut, on December 25, 2011, three children and grandparents died in a fire as their mother, an accomplished ad executive, screamed for help. The grandfather, retired from work that included overseeing building safety and now enjoying his retirement by playing Santa at Saks, was trying to help the children escape when they perished. The cause of the fire was determined to be fireplace embers that were placed as trash just outside or perhaps inside the house. Fire alarms may not have been working.[161]

Children Playing with Space Heater Caused Fire
In Memphis, Tennessee, on January 30, 2011, a fire was started when children were playing with paper and a space heater. The mother was able to save four of her children; the fifth, her toddler daughter, perished in the house.[162]

Of course, the major recommendation here is to make sure that you have working **photoelectric and ionization** detectors. Consumer Reports summarized their findings: "Smoke alarms that use ionization technology were great at detecting a fast, flaming fire such as burning paper, but poor at detecting a smoldering fire, as in a couch or mattress. The opposite was true of photoelectric smoke alarms."[163] These two technologies detect very different fires, and the smoldering fire (photoelectric) is apparently the more common type. I learned this recently when I went on Amazon.com to purchase new detectors and found a review that made my eyes pop,[164] explaining how we should all be immediately using photoelectric sensors. Everything I have read since suggests that both detectors are needed, since they capture different types of dangers. Consumer Reports provides a thorough buying guide and recommendations on placement. Some new detectors even allow for recordings of Mom or Dad's voice to help guide children.

Having working detectors also means having ones that don't have the batteries ripped out because they kept going off while you were basting the turkey (I've been there!). I read one person's solution was to put the photoelectric detector closest to the kitchen and the ionization detector farther down the hall.

The next most important recommendation, particularly for one- to four-year-olds, is to have a fire emergency plan that you practice as a family. Since a year is a lifetime to some of these children, practicing the plan once a year may be too little. Practice two ways out of every room. If you are above the ground floor and need a ladder, get one and practice using that, too. Remember that the ladder needs to be in a place where you can find it easily in the dark.

The recommendations here are mostly those you have heard before: don't overload extension cords, keep everything at least three feet from heaters, store fireplaces ashes in a sealed metal container outside and away from the house, and keep matches/lighters away from children. But here are some that seemed to say something beyond what I've heard before:[165]

- Buy electrical products (including heaters) evaluated by a nationally recognized laboratory, such as Underwriters Laboratories.

- Immediately shut off, then professionally replace, light switches that are hot to the touch and lights that flicker.

- Check to make sure the portable heater has a thermostat control mechanism, and will switch off automatically if the heater falls over.

- For fireplaces, clean chimneys annually and use a fireplace screen heavy enough to stop rolling logs and big enough to cover the entire opening of the fireplace to catch flying sparks. Don't burn paper, trash, or green wood.

- Teach children that fire is not a toy and not to pick up matches or lighters they may find. Instead, they should tell an adult immediately.

- Replace mattresses made before the 2007 Federal Mattress Flammability Standard. Mattresses made since then are required by law to be safer.

- Don't use candles for light; use free-standing flashlights or battery-powered lanterns. Keep extra batteries on hand.

Choking: 3 Minutes

Choking occurs when the airway is blocked by food or other objects, such as small toys. What causes choking? Within the food culprits, it seems that hot dogs are likely number one. One study looked at ten years of injury data from twenty-six hospitals in the US and Canada in the 1990s and found that hot dogs led in choking fatalities (1.6 deaths per year), followed by candy (1.0), grapes (0.8), meat (0.7), peanuts (0.7), carrots (0.6), cookies (0.6), apples (0.5), popcorn (0.5), and bread (0.4). Peanuts were reported to cause the most injury, but hot dogs were more likely to be fatal. [166]

Of course, these are all foods that children tend to eat more often, and I didn't find a way to account for the ratio of choking incidents to consuming incidents.

Although coins are frequent causes of emergency room visits, studies have long pointed to latex balloons as standing out and causing about 30 percent of nonfood choking deaths. Balloons are also a danger as children get older, not just for younger children, who put things in their mouths indiscriminately. I admit that I had a very hard time finding examples of stories in the media from recent years or finding examples in the data sets of balloon deaths, although I did find a Mylar balloon death. It sounds like it may be time for another study.

I also did a very quick analysis using the National Electronic Injury Surveillance System of the Consumer Product Safety Commission and ran the data for two separate years. While I didn't find any deaths in the samples, which is indicative of the rarity of these events, I did find what I suspect is an emerging trend that deserves attention: ingestion of batteries, including children putting "button" batteries—those cute little batteries from greeting cards, remote controls, garage door openers, and, yes, children's books—in their mouths and more often up their noses (and from there into their systems).

In May of last year, the *New York Times* covered a story about thirteen-month-old Aidan Truett of Hamilton, Ohio, who developed what seemed like an upper respiratory infection. After nine days of Aidan's getting worse, the doctors took an X-ray to check for pneumonia and instead found that the child had ingested a button battery. "The battery was surgically removed the next day, and Aidan was sent home," they reported. "But what neither the doctors nor his parents realized was that the damage had been done. The battery's current had set off a chemical reaction in the child's esophagus, burning through both the esophageal wall and attacking the aorta. Two days after the battery was removed, Aidan began coughing blood, and soon died from his injuries."[167]

The *Times* also reported that data from the National Capital Poison Center in Washington found a sevenfold increase in severe complications from button-cell ingestions recently and that "moderate to severe cases have risen from less than a half percent (about a dozen cases per year) to about 3 percent (nearly one hundred cases per year), based on a review of fifty-six thousand cases since 1985." The batteries that pose the greatest risk are the larger ones that begin with the number twenty (for twenty millimeters). Batteries numbered 2032, 2025, and 2016 are responsible for more than 90 percent of serious injuries.[168]

Story Box: Choking, Ages One to Four

Toddler Dies after Swallowing Game Battery
A two-year-old girl was rushed to the hospital after telling her parents her chest hurt. X rays revealed that she had swallowed a button battery. Three weeks later, she bled to death from an esophageal hemorrhage due to erosion of her esophagus and aorta.

Suffocation: 1 Minute

Half of the suffocation incidents occurred in the child's bed. Almost all of these are cases of positional asphyxia, when children under the age of two get trapped between the (adult) bed and the wall. In some cases, these children fell off the bed and into dangerous things, such as stacks of clothing, dry cleaning, stuffed bags, or even bowls with sufficient amounts of liquid to drown the child.[169]

Children can also get strangled in things sticking out of the bed or around the bed. This is where the prohibition against using old cribs comes from. Older cribs are more likely to have protruding objects, such as hardware, that children's clothing can latch onto, strangling them. I came across a recent incident where a child was found dangling from a bunk bed, her pajamas having gotten stuck on the top bunk.

Window blinds have also been the source of injury in many cases. The issue with blinds is not just the pull cords on the side, but also the string through the middle of the blinds (see story box). Manufacturers of blinds have gotten a lot of pushback, and the *New York Times* reported in 2011 that changes may be coming.[170]

Poisoning: 1 Minute

Most poisonings are children getting a hold of their parents' or other household members' drugs, half of these being illegal drugs and half being legal (prescription or over-the-counter) drugs, which total about half a minute on the clock. See breakout below.

Drugs (illegal and legal)	*30 seconds*
Gases and vapors	*20 seconds*
Other	*10 seconds*

The next most common incident is from gases and vapors. Although this data set doesn't specify which gases were the culprits, chances are good that carbon monoxide is a factor, since 3 percent of these deaths occur in this age group. The source of the carbon monoxide is apparently virtually always a fuel-burning product. The CPSC warns, "Poor product maintenance by professionals or consumers, inadequate ventilation, faulty exhaust pathways, and poor user judgment in operating these products can result in fatal scenarios."[171]

Falls: 1 Minute

Falls come in at just one minute of the Worry Clock. To put this in perspective, the number of falls equaled half the deaths of fires by open flames (primarily candles) and just a few more than deaths from hyperthermia from being left in a car. The breakdown appears below.

Fall from or through building	*30 seconds*
Falls from one level to another in house	*25 seconds*
Falls from furniture in home	*15 seconds*
Stairs	*5 seconds*
Other	*15 seconds*

Most of these falls do not involve stairs; most deadly falls happen when children fall from buildings, or from one level to another within a building. Almost three times as many children died from dog attacks as from falling down stairs, although both numbers were so low as to be flagged as unreliable.

Falls from furniture were about half beds and half other furniture in the home. Other falls included a collection of rare incidents, such as slipping and tripping in the home and falling from playground equipment, both extremely rare and low.

Other Incidents: 5 Minutes

Finally, a collection of uncoded incidents, along with other incidents that did not lend themselves to a group of more than one minute, make up the "other" category. For two of the six minutes, we do not know the causes of death, as it was coded by the doctor as "unspecified" or "other." It is likely that these incidents reflect what has already been covered. For the remaining miscellaneous causes of death, there were not many incidents that leapt out, but below are a few.

Other or unspecified	2 minutes
Struck by thrown or projected object	*45 seconds*
Complications of medical care	*40 seconds*
Exposure to excessive heat or cold	*35 seconds*
Firearm related (e.g., accidental discharge)	*30 seconds*

The remaining minute and a half is the sum of all the miscellaneous categories that make up very low numbers of deaths, such as those that appear in the next section. They are those accidents that did not make the clock for this age group.

What Doesn't Appear on the Clock

Below are a few causes of death that I singled out for a special look, either because they had no findings or because of how they compared to other findings (but didn't occur frequently enough to talk about in the main section of the chapter). For example, take a look at the estimate for dogs killing toddlers; it is twice the number of deaths by electrical current (e.g., a fork in an outlet).[172] I can hear the Dog Whisperer saying that this is just an extension of the human homicide category, since dogs are just extensions of the people around them, and it is the people who need the training.

Although many incidents on this table are very low, their appearance does not mean that your child is necessarily safe from these causes of death. Your child may have a particular susceptibility to bees, for example, that is not taken into account here. What this table does show is that across the country over many years, these incidents were incredibly rare. Similarly, although exposure to electrical current (sticking fingers or objects into outlets) and contact with hot fluids are low, it is important to remember that we are only covering deaths; injuries, such as burning a hand, are not a part of this measure.

Miscellaneous Causes of Death, Ages 1–4	Worry Clock
Dog (bitten or struck by ~)	*12 seconds*
Other mammals (bitten or struck by ~)	*6 seconds*
Venomous snakes, lizards, and other reptiles	**
Insects (bees, hornets, scorpions, etc.)	**
Exposure to electric current	*6 seconds*
Fall from playground equipment	**
Contact with powered lawnmower	*3 seconds*
Contact with hot tap water	*3 seconds*
Contact with other hot fluids	*2 seconds*
Contact with hot drinks, food, fats, and cooking oils	**
Cataclysmic storm or flood	*6 seconds*
Lightning	**
Foreign body entering through eye or orifice	*3 seconds*

** The government says this number is too small to estimate accurately.

Since dogs are such a part of our lives, I wanted to go into more depth to understand those numbers. I found one study cited by the CDC[173] that looked at this issue over a twenty-year period. They found most cases (67 percent) involved unrestrained dogs on the owners' property and were the result of one dog. But 30 percent involved one or more dogs, usually unrestrained dogs away from any owner's property.

This study also looked at the breeds accountable. Rottweilers and pit bulls were involved in approximately 60 percent of the deaths. Other breeds with multiple deaths listed are, in descending order, German shepherd, husky, malamute, Doberman pinscher, chow chow, Great Dane, and Saint Bernard. This study did not account for how many of each breed are out there in the world, which is a serious limitation of the study. For example, let's say there are very few chow chows relative to all the other breeds. If there were as many chow chows as Rottweilers, they might have quadruple the number of deaths attributable to them. Having said that, I do know that golden and Labrador retrievers are very popular, but I do not see them on the list. So the study still tells us something.

To prevent dog bites, the CDC advises you to teach your children:
1. Do not approach an unfamiliar dog.
2. Do not run screaming from a dog.
3. Remain motionless ("be still like a tree") when approached by an unfamiliar dog.
4. If knocked over by a dog, roll into a ball and lie still ("be still like a log").
5. Do not play with a dog unless supervised by an adult.
6. Immediately report to an adult stray dogs or dogs displaying unusual behavior.
7. Avoid direct eye contact with a dog.
8. Do not disturb a dog that is sleeping, eating, or caring for puppies.
9. Do not pet a dog without allowing it to see and sniff you first.
10. If bitten, immediately report the bite to an adult.

Before you get a dog, consider the following:
1. Consult with a professional (e.g., veterinarian, animal behaviorist, or responsible breeder) to learn about suitable breeds of dogs for your household.
2. Dogs with histories of aggression are inappropriate in households with children.

3. Be sensitive to cues that a child is fearful or apprehensive about a dog and, if so, delay acquiring a dog.
4. Spend time with a dog before buying or adopting it. Spay/neuter virtually all dogs (this frequently reduces aggressive tendencies).
5. Never leave infants or young children alone with any dog.
6. Do not play aggressive games with your dog (e.g., wrestling).
7. Properly socialize and train any dog entering the household. Teach the dog submissive behaviors (e.g., rolling over to expose its abdomen and relinquishing food without growling).
8. Immediately seek professional advice (e.g., from veterinarians, animal behaviorists, or responsible breeders) if the dog develops aggressive or undesirable behaviors.

Quiz Time for Ages One to Four!

Here's a chance to test your ability to keep all these statistics in your head. After the quiz, I propose a top ten list of action steps to give you some idea of where to start.

1. What is the number-one cause (major category) of death for ages one to four?

2. Which is more likely, pedestrian accidents or children falling, and by roughly how much—3, 5, 7, or 9 times? (circle one)

3. Which is more likely: dying from electrocution from an outlet or dying from a dog attack?

4. Which food poses the biggest choking risk?

5. Which nonfood poses the biggest choking risk?

6. Which is more likely, drowning in a pool or dying from fire or smoke?

7. True or false: Children are OK left alone in the car if the errand is less than fifteen minutes and the temperature is less than eighty degrees.

8. Which is more likely, drowning in the bathtub or getting run over in or near the family driveway?

9. Which is more likely, drowning in natural water (a lake or stream) or dying from poisoning, and by how much—3, 5, 7, or 9 times? (circle one)

10. Which is more likely, drowning in utility buckets or in toilets?

Answers to Quiz:

1. Drowning (thirteen minutes).

2. Pedestrian accidents (seven minutes) are seven times more likely than death through falls (one minute).

3. The reported numbers show that dying from a dog attack is actually more likely; however, if you said there was no difference, that is technically an even better answer because the numbers are so small that there may be issues of reliability in the size differences.

4. Hot dogs.

5. Latex balloons.

6. The chances of dying in a fire, at seven minutes, are greater than drowning in a pool, at six minutes.

7. False and false. Never leave children in the car for any reason because children will play and may, for example, asphyxiate even on a stationary open window or with a seat belt. Also, heatstroke can happen even on mild days (in the seventies) with windows partially opened.

8. Getting run over in or near the family driveway (about one and a half minutes on the clock) was more likely than drowning in a bathtub (one minute).

9. Drowning in natural water (two minutes) was about three times more likely than dying from poisoning (forty-five seconds).

10. Five-gallon buckets (utility buckets) with liquid in them were more dangers than toilets.[174]

Top Ten for Toddlers

You made it through all the data, now where to begin? If you feel overwhelmed and don't know where to start, here are some suggestions based on the most frequent causes of death in the past data. As you are keenly aware, doing these things doesn't guarantee a safe child, but they give you a place to start.

Top ten suggestions for increasing safety for ages one to four:

1. **Use seat belts from startup and obey other driving laws.** Always, always make sure the children wear seat belts from the time the car is turned on until after it is turned off. Obey other driving laws, including speed limits, cell phone use, and no drinking while driving. Speed, drinking, and distraction are the big bad guys.

2. **Minimize distractions.** Keep your electronic toys out of the driver's area and make sure that whatever children need for the journey is accessible before you turn on the car.

3. **Learn how to cope with inconsolable crying, and teach anyone who cares for your child that it happens and what to do.** Crying will happen, probably at the worst time, when you or your caretaker is already tired and frustrated.

4. **Use touch (or very close) supervision while in and around the pool.** Do not do other things when your child is swimming. Do not rely on others to identify if the child is in trouble, since the child will not make noises while drowning. Make clear which parent is on or off, so there is no diffusion of responsibility.

5. *If you have a pool or spa,* **block off that area with a four-sided locked gate**. If you cannot block it off (e.g., you house forms one side of the fence), put an alarm or childproof lock on that door (while ensuring that in a fire there is a way out). *If you are visiting a house with a pool* (or pond/stream/spa), even if you are planning to stay inside, practice touch supervision. Remember that children who drowned were most often last seen in the house and not expected to be out near the pool.

6. **Give your child swimming lessons as soon as possible.** One source estimated that participation in formal swimming lessons could reduce the risk of drowning by 88 percent among children ages one to four.[175]

7. **Get the right fire equipment now**, which includes *working* photoelectric *and* ionization detectors and escape rope ladders for rooms that need them. Your place probably has ionization detectors but may not have photoelectric ones, which detect a more common type of fire. You may also want to install detectors in your child's room that allows for your voice to be recorded, giving instructions to the child in case of fire.

8. **Don't use candles for light** or anytime you might fall asleep with them on; use free-standing flashlights or battery-powered lanterns. Keep extra batteries on hand.

9. **Do whatever you can to keep children away from cars.** Make the driveway a no-play zone, or make the transition clear (with movable fences, for example). Keep all toys off the driveway. Lock car doors. Put barriers between children and roads whenever possible, and don't assume that your child will always be logical around cars. Hold on tightly.

10. Know that the top categories for breathing trouble appear to be choking on hot dogs or latex balloons and suffocation of a child on an adult bed. Cut up those hot dogs or teach children how to eat them carefully. Switch to Mylar balloons. And make sure that children cannot get wedged between the bed and the wall or fall off the bed into anything dangerous (e.g., bags of any kind).

Conclusion

You may have noticed throughout this chapter that many of the incidents happened primarily to the younger children in this age group, the one- and two-year-olds. By the time children are four, they are getting pretty savvy about themselves and their surroundings, and they can follow directions better. In the next chapter, we welcome you to the golden ages of five to nine.

Welcome to the relatively worry-free zone of having children ages five to nine! Only one in ten thousand children die during this time, the lowest rate of any of the age groups.

Your child knows how to talk—and negotiate—by now, and you can take a moment to breathe before the "tweens" (the ages in between being a child and a teen, roughly ten to twelve years old) hit. The pie graph is here as a visual reminder of how few children die for any reason (e.g., cancers, diseases, *and* accidents).

Percent of Children Aged 5-9 Who Died
(CDC Mortality Rates, 1999-2007)

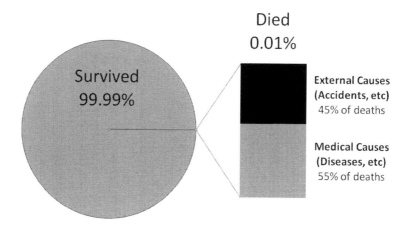

Accidents are about half (45 percent) of that slice (see bar), so we will spend the remainder of this chapter focused on just a half (the black portion) of that tiny slice.

Lessons from the young children age group include:
- The vast majority of children killed in car crashes was either not wearing seat belts or were sitting in the front seat.
- Pedestrian accidents account for nearly four times as many deadly accidents as bicycles, but the patterns are fairly similar: mostly, they are boys and a significant percentage of girls (36 percent) who dart into or fail to yield to traffic.
- All-terrain vehicles (ATVs) make a significant showing for this age group (the same death rate as bicycle deaths), and two out of three

ATV deaths occurred when children were riding as passengers, which the government specifically discourages.

- Gun accidents (accidental firearm discharge, not including those used in homicide) make their debut as a unique category on the Worry Clock, with handguns accounting for about 70 percent of all unintentional firearm-related deaths.

Below I review the Worry Clock for Ages Five to Nine and then provide more detail on each category, including recommendations on how to prevent these accidents.

The Worry Clock for Ages Five to Nine

Let's look at the Worry Clock for Ages Five to Nine. The first thing to notice is that there is just more going on in this clock than in the toddler clock. We see three new categories: bicycles, ATVs, and gun accidents.

The next change that leaps out is the doubling of minutes for motor vehicle accidents; they are now worth twenty minutes of your time. Transportation-related accidents overall, including motor vehicle (twenty minutes), pedestrian (seven minutes), ATV (two minutes), bicycle (two minutes), and other types (one minute) consume over half (thirty-two minutes) of your worry time for this age group (see darker, right side of clock).

Fire-related incidents remain at seven minutes of your worry, while drowning and homicide drop by nearly half to seven and six minutes, respectively. Gun accidents make their first appearance on the clock, with one minute of worry. Breathing worries fall by half. Finally, falls and poisoning each have one minute of worry.

Reminder: Very few children die. The entire Worry Clock for Ages Five to Nine is based on half of that tiny slice of the pie at the beginning of the chapter and is an average of about 1,350 deaths per year, which means each minute represents about twenty-three deaths.

As in all chapters, these data and recommendations do not tell you what will happen or guarantee against something happening. These data are for you to consider and talk to your health care providers about in deciding what is right for your child.

Worry Clock for Ages Five to Nine

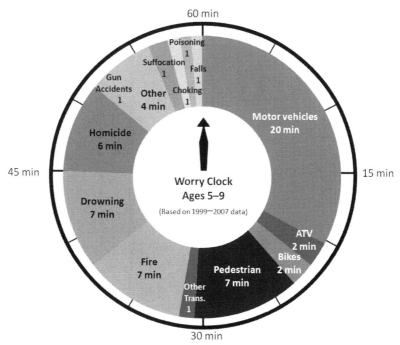

The following sections give more detail on the causes within each of the major components of the Worry Clock and provide recommendations for what to do about them.

First we will take a look at all the transportation-related incidents, since these total about half your worry. Then we will turn to the non-transportation-related accidents.

Motor Vehicle Accidents: 20 Minutes

Motor vehicle accidents—i.e., deaths of child passengers (or child drivers!) of motor vehicles—take up twenty minutes, twice as many minutes as in the toddler years. Note that these accidents include cars, minivans, and trucks, but do not include ATVs, which have so many accidents that they have a separate grouping.

The best available data indicate that approximately half of the children who died were not wearing any seat belt or other restraint. Just as in the toddler chapter analysis, a separate analysis here of 2008 and 2009 data[176] finds that again about half of the children who died were not wearing a seat belt or restraint of any kind.[177,178] Another 20 percent of the children who died were wearing seat belts but were sitting in the front seat.

Motor Vehicle Point #1: About 70 percent of the children killed in crashes were either not wearing *any* form of seat belt or were wearing one but sitting in the front seat.

So, to reverse this lens, only about 30 percent of children who died in crashes were sitting in the back seats and belted—though perhaps not properly belted. If we focus on this small group of children, we find a number of driver-related primary factors (there may have been secondary factors in addition to these) cited in the fatality records, summarized in the table below. The summary point is that about one-third of the time there was no driver error; if there was, the two big errors were failure to keep in the proper lane and failure to yield the right-of-way.

Primary Driver Factors Driver Error Contributions to Motor Vehicle Accidents in Which Children Were Seated in the Back & Wearing Seat Belts	
None; no driver factors	*37%*
Failure to Keep in Proper Lane	13%
Failure to Yield Right-of-Way	11%
Operating the Vehicle in Careless or Inattentive Manner	6%
Under the Influence of Alcohol, Drugs, or Medication	4%
Making Other Improper Turn	4%
Ice, Snow, Slush, Water, Sand, Dirt, Oil, Wet Leaves	4%
Drowsy, Sleepy, Asleep, Fatigued	3%
Failure to Obey Actual Traffic Sign, Stop Lights, Etc.	3%
Driving on Wrong Side of Road (Intentionally or Not)	3%
Overcorrecting	2%
Tire Blowout or Flat	1%
Stopped or Stopping in Roadway	1%
Following Another Vehicle Improperly	1%
Improper or Erratic Lane Changing	1%
Unknown or Other	6%

These two driver errors, failure to keep in the proper lane or yield right-of-way, appeared frequently in my analyses of crashes. Changing lanes on a highway and not seeing a car already in the lane, or making a left in front of an oncoming vehicle that doesn't have time to stop, are two examples of these incidents. And how many people even remember the rules for right-of-way? (See the recommendations section if you don't.)

Blind spots—of the driver of the child and of others—may be a large source of originating error in both cases. Twenty percent of the motor vehicle accidents in this group (children belted in the back seat) involved heavy trucks, which have enormous blind spots. Be aware that a heavy truck's blind spot can be three lanes wide and more than the length of the truck on the right side. Passenger vehicles are now coming equipped with systems that let you know when there is someone in your blind spot. If your car doesn't have one of these systems, you might consider an additional blind spot mirror (an easy add-on, but takes some getting used to).

Driver errors may also be related to contributing factors such as drowsiness or alcohol or drug impairment. Note that these categories refer to the condition of the driver of the vehicle containing the child. In fact, a CDC analysis found that in alcohol-related crashes, more than two-thirds of fatally injured children were killed while riding *with* a drunk driver.[179] Yes, that's right—the fault wasn't someone else's; it was the child's own driver's mistake.

I found some perhaps trivial but interesting things that were not cited as driver factors, such as live animals in the road, emotional upset, and driving more slowly than the posted minimum. I am not saying that these things are not issues; I am only pointing out that they were not cited in these data as factors related to the crash.

Motor Vehicle Point #2: Drivers' failure to keep in their lane and to yield right-of-way were the two major factors in fatal accidents in which children were properly placed and restrained. Heavy trucks (e.g., tractor trailers) were involved in 20 percent of the accidents.

I also found a lot of research related to lane-shifting by older drivers, relevant just for the increasing relative size of this demographic group, which is expected to increase by more than 70 percent between now and 2030. Not surprisingly, the percentage of accidents attributable to this group is also expected to increase. According to a piece in *USA Today* on older drivers, "Road safety analysts predict that by 2030, when all baby boomers are at least sixty-five, they will be responsible for 25 percent of all fatal crashes. In 2005, 11 percent of fatal crashes involved drivers that old."[180]

A federal study found five crash types where older drivers were most strongly overrepresented:

1. The driver turned left at an intersection with stop-sign control where cross traffic does not stop.
2. The driver turned left at an intersection with signal control where the permissive (not protected) green phase was displayed during the driver's approach.
3. The driver turned right at an intersection controlled by a yield sign, in a channelized right-turn lane, merging with traffic approaching from the left on a principal arterial with operating speeds of forty to forty-five miles per hour.
4. The driver merged onto a limited-access highway on a ramp/acceleration lane controlled by a yield sign.
5. The driver changed lanes on a multilane roadway (four-plus lanes).

All of these data point to a need for drivers to focus on driving defensively, which is a central part of the recommendations below.

Story Box: Motor Vehicle Accidents, Ages Five to Nine

Seven-Year-Old Dies in Speeding Car
On October 30, 2012, in Everett, Washington, a BMW was seen speeding and weaving before crashing into a minivan. People heard the thirty-year-old BMW driver screaming about a boy. Rather than being seated in the back in the available car seat, the child was in the front seat and had been crushed by the impact. The seven-year-old died at the scene.[181]

Five-Year-Old Dies When Minivan Collides with Bus
On November 2, 2012, in San Antonio, a minivan driver collided with a VIA bus, killing the minivan driver's child on impact.[182]

Packed SUV Flips, Kills Five En Route to Water Park
On August 22, 2012, on route to a Canton, Texas waterpark, the right rear tire of an SUV exploded. The driver attempted to gain control of the vehicle but overcorrected, causing the vehicle to flip. Five children, ages two, three, six, seven, and thirteen, died. None of the children was wearing a seat belt. The fifteen-year-old, who was wearing a seat belt, walked away uninjured.[183]

Mother, Allegedly DUI, Survives Crash That Kills Two Daughters

On August 6, 2012, in Otay Mesa, California, a mother lost control of her car and drove off an embankment into a reservoir. Her two daughters were restrained in the back seat and did not make it out alive. The mother was charged.[184]

Father and Son Die in Morning Crash

A little after ten a.m. on September 30, 2012, in Middletown, New Jersey, a father and son were killed when another vehicle struck the side of their hatchback.[185]

Three Children Die in Two-Car Collision When Oncoming Vehicle Fails to Yield at Stop Sign

On July 23, 2012, in Montana Vista, Texas, three children from Dallas who were visiting their grandfather were killed when another vehicle failed to brake at a stop sign and struck the side of the car. The impact was so great that it flipped the children's car.[186]

Pickup Smashes into Side of Left-Turning Car, Splitting Car in Two and Killing Seven-Year-Old Boy

On the morning of October 29, 2012, in Augusta, Georgia, a seven-year-old boy was traveling in a car that was attempting to make a left turn at an intersection. An oncoming pickup hit the car, splitting it in two and killing boy.[187]

These are recommendations based on those from the CDC[188] and others as noted:

1. **Always have kids buckle up.** A reminder about the current guidelines (check the CDC website to ensure you are up to date with the standards, http://www.cdc.gov/motorvehiclesafety/child_passenger_safety/cps-factsheet.html):
   a. **Between Ages 4 and 8 OR until 4" 9" Tall** – Booster seat. Once children outgrow their forward-facing seats (by reaching the upper height and weight limits of their seat), they should ride in belt-positioning booster seats.
   b. **After Age 8 AND/OR 4" 9" Tall** – Seat belts. Children should use booster seats until adult seat belts fit them properly. Seat belts fit properly when the lap belt lies across the upper thighs (not the stomach) and the shoulder belt fits across the chest (not the neck). When adult seat belts fit children properly, kids can use the adult belts without booster seats.

2. **Seat kids in the back seat, always.** This entire age group should still be in the back seat of the car. Ideally, they should be in the middle of the back seat because it is the safest spot in the vehicle.

3. **Know when it is safe to change lanes by…**

   a. **Getting a blind-spot mirror** addition to your car (see the Automobile Safety Foundation's "Safe Mirrors Now!" campaign at http://www.carsafe.org/mirrors.php for more on mirror inserts).

   b. **Getting a car with technology that addresses the blind spot.** Ford, GM, Volvo, and others are putting out technologies that provide drivers with different levels of information and even alerts, such as lights that come on, when vehicles are traveling in your blind spot.

4. **Know how to drive around trucks.** The American Trucking Association's Share the Road Safety Guidelines for Motorists offers some key points:

   a. **Always pass trucks on the left.** The driver has a much bigger blind spot on the right side—three lanes wide and tractor-trailer length long.

   b. **Move back into the truck lane only when you can see both of the truck's headlights in your rearview mirror.** A fully loaded tractor-trailer weighs eighty thousand pounds. That is the equivalent to twenty-five cars. It takes a fully loaded tractor-trailer three hundred feet—the length of a football field—to come to a complete stop.

   c. **Know when you are in a truck driver's blind spot and don't stay there.** If you are following a truck and you can't see the driver's face in the truck's side mirrors, the truck driver can't see you.

5. **Never stay in any car's blind spot.** Be aware when you are traveling in someone else's blind spot and avoid staying there.

6. **Know the right-of-way rules at intersections.** Yielding to traffic in intersections follows four rules, according to guidance from the NHTSA:[189]

   - **First to Stop = First to Go.** This is the base rule. The first vehicle at the intersection goes through the intersection first.

   - *If the base rule doesn't apply:* **Farthest Right Goes First.** When two vehicles get to the intersection at the same time, the vehicle on the right goes first; it has the right-of-way.

   - *If neither the base rule or farthest right rule apply:* **Straight Traffic Goes First.** When two vehicles are directly across from each other, and one is turning left, the one that is going straight goes first.

   - **When in Doubt, Bail Out.** This trumps all rules. Even if you have the right-of-way, if for any reason you feel uncomfortable or that your safety is threatened, let the other traffic go ahead. Your safety always comes first.

7. **Know the general other rules for when to yield, such as:**
   a. Generally, drivers coming from a smaller road (e.g., driveway, side street, or access road) onto a larger road yield to the vehicles on the larger roadway.
   b. At modern roundabouts (newer, better versions of traffic circles that apparently are significantly safer than regular intersections),[190] those coming into the circle yield to those already in the circle.
8. **Be prepared for others to make mistakes.** For example, a common error that is likely to increase as our population ages is for people to turn left without yielding. Being prepared for this error may ensure, for example, that you notice slight vehicle movements faster and go slowly enough that you are able to stop.
9. **Take a defensive driving course.** Here are a few resources cited by NHSTA:
   - AARP 55 ALIVE Driver Safety Program, (888) 227-7669
   - AAA: Call your local AAA club to find a class near you
   - National Safety Council Defensive Driving Course, (800) 621-7619
   - Driving School Association of the Americas, Inc., (800) 270-3722

ATVs: 2 Minutes

This category includes all motorized wheeled vehicles designed for off-road use. As I mentioned in the last chapter and will mention in the next (although, interestingly, not in the teen chapter), ATVs are viewed as so potentially dangerous that the federal government has developed a special site for ATV safety, www.atvsafety.gov.

For this age group, these accidents are mostly (70 percent) nontraffic; that is, they do not hit other vehicles. Only about 30 percent are from hitting other vehicles, often on paved roads.

About one in three of these children was driving the ATV. The rest were passengers, which the government specifically recommends against (see below).

ATV Point #1: Children should never ride as passengers in an adult-size ATV (like when you visit you uncle in Colorado and think one ride cannot hurt). Any child who is permitted to ride in a youth-size ATV should wear prescribed protective gear and should NOT ride on paved surfaces, which are actually less safe.

Story Box: ATV Accidents, Ages Five to Nine

Five-Year-Old Girl Dies Driving ATV at Grandparents' House
On October 16, 2012, in Jefferson County, Idaho, a five-year-old died when the ATV she was driving fell on top of her.[191]

Recommendations from www.atvsafety.gov include:

- **Every rider should take a hands-on safety course.** Formal training teaches drivers how to control ATVs in typical situations. Drivers with formal, hands-on ATV training have a lower injury risk than drivers with no formal training.

- **Always wear protective gear—especially a helmet—when riding an ATV.** Select a motorcycle or other motorized sports helmet and make sure it is certified by the US Department of Transportation and/or the Snell Memorial Foundation.

- **Do not drive an ATV with a passenger or ride as a passenger.** The majority of ATVs are designed to carry only one person. ATVs are designed for interactive riding—drivers must be able to shift their weight freely in all directions, depending on the situation and terrain. Interactive riding is critical to maintaining safe control of an ATV, especially on varying terrain. Passengers can make it difficult for drivers to control the ATV.

- **Do not drive ATVs on paved roads.** Because of their design, ATVs are difficult to control on paved roads. Many fatalities involving ATVs occur on paved roads.

- **Do not permit children to drive or ride in adult ATVs.** Children are involved in about one-third of all ATV-related deaths and hospital emergency room injuries. Most of these deaths and injuries occur when a child is driving or riding on an adult ATV. Children under sixteen riding adult ATVs are twice as likely to be injured as those riding youth ATVs.

- **Do not drive an ATV while under the influence of alcohol or drugs.** Alcohol and drugs impair reaction time and judgment, two essential skills for safe ATV use.

Bicycles: 2 Minutes

This is often the age when children and bicycles cement a lifelong relationship. Bicycles, however, are far from the safest form of travel or exercise. According to the Pedestrian and Bicycle Information Center, for all ages (including adults), "bicycle fatalities represent just fewer than 2 percent of all traffic fatalities, and yet bicycle trips account for 1 percent of all trips in the United States."[192] Even with a drop of 25 percent in fatalities since 1995,[193] bicycling still has a ways to go in terms of safety.

Although everyone is getting better about wearing helmets, only about 20 to 25 percent of all bicyclists do. Yet bicycle helmets are estimated to be more than 85 percent effective in mitigating head and brain injuries, says the NHTSA, "making the use of helmets the single most effective way to reduce head injuries and fatalities resulting from bicycle crashes."[194] Of all fatal bicycle crashes, nearly 70 percent involve head injuries.[195] Only 10 percent of the children in my data set who died in bicycle accidents were wearing helmets.

Bicycle Point #1: Nearly 70 percent of fatal bicycle crashes involve head injuries, and only one in ten victims wore a helmet.

Most (75 percent) of bicycle deaths were from child cyclists colliding with cars, vans, and pickup trucks. An additional 10 percent of deaths were collisions with heavier vehicles, such as trucks and buses, a number that seems high if you assume children spend on average less than 10 percent of their bike-riding time around heavier vehicles.

In my analysis of 2008–2009 data, no bicycle fatalities were reported linked to school buses. In fact, according to the US Department of Transportation, school buses are the single best way for students to get to school, fifty times safer than if they (later in teen years) drive themselves and even safer than if you drive them.[196]

In the majority of the cases,[197] it appears that the child cyclist is darting out into the traffic lanes (25 percent); failing to yield to traffic (19 percent); or disobeying signs or otherwise improperly crossing or using the roadway (22 percent). So two-thirds of the time, the accidents are driven by the behavior of the cyclist.

The accident locations will not surprise you. About half (48 percent)[198] of the accidents occurred away from any intersection or driveway; intersections accounted for about another 40 percent, and driveways added another 14 percent.

Two-thirds of these deaths were boys,[199] a figure consistent with pedestrian deaths as well. Other studies have found the disproportionality to go up to 80 percent boys if we also include children up to age fourteen.[200]

Bicycle Point #2: Accidents occur when children, usually boys, dart out into the traffic, sometimes in front of trucks that cannot stop.

Story Box: Bicycle Accidents, Ages Five to Nine

Boy Falls Off Balance, Dies under Truck
In 2012, in Las Vegas, a five-year-old boy was riding his bicycle around the strip mall with his brothers while his parents shopped. The boy lost his balance on the bicycle and fell into a nearby alley and under a garbage truck. The driver didn't see the boy as he pulled out of the alley, and the boy's brothers, who were watching, were too far to signal an alarm.[201]

The following recommendations are based on the suggestions from the American Academy of Pediatrics[202] and the Pedestrian and Bicycle Information Center (Bicyclinginfo.org), a technical assistance center supported by the federal government:

1. Establish the helmet habit early. It's important to wear a helmet on every ride, no matter how short.
    a. Wear a helmet yourself. The most important factor influencing children to wear helmets is riding with an adult who wears a helmet.
    b. Talk to your children about why helmets are important.
    c. Reward your kids for wearing helmets. Notice when they wear their helmets without having to be told.
    d. Encourage friends to wear helmets, too.
2. Keep your young cyclists off the roads. The CDC recommends that children in this age group stick to cycling on sidewalks only.
3. Teach your young rider these basic riding skills (see Bicyclinginfo.org for more on these):
    a. Cycle with traffic, *not against it*. Like all cyclists, children should ride on the right side of the road, with traffic.
    b. Understand and obey traffic signs, signals, and other markings.
    c. Teach children to look behind themselves for approaching traffic, while simultaneously cycling in a straight line.
    d. Recognize what can cause a fall and how to control a fall. Kids should learn how to spot hazards and avoid them.

e. Ride carefully on sidewalks, wet roads, and trails. Explain the dangers of night riding and have children avoid riding at night.

f. Assess a good bike route and differentiate bike lanes and bike routes.

g. Cross an intersection or crosswalk correctly. Children in this age group should dismount and walk the bike across, taking care to watch for vehicles.

h. Communicate and negotiate with drivers. Show kids how to use standard hand signals and to make eye contact before moving in front of a car.

And sure, why not put out one of those signs alerting drivers if your kids are riding around near your house?

Pedestrian Accidents: 7 Minutes

Take the bicycle safety worry and multiply it by three to four times and you will have the proportional amount of appropriate worry for pedestrian accidents.[203] That's right—your five- to nine-year-old is three to four times more likely to die as a pedestrian than as a bicyclist. This may not be too surprising if you consider how much more time we spend walking than riding bicycles.

The patterns for who, when, and where pedestrian accidents happen[204] are fairly similar to those of the bicycle accidents at this age. Boys are disproportionately represented (about 64 percent). A significant portion (32 percent) of accidents was at intersections. More than half of the deaths (59 percent) were in part attributed to actions of the child, such as darting out into traffic (22 percent), improperly crossing the road (14 percent), walking with traffic (9 percent), or failing to yield right-of-way (5 percent). Invisibility to drivers, a common concern of parents, contributed to 3 percent.

Pedestrian Point #1: Pedestrian accidents account for nearly four times the deadly accidents as bicycles, but the patterns are fairly similar: they are mostly boys who dart into or fail to yield to traffic.

Here are some recommendations based on those from the National Highway Traffic Safety Administration:[207]

1. **Make sure your child understands that these are myths:**
   a. **Myth:** A green light means that it is safe to cross. (Truth: Look left-right-left first.)
   b. **Myth:** You are safe in a crosswalk. (Truth: Look left-right-left first.)
   c. **Myth:** If you see the driver, the driver sees you. (Truth: Wait for the driver to stop.)
   d. **Myth:** The driver will stop if you are in a crosswalk. (Truth: Wait for the driver to stop.)
   e. **Myth:** Wearing white at night makes you visible to drivers. (Truth: Reflectors and lights are needed.)
2. **Preschoolers should NOT be allowed to cross the street alone.** Teach them who can help them cross the street safely (generally adults or siblings over the age of twelve). Always hold the hand of a preschooler when crossing the street.
3. **When walking, always:** Walk on the sidewalk, if one is available. Walk *facing* traffic if no sidewalk is available. Note that this is the *opposite* procedure from bicycling.
4. **When crossing the street, always:** Cross at a corner or crosswalk with the walk signal. Stop at the curb. Exaggerate looking LEFT-RIGHT-LEFT for traffic in all directions before and while crossing the street. Explain that you are looking for either no traffic, or that traffic has stopped for you to cross safely. Hold your child's hand when crossing the street. Keep looking for cars as you cross.
5. **Teach by explaining.** Explain to your child the safe way to cross a street. Say, "When I cross a street, I always stop at the curb. I look and listen for cars. I look left for any traffic coming, and then I look

right for traffic coming that way. Then I look left again for any traffic coming. When it is clear, I cross the street, and keep looking left and right and listening for cars coming."

6. **Teach by example—be a role model.** Your child watches and notices your actions as an adult. Practice what you teach at *all* times.

The Federal Highway Administration[208] identified and is supporting initiatives in the states and cities with the highest numbers or rates of pedestrian fatalities. States with high pedestrian fatality rates in 2010, in order, were Florida, Delaware, Arizona, South Carolina, and Hawaii.[209] The cities with the highest rate of fatalities in 2011 were Orlando, Tampa, Jacksonville, and Miami, all in Florida; Riverside, California; and Las Vegas, Nevada.[210]

Fire: 7 Minutes

The same issues that were presented in the toddler chapter still hold, except that unlike toddlers, young children have less trouble getting out of a dark and smoke-filled house. The recommendations given in the last chapter, such as having photoelectric and ionization detectors and a practiced family plan for fire emergencies, also remain the same.

Story Box: Fire, Ages Five to Nine

Fire Claims Eight-Year-Old; Grandmother Unable to Escape with Family
On October 30, 2012, in Lakeland, Florida, a mother, father, and two children were pulled from a house fire by a passing neighbor, but an eight-year-old boy and his grandmother did not escape. The fire apparently started in the carport and spread to the house.[211]

Four Children and Mother Die in Electrical Fire
On April 27, 2013, a mother awakened her eleven-year-old daughter and told her to get out of the house because there was a fire. It was so dark in the house (due to lights not working and smoke) that they bumped into each other and had to feel their way around the house. The eleven-year-old was the only survivor. The mother, her two other children, and two additional children staying in the house perished. A faulty breaker in the electrical box started the fire.[212]

Drowning: 7 Minutes

In the previous age group, drowning was the number-one cause of worry. It was largely attributable to wandering toddlers who were last seen in the house. If the two stories in the box below are any indication, the wandering child may still be a major issue. However, many children in this age group are learning to swim by now, and the worry time drops by half to only seven minutes, the same amount as pedestrian and fire deaths. Again, the worry comes from pools, lakes, etc., where there is no formal supervision (such as a lifeguard). For more, review the section on drowning in Chapter 2.

At this age, pools and natural bodies of water, such as lakes or streams, account for equal amounts of worry time. Bathtubs barely rate a mention.

Drowning or Water-Related Deaths		Worry
Swimming Pool		2 minutes, *15 seconds*
	Swimming in pool	2 minutes, *5 seconds*
	Falling into pool	*10 seconds*
Natural Water		2 minutes, *0 seconds*
	Swimming in natural water	1 minute, *30 seconds*
	Falling into natural water	*30 seconds*
Bathtub		*20 seconds*
	Bathing in bathtub	*20 seconds*
	Falling into bathtub	*0 seconds*
Unspecified/other		2 minutes, *25 seconds*

Boy Wanders from Porch, Drowns in Nearby Canal
On October 16, 2012, in Sugarloaf Key, Florida, a mother went inside to feed her newborn and left her six-year-old son eating pistachios on their home's porch. The boy was later found unresponsive in a local canal.[214]

Homicide: 6 Minutes

Homicide starts to take on new horrifying dimensions in the five- to nine-year-old group. Firearms are the most common method of killing (over two minutes), even at this age. The remaining methods of homicide—due to strangulation, knives or other sharp objects, and fire—are about equal and together do not total the amount of worry time for guns.

Method of Homicide	%	Worry Clock
Firearm	39%	2 minutes *20 seconds*
Strangulation/suffocation	10%	*36 seconds*
Sharp object	10%	*36 seconds*
Smoke and fire	9%	*32 seconds*

The number of deaths in this age group foreshadows the incredibly high rates of homicide we will see in the preteen and teen years, so these issues are addressed more fully in the next chapter.

Story Box: Homicide, Ages Five to Nine

Upper West Side Nanny Stabs Children to Death
On October 25, 2012, in Manhattan, a mother took her three-year-old to swimming lessons at the neighborhood YMCA, leaving her two- and six-year-old at home with a nanny. She returned home to find her other children together in the bathtub, both with knife wounds. Upon seeing the mother, the nanny turned the knife on herself.[215]

Five-Year-Old Killed by Mother's Live-In Boyfriend
On November 8, 2012, in Knoxville, Tennessee, a man was charged with murdering his girlfriend's son, who died after several days in the hospital from his injuries. The man was charged with felony murder, aggravated child abuse, and possession of drugs.[216]

Gun Accidents: 1 Minute

Gun accidents make their debut as a distinct category on the Worry Clock beginning with five- to nine-year-olds. This category refers to the accidental discharge of handguns, rifles, and other firearms. Handguns account for about 70 percent of all unintentional firearm-related injuries and deaths.[217]

Gun accidents are problematic because of the effectiveness of the guns. One out of every five children wounded by a gunshot died from that injury.[218]

Gun Point #1: Seventy percent of accidental firearm shootings within this age group are handgun accidents, and one out of every five children shot died.

Since one out of every three American households contains at least one gun,[219] children at this age should be taught what to do if they see a gun:[220]

- Don't touch it.
- Immediately leave the area.
- Immediately tell an adult what they found.

If their friend tries to show them a gun, they should be told to exit the room immediately and go find an adult.

Suffocation & Strangulation: 1 Minute

For this age group, strangulation accidents are four times more common than suffocation. Accidental strangulation entails various items getting caught around children's necks. The three examples I found in the Consumer Product Safety Commission database were blind cords, a belt removed from pants, drawstrings (like in older sweatshirts), and a jump rope. Although it wasn't always clear what game or other activity led the children to put these things around their necks, it was clear that these were terrible accidents.

When suffocation was to blame, a cited reason was "cave-in" or "falling earth," suggesting holes had been dug that were big enough to bury a child.

Choking: 1 Minute

Choking clocks in at one minute, with objects (like toys) nearly two times as likely as food to be causing the blockage.

Objects	*35 seconds*
Food	*20 seconds*
Vomit	*5 seconds*

It is difficult to say what objects are the most common in this age group. A review of the CPSC annual reports points to the usual culprits, such as balloons.

Poisoning: 1 Minute

The poisonings in this age group are nearly equally divided between drugs and gasses. The drugs were primarily hallucinogens and other "unspecified" drugs. No additional detail could be found specific to this age group.

As usual, carbon monoxide (CO) appears to top the list of killer gases. As a reminder, CO is an insidious poison that is a naturally occurring byproduct of the incomplete combustion of carbon-based fuels. Because CO is colorless, tasteless, odorless, and nonirritating, its presence usually is not detected. So where is CO a problem? Here are some examples I found:

- Snow blocking a vehicle's tail pipe (for example, after shoveling snow with her parents, a girl took a nap in the running car and got CO poisoning because the tail pipe was blocked with snow)[221]
- Children riding in the back of pickup trucks[222]
- Generators improperly vented in houses, boats, or houseboats (cited as specific concerns[223])

Carbon monoxide detectors are easily purchased for both the home and the car (battery operated).

Falls: 1 Minute

The falls in this age group have now shifted to being almost entirely larger falls, either from one level of a building to another, or out of a building.

The recommendations for earlier age groups regarding fall prevention apply here. Because many of these cases are falls from a building or between levels, talking to children about the dangers of leaning out windows or over balconies, or otherwise limiting this behavior, appears to be a logical, although not an evidence-based, recommendation.

What Doesn't Appear on the Clock

Below are a few causes of death that I singled out for a special look, either because they had no findings or because of how they compared to other findings.

Although many incidents on this table are very rare, your child is not necessarily safe from these causes of death. Your child may have a particular susceptibility that is not taken into account here. What this table does show is that across the country over many years, these incidents were relatively rare. Similarly, although some numbers may be low, it is important to remember that we are only covering deaths; injuries are not a part of this measure.

Miscellaneous Causes of Death for Five- to Nine-Year-Olds	Worry Clock
Bitten/struck by dog	9 seconds
Bitten/struck by other mammals	7 seconds
Snakes	**
Spiders	**
Fall from tree	**
Fall from playground equipment	**
Aircraft accident	15 seconds
Bus occupant	**
Train (railway)	**
Exposure to electric current	12 seconds

Suicide	*11 seconds*
Foreign body entering into or through eye or natural orifice	**

** The government says this number is too small to estimate accurately.

Exposure to electrical current is actually worth more worry in this age group than it was for toddlers. Being bitten by a dog or other mammal remains about the same level.

Deaths due to spiders, snakes, and falling from trees or playground equipment did not make the clock. These incidents did not happen frequently enough that the government could put a reliable number to them.

Suicide foreshadows the grim numbers of the next age group. Nearly all of these children chose hanging, a trend that continues into the early teens but shifts for the later teens.

Quiz Time for Ages Five to Nine!

Here's a chance to test your ability to keep all these statistics in your head. After the quiz, I propose a top ten list of action steps to give you some idea of where to start.

1. What is the number-one cause (major category) of death for five- to nine-year-olds?

2. Give three safety rules for a youth this age riding an ATV, other than wearing a helmet and not drinking alcohol.

3. Which of these is more common than poisoning, falls, choking, and bicycle accidents combined?
   ☐ Fires ☐ Pedestrian accidents ☐ Homicide ☐ Drowning

4. Name the two most common driver mistakes (in cases in which kids were wearing seat belts in the back seat).

5. True or false: In cycling accidents for this age group, the cyclist is most likely responsible for the accident.

6. Which is most common: accidents due to ATVs, drowning in pools, or drowning in natural water—or are all three about the same?

7. When a child is killed in a crash that involved alcohol, is it the driver of the child or the driver of the other vehicle who is more likely to have been drinking?

8. Which is more likely, aircraft accidents or pedestrian accidents, and by how much?

9. Which is more likely based on these data: death by an accidental gunshot, a fall, or poisoning?

10. True or false: Being killed by a mammal (including dogs) was about as likely as being killed in an aircraft.

Answers to Quiz:

1. Motor vehicle accidents.

2. Any three of the following: take a safety course, do not ride as a passenger, do not take passengers, do not ride on pavement, and ride a youth-sized (not adult) ATV.

3. All four are worth more on the clock.

4. Failure to keep in proper lane and failure to yield right-of-way.

5. True.

6. All three are about the same, at two minutes.

7. The child's driver.

8. Aircraft accidents, at fifteen seconds, did not compare to pedestrian accidents, at seven minutes. Pedestrian accidents were twenty-eight times more likely.

9. All three are about the same.

10. True.

Top Ten for Five- to Nine-Year-Olds
You made it through all the data, now where to begin? If you feel overwhelmed and don't know where to start, here are some suggestions

based on the most frequent causes of death in the past data. As you are keenly aware, doing these things doesn't guarantee a safe child—and you have to decide if these are even appropriate for your child—but they give you a place to start.

Top ten suggestions for increasing safety for five- to nine-year-olds:

1. **Address the blind spot.** Get either a technological fix or a blind-spot mirror that ensures that you won't be the one missing the cars near you.
2. **Avoid others' blind spots.** Others will not have fixed their blind-spot problems; do not give them the chance to not see you.
3. **Know how to drive defensively, and live it.** Whatever "justice" you think you might be enforcing on the road (and I've been there), it's not worth it. Raging at another driver gets you nothing and endangers your children. Know the mistakes other drivers are likely to make and be prepared to deal with them.
4. **Require helmets,** always, on ATVs, bicycles, or anything else that moves with a child on it.
5. **Follow ATV guidelines.** Don't allow two people to ride together on an ATV, or have children ride youth-sized ATVs.
6. **Know that children make bad choices on bicycles and while walking and will dart out in front of cars.** Consider this in deciding who should walk your kids to school, where they play, etc. The issue is usually not that kids aren't seen; it's that they do something not predicted by the drivers.
7. **Always watch swimmers.** Never let children swim alone, even if they are very capable swimmers.
8. **Be aware that accidental strangulation accounts for about one minute on the clock.** Note the potential hazards in your child's environment. Consider if talking to your child about not putting things around his neck would discourage rather than encourage him from playing this way.
9. **Test your fire alarm batteries.** If you bought the dual-sensor detectors way back when, make sure that they are running properly.
10. **Get carbon monoxide detectors for your home *and* car.** Home carbon monoxide detectors are ready available, and you can even get a portable battery-operated detector for your car.

The Worry Clock for Ages Ten to Fourteen begins to foreshadow some of the horrors of the later teenage years, but the rates of death are not nearly as high yet. But let's begin with the important reminder that few kids die from any cause (see pie graph). Just .02 percent of children die for any reason, and about half of these deaths are accidents or more controllable events, which we will explore in this chapter.

Percent of Children Ages 10–14 Who Died
(CDC Mortality Rates, 1999–2007)

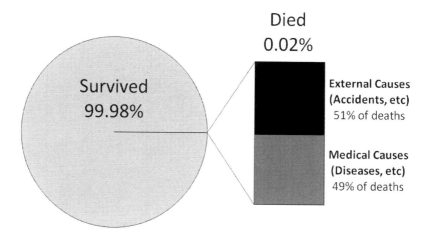

Here are some of the lessons in this chapter:
- Diagnosable mental illnesses begin to appear and should be addressed immediately because suicide, linked to many of the most common disorders, is a whopping eight minutes of worry time.
- Watching for alcohol use becomes important as alcohol begins to play a significant role in many forms of death including suicide, homicide, and transportation deaths.
- Motor vehicles begin to play a prominent role as these young teens— and their older peers—start driving.

First I review the Worry Clock for ages ten to fourteen, which presents the main causes of death, and then I go into each category in more detail and pass along recommendations primarily from the government on how to prevent these accidents.

The Worry Clock for Ages Ten to Fourteen

The first thing you may notice about the Worry Clock for this age group is the addition of the sobering new category of suicide, which leaps from zero worry in the previous age group to a whopping eight minutes of your worry time. And this is the beginning of a trend that steepens in the later teen years.

Transportation continues to account for just shy of half of your worry. Motor vehicle accidents remain the largest chunk of the transportation accidents (eighteen minutes here and twenty in the previous age group), while pedestrian accidents drop slightly to five minutes. ATV accidents increase by 50 percent, while bicycle and other transportation accidents remain at two and one minutes, respectively.

Worry Clock for Ages Ten to Fourteen

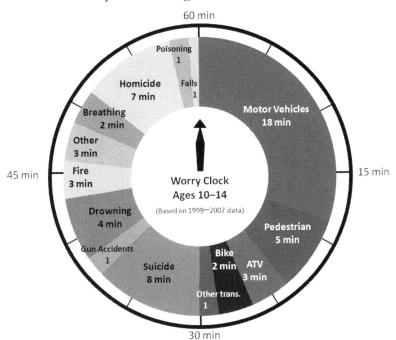

Homicide edges up one minute to seven. Guns accidents remain at one minute, and drowning drops another few minutes to four.

Reminder: The number of children who die is small. The entire Worry Clock for Ages Ten to Fourteen is based on half of that tiny slice of the pie at the beginning of the chapter and is an average of about 1,980 children per year, which means each minute represents about thirty-three deaths.

As in all chapters, these data and recommendations do not tell you what will happen or prevent something from happening. These data are for you to consider and use when talking to your health care providers about what is right for your child.

The following sections give more detail on the causes within each of the major components of the Worry Clock and provide recommendations for what to do about them.

Motor Vehicle Accidents: 18 Minutes

Motor vehicle accidents account for over one-quarter of your worry. They continue to be the largest chunk of worry, and we will only see that grow in the next chapter. Most of these accidents were in cars, minivans, trucks, and similar vehicles, but a significant group (about three minutes of the eighteen) died on motorcycles. Since motorcycles have different issues than these other vehicles, motorcycles are addressed separately, at the end of this motor vehicle accident section.

By now you know that the first question to ask is what percent of victims were wearing seat belts. Consistent with other age groups, the majority (about 60 percent) of children who died in car accidents were not wearing any form of seat belt. Another 6 percent were wearing them partially or improperly (e.g., just a shoulder belt). Only 34 percent were wearing seat belts properly. About 80 percent of teens (albeit a slightly older comparison group) wear seat belts, and although that rate is the lowest of any other age group, it is high compared to the one-third who died belted.[224]

The children were seated throughout the vehicles. About 10 percent of the children who died in motor vehicle accidents were either driving the vehicle (4 percent) or in a "seat" not meant for people (e.g., cargo area of a pickup, 6 percent). The remaining youth were positioned either in a back seat (50 percent) or in the passenger side of the front seat (35 percent).

> **Motor Vehicle Point #1:** Again, the majority (60 percent) of those who died were not wearing seat belts. One in ten youths were either driving (if in a state where fourteen-year-olds can legally drive) or riding in a nonseat (e.g., back of a pickup), and one in three was in the front passenger seat.

The most common types of accidents were:

Hitting another motor vehicle	45%
Rolling over	31%
Hitting a tree	10%

The youth who die are likely to be in a car with several to many others (see pie graph), a pattern we will see again in the teen years. Three-quarters of those who died were in vehicles with *more than two people in the car*. These young individuals may be driving with their older, driving (yet inexperienced) siblings or peers, and there is good evidence that the more teens in a car, the greater the likelihood of something going wrong (see the teen chapter for more).

Another potential issue for inexperienced drivers is ignorance of what to do in an accident; they can panic and turn a minor accident deadly. For example, a youth new to driving might survive a crash only to be killed after exiting the car (see story box for an unusual version of what is too common a story). To ensure that youth stay safe after accidents, KidsHealth (KidsHealth.org) offers advice directly to young,

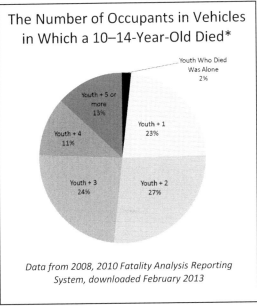

The Number of Occupants in Vehicles in Which a 10–14-Year-Old Died*

- Youth Who Died Was Alone 2%
- Youth + 5 or more 13%
- Youth + 4 11%
- Youth + 1 23%
- Youth + 3 24%
- Youth + 2 27%

Data from 2008, 2010 Fatality Analysis Reporting System, downloaded February 2013

new drivers for after they get into an accident, including:

- **"Take some deep breaths to get calm.** After a crash, a person may feel a wide range of emotions—shock, guilt, fear, nervousness, or anger—all of which are normal. But take a few deep breaths or count to ten to calm down. The calmer you are, the better prepared you will be to handle the situation."
- **"Keep yourself and others safe.** If you can't get out of your car—or it's not safe to try—keep your seat belt fastened, turn on your hazard lights, then call 911 if possible and wait for help to arrive. If the collision seems to be minor, turn off your car and grab your emergency kit. If it's safe to get out and move around your car, set up orange cones, warning triangles, or emergency flares around the crash site."

Motor Vehicle Point #2: Three-quarters of these youth were riding with more than one other passenger, which, as we will see in the teenage years, may be problematic.

Recommendations for avoiding fatal motor vehicle accidents (based mostly on CDC advice) are the same ones cited in other chapters, including:

- Don't ever put children (or anyone else) in the cargo areas of trucks or other areas not meant for passengers.
- Practice and teach defensive driving. Know some of the major mistakes other drivers are likely to make, including changing lanes due to blind spots and failing to yield when making left turns.
- If you are in one of those states where kids can start driving at fourteen, follow the advice in the teen chapter on making sure you teen gets lots of daytime driving practice first and limiting the number of other teens in the car.
- If your child is going to be driven by another teen, make sure that teen is following those guidelines, too. Ideally, don't let your child ride with another teen until that teen has been driving for six months or, better, one year.
- Make sure your teen knows what to do if there is an accident and how to assess whether it is safe to exit the car. (Cars.com also has some good advice on a step-by-step process for what to do after a crash, at
  http://www.cars.com/go/advice/Story.jsp?section=maintenance &subject=autodisasters&story=single-car-crash-disaster&referer=&aff=national).
- Always wear a seat belt and don't move until your children have theirs on, too. Make it a habit for everyone.
- Don't drink, speed, or commit any of the other duh mistakes.

Although included in the motor vehicle category, motorcycles pose different issues and require different recommendations, such as wearing helmets. Per vehicle mile traveled, motorcyclists are over thirty times more likely than passenger car occupants to die in a traffic crash.[225]

About half of those who died from motorcycle accidents in this age group were not wearing helmets.[226] Unhelmeted riders are 40 percent more likely to die from a head injury than someone wearing a helmet.[227]

Half were drivers and half were passengers. So it's likely that it is deadlier to be a passenger (one would expect the number of individual riders to be higher than the passenger numbers because people would travel alone more often than with a passenger). Roughly 80 percent of those who died were male.

In case you were wondering how motorcycles compare to ATVs, they have one-third the deaths. Note that I have no way to account for frequency of driving. If ATVs are driven three times more than motorcycles by these teens, then these two are equally deadly. However, if ATVs are driven the same amount as motorcycles, then per mile driven, ATVs are three times as deadly (perhaps because youth are less likely to wear helmets on ATVs).

Motor Vehicle Point #3: Youth who died on motorcycles were equally divided between drivers and passengers, so even if your family doesn't own a motorcycle, you may want to talk to your child about the importance of wearing a helmet.

The CDC offers some suggestions for motorcycle safety:[228]

- **Always wear a DOT-approved helmet.**
- **Never ride your motorcycle after drinking.** Alcohol greatly impairs your ability to safely operate a motorcycle. If you have been drinking, get a ride home or call a taxi.
- **Don't let friends ride impaired.** Take their keys away.
- **Wear protective clothing that provides some level of injury protection.** Upper-body clothing should also include bright colors or reflective materials so that other motorists can more easily see you.
- **Avoid tailgating.**
- **Maintain a safe speed and exercise caution when traveling over slippery surfaces or gravel.**

Story Box: Motor Vehicle Accidents, Ages Ten to Fourteen

Sixth-Grader Is Only Death in Eighty-Six-Car Pileup
On January 21, 2013, in Mason, Ohio, a quickly approaching, blinding whiteout snow caused an eighty-six-car pileup in the freeway. A twelve-year-old then exited her damaged car to stand in the median, where she was struck and fatally injured by a cable median barrier.[229]

Eleven-Year-Old Girl Dies during Ride with Two Seventeen-Year-Olds
On October 25, 2012, in Walworth County, Wisconsin, an eleven-year-old was riding in the back seat of a vehicle with two seventeen-year-olds in the front, one of whom was driving. The car swerved off the road and hit a utility pole, causing severe damage to the car. Drugs and alcohol were not expected to be involved, and all were wearing their seat belts.[230]
Overcorrection Accident Kills Thirteen-Year-Old

On July 30, 2011, in Miller County, Missouri, a thirteen-year-old was killed when the adult driver of the car he was in overcorrected, then traveled off the roadway, hit an embankment, flipped, and hit several trees. Neither was wearing a seat belt.[231]

Younger Brother Dies When Being Driven to School by Older Brother

On January 24, 2013, in Homes County, Ohio, a twelve-year-old boy was being driven to school by his older brother, eighteen, when the car went off the road and hit an embankment, then a tree. Both were wearing seat belts.[232]

Boy Killed in Family Minivan after Being Struck by Car Escaping Police

On Christmas night, December 25, 2012, in Daly City, California, an eleven-year-old was killed when a car rushing to escape police hit his family's minivan.[233]

Eleven-Year-Old Dies in Motorcycle Wreck

On February 12, 2013, in Fort Worth, Texas, an eleven-year-old-boy died when his motorcycle crashed into a fence. He died from neck injuries.[234]

Pedestrian Accidents: 5 Minutes

More than three-quarters of the pedestrian accidents in this age group[235] result in part from some action of the pedestrian. In other words, most of the time, the accident is the pedestrian's fault to some degree. The most commonly noted pedestrian mistake is to dart or dash out into the roadway (see table).[236] Two of the five minutes of worry are linked to a youth darting out into the road. This is a change from the much earlier years, when accidents occurred in driveways, parking lots, or alleys; few accidents now occur in those places.

Pedestrian Accidents Breakdown, Ages 10–15	Worry Clock Estimate
Pedestrian Did Nothing	**1 Minute**
Pedestrian Contributed to Accident	**4 Minutes**
Darting into road (e.g., mid-block)	2 Minutes
Not yielding to cars or jaywalking	1 Minute
Playing, lying, or otherwise behaving inappropriately in road	*30 seconds*

Walking wrong way	*10 seconds*
Inattention (talking, eating, etc.)	*5 seconds*
Other	*15 seconds*

These youths differ from adults, whose pedestrian accidents occur mostly at intersections. For the youths, accidents tend to take place mid-block or just after an intersection. About two-thirds of the accidents occur mid-block, and three-quarters total occur away from intersections (see table below).

Location of Pedestrian Accidents	Percent
Nonintersection—On roadway, not in crosswalk	66%
Nonintersection—On roadway, in marked crosswalk	0%
Intersection—In marked crosswalk	15%
Intersection—Not in Crosswalk	10%
Shoulder/Roadside	4%
Sidewalk	2%

As you would expect from earlier sections of this book, boys are more likely than girls to be in these fatal accidents. In an analysis of the most recent years, boys represented 62 percent of youth pedestrian deaths.

Alcohol use (by either the driver of the pedestrian) plays a role in anywhere from 5 to 50 percent of the pedestrian accidents.

For pedestrian safety, the NHTSA and the CDC recommend:
- When possible, cross the street at a designated crosswalk.
- Increase visibility at night by carrying a flashlight when walking and by wearing retro-reflective clothing that helps to highlight body movements (i.e., get your child clothing, especially winter jackets, that have a chance to be seen).
- Walk on a sidewalk, where it is much safer. If you must walk in the street, walk facing traffic.

Pedestrian Accidents Point #1: Dashing out mid-block or near intersections is once again the number-one cause of pedestrian deaths.

ATV Accidents: 3 Minutes

The relative amount of worry for ATVs jumps for early teen youth, to three minutes. About 75 percent of the time, the youth who died was the driver of the ATV.[239] When the driver died, the accidents were about equally divided between collisions (e.g., hitting another ATV) and noncollisions (e.g., flipping the lone ATV). Of those who died, only about one in five (20 percent)[240] was wearing a helmet.

ATV Point #1: Only one in five (20 percent) of youths who died driving (75 percent) or riding (25 percent) ATVs was wearing a helmet.

The ATV recommendations are the same as always: wear helmets; only have one person on the ATV, which should be youth-sized; and don't ride on paved surfaces.

under fourteen from riding ATVs unless there is a sanctioned event or other exemption, and toughened penalties against adults who allow children to ride such vehicles. The law, considered one of the toughest in the country, passed in 2010."[241]

Bicycles and Other Transportation: 3 Minutes

Unlike pedestrian accidents, in which one-quarter of the walkers did nothing to contribute to their demise, bicycles always had some reason coded for what the cyclist did. About half of the actions noted as contributing were classified as a failure to obey traffic signals or signs (e.g., riding through a stop sign or red light). An additional 20 percent were for entering traffic from between parked cars, and about 5 percent were from inattentiveness.

Almost all (95 percent) of the youths who died in bicycle accidents[242] were not wearing helmets.

Bicycle accidents showed an even greater gender disparity than pedestrian deaths, with about 80 percent of fatalities being boys.

Bicycle Point #1: Almost none of the bicycle accident victims wore helmets, most were boys, and about half ignored traffic signs.

The recommendations for increased safety on bicycles are straightforward and continue from the younger years. Hopefully, you've already established that the child always wears a helmet and obeys traffic rules, all by habit. The next task is to make sure that the child is seen by cars, by putting lights (white in front and red in back) and many orange reflectors on the bicycle, and easily seen clothing on the rider. There is some evidence, as with cars, that daytime running lights increase safety, too.[243]

Story Box: Bicycle Accidents, Ages Ten to Fourteen

Ten-Year-Old Bicycle Rider Hit, Killed by SUV While Mother Jogged Beside Him
On July 6, 2012, in Meridian, Idaho, a ten-year-old boy was riding his bicycle next to his mother. They were crossing in a crosswalk together when they were struck by an SUV. The crosswalk was just after a traffic circle that had lots of landscaping that may have obscured views. The boy was not wearing a bicycle helmet.[244]

Within this age group, most suicides occur in the older half, between ages twelve and fourteen. Suicide rates, in fact, will increase markedly in the late teens and continue to rise until the early twenties.[245]

Why does suicide suddenly appear in these early teen years? A recent study suggests, "The consensus in empirical research is that mental disorders and substance abuse are the most important risk factors in both attempted and completed adolescent suicide."[246] In other words, depression (primarily) and abuse of drugs and alcohol appear to be the two main predictors for suicide in adolescents.[247] And not coincidentally, those precursors begin to appear in significant numbers in early adolescence.

Depression and other forms of mental illness are common in this country, and for many of us, they start in adolescence. About 30 percent of high school–age teens reported feeling sad or hopeless almost every day for two or more weeks in a row in the last year,[248] which is consistent with estimates from the research on the prevalence of depression.[249] One out of every seventeen Americans suffers from a severe mental illness, and half of these individuals begin showing symptoms by the age of fourteen.[250] The Office of Adolescent Health reports that one in five adolescents has a diagnosable mental disorder, such as depression and "less than half of adolescents who need mental health services receive them."[251]

There is no question of a link between mental illnesses and suicide. Of those adolescents who die by suicide, 90 percent demonstrated behaviors diagnosable under at least one psychiatric disorder.[252] Depression and related depressive disorders are consistently the most prevalent among adolescent suicide victims, ranging from 49 to 64 percent. Many of these disorders co-occur with an anxiety or substance abuse disorder.[253]

Suicide Point #1: Suicide rates spike as children become teenagers, and 90 percent of the children who commit suicide are diagnosable with at least one psychiatric disorder.

Alcohol and drug abuse are also related to increased depression, disorders, and suicide.[254] For example, sixteen- to nineteen-year-old females are more than six times as likely to experience depression if they abuse alcohol than if they do not.[255] Although they are consistently documented as co-occurring, it is unclear whether depression drives the alcohol abuse or the alcohol fuels the depression, or both. Whatever conclusions you decide to draw, the point here is that the combination of depression with drug/alcohol abuse, which are the most common co-occurring disorders in adolescence, puts youth at even greater risk of suicide.

> **Suicide Point #2:** Substance abuse (alcohol and other drugs) increases the risk of suicide, particularly when in combination with depression.

Suicide attempts should not be ignored; estimates are that as many as one-third of those who commit suicide have at least one prior attempt. The National Institute of Mental Health warns, "A history of a prior suicide attempt is one of the strongest predictors of completed suicide, conferring a particularly high risk for boys (thirty-fold increase) and a less elevated risk for girls (three-fold increase)." [256]

As many know, homosexual and bisexual youth are also at increased risk—they have a two- to six-fold increased risk of nonlethal suicidal behavior.

Youth who commit suicide at this age make slightly different choices in methods compared to their older peers. More than 60 percent of these ten- to fourteen-year-olds chose hanging, strangulation, or suffocation; only 30 percent chose firearms. During the teen years, this trend reverses, with half of teens choosing guns.

Method of Suicide	
Hanging, strangulation, and suffocation	5 minutes
Firearms (handgun, rifle, or shotgun)	2.5 minutes
Poisoning	*20 seconds*
Jumping from a height or lying before a moving object	*5 seconds*
Other	*5 seconds*
Total	**8 minutes**

There is no question that there is a biological basis to suicide. Studies have found that first-degree relatives of those who have committed suicide have more than twice the risk of the general population, and the rates are much higher in identical twins.[257] Brain researchers now have twenty-five years of evidence for serotonin's role, and geneticists are seeking to pinpoint the exact genes that predispose one to be more at risk for suicide.

That is not to say that biology is everything. Social support and connection are major buffers. Researchers found, for example, that "students who described family life in terms of a high degree of mutual involvement, shared interests, and emotional support were 3.5 to 5.5 times less likely to be suicidal than were adolescents from less cohesive families who had the same levels of depression or life stress."[258]

The recommendations are the same as they are for the teens and are covered in the next chapter under the teen suicide section.

Homicide: 7 Minutes

Homicide in this age group looks a lot like it does in teenage years except with relatively less gun involvement, similar to the pattern seen for suicide. Firearms are number one, used in almost 70 percent of the homicides (see below). Strangling and suffocation are just under 10 percent, and arson-related homicide is just over 5 percent.

Firearms	67%	5 minutes
Knives or other sharp objects	8%	*30 seconds*
Strangling, suffocating, or hanging	6%	*20 seconds*
Fire, smoke	3%	*10 seconds*
Unspecified	15%	1 minute

Homicide by a blunt object (e.g., hitting someone over the head with a heavy object) doesn't make the list, nor do drugs or poisoning.

Drowning: 4 Minutes

Most of the drowning incidents now occur during swimming in natural water. About 10 percent of these accidents are from *falling into* natural water and then drowning, such as boating accidents (see box for more on boating). Deaths from injuries that occur while jumping into water (e.g., hitting head on rocks in a quarry) are such a small fraction that these numbers are unreliable.

Swimming pool accidents are half as common as natural water incidents.

Bathtubs are still not entirely out of the picture, contributing less than 10 percent to the total.

If your children don't know how to swim, it is never too late to teach them. If they like to swim in natural water, such as beaches or quarries, try to take a swim class related to the venue.

Boating Safety for All Ages

Motor boats, a very common form of boat, account for the vast majority of boating deaths (see 2012 data below). Blow boaters may rest easier knowing that sailboats, although commonly used, come in after canoes, kayaks, and inflatables. Alcohol is involved in one third of all (all ages) boating fatalities. In boating deaths involving alcohol use, over half of the victims capsized their boats and/or fell overboard. And drink for drink, a boat operator is likely to become impaired more quickly than a driver.[259] Drowning is the cause of death for more than 70% of boating deaths, and most of these drowning were precipitated by unexpected entry into the water (e.g., boat collision or capsizing event throws people overboard). Over 80% of drowning victims were not wearing life jackets when found, yet most of those victims could have been saved had they been wearing a life jacket before the mishap occurred.[260] The 20% who were wearing life jackets, but still died tended to be canoe or kayak operators caught underwater, for example. [261]

Lessons applicable to children?
Boat operators should know that alcohol is more likely to affect them on sea than on land and, ideally, not drink all together (especially if the person lacks significant experience operating that boat). Also, get into the life jackets habit; you won't have warning for when you should put one on (e.g., hitting a rock, for example, provides no warning.

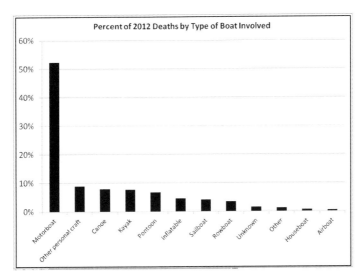

US Coast Guard (2013). 2012 Recreational Boating Statistics. Us Coast Guard, Washington DC, COMDTPUB P16754.26,

Fire: 3 Minutes

About 90 percent, or almost all, of the worry goes to uncontrolled fires in buildings, so all those same lessons from the toddler section on fire apply here.

One of the issues that we will see in the teen chapter begins to pop up at this age: the youth victims are often the ones who start the fires. If you have a child who likes to start even small fires, check in with a mental health professional.

The remaining 10 percent of fire-related deaths are attributed not so much to what you might associate with youth, such as fireworks, but to exposure to the ignition of other flammable materials.

Breathing-Related Accidents: 2 Minutes

Again, most of these deaths (66 percent) are from accidental hanging or strangulation. Examples of actual accidents I read about included a child being strangled when his helmet got caught in a homemade zip line and another boy whose neck was caught in a rope swing. The last third of breathing-related accidents are due primarily to choking (mostly on nonfood) and cave-ins (e.g., a child climbs in a hole dug in the sand at the beach, only to have the sides cave in). Most of these are fairly unusual accidents, but it does appear that many may have been prevented with closer supervision.

Firearms: 1 Minute

The incidents in this category are the purely accidental deaths due to guns, such as from an accidental discharge during cleaning. Unlike in the other categories of deaths by guns, handguns were not the most frequent culprit. Instead, rifles, shotguns, and the like were used about 40 percent more often than handguns. This may indicate that these youth are the ones handling the guns.

As a reminder, one-third of the homes in the US have at least one gun, so chances are your child will be in a house with guns. Make sure they know to leave the area if they see a gun. Teens may like holding the guns, but in the natural holding position, their finger is on the trigger, which it should not be unless they intend to shoot. The NRA has three basic rules:

1. Always keep the gun pointed in a safe direction.
2. Always keep your finger *off* the trigger until you are ready to shoot.
3. Always keep guns unloaded.

Story Box: Gun Accidents, Ages Ten to Fourteen

Teen Accidentally Shoots Best Friend with Brother's Gun
On November 3, 2012, in Indianapolis, a teen called a friend over and, as a prank, took out a gun just purchased online by his eighteen-year-old brother. He pointed it at his friend and then accidentally pulled the trigger. The friend died from his injuries.[264]

Falls: 1 Minute

For the first time, the top incidents in falls are sports-related accidents, specifically those associated with skiing, snowboarding, ice-skating, and similar activities. There is little information on these incidents, although some suggest that skiing accidents tend to be young men who are going very fast and hit immovable objects, such as trees.[265] This is apparently one reason why, despite increasing helmet use, the number of deaths has not changed; helmets are not enough protection for these head-on collisions. I could not find any examples of ice-skating deaths at younger ages (head injuries were reported in older teens), except for drowning that occurred from attempted ice skating on an incompletely frozen lake.

Having said all that, these sports accidents only account for about fifteen seconds on the Worry Clock, comparable to some of the categories that didn't make the clock, which are presented in the section describing what's not on the clock.

Cause of Death by Falling	Percent within Falling	Seconds on the Worry Clock
Fall involving skates, skis, etc.	26%	*15 seconds*
Other fall from one level to another	21%	*13 seconds*
Fall from/through building or structure	14%	*8 seconds*
Fall from tree or cliff (50 percent each)	14%	*8 seconds*
Other fall on same level	12%	*7 seconds*

Poisoning: 1 Minute

The two major culprits for poisoning are gasses and narcotics, each responsible for about one-third of deaths:

Gasses   32%

Narcotics   36%

The gas primarily responsible for deaths is carbon monoxide—and it may not kill in the same way you think. In 1975, catalytic converters, which turn most of the deadly carbon monoxide into harmless carbon dioxide, minimized the amount of the poison to such a degree that suicide rates supposedly fell as people found that running the car in a closed garage didn't achieve the desired result.

So what does cause carbon monoxide poisoning? Lots of the things that happen in winter, including: a furnace not installed or working properly (including a blocked outside vent), a blocked chimney, a car or gas-powered snow-blower (or other gas operated equipment that doesn't have a converter) left running, or a blocked car tail pipe.

Twenty-five states have statutes that require carbon monoxide detectors in certain residential buildings.[266] Although having carbon monoxide detectors in your home is definitely recommended, having a detector in your car is also important; snow, mud or anything that blocks the tail pipe is potentially deadly.[267]

For the one-third of incidents that were drug induced, narcotics and psychodysleptics (hallucinogens) topped the list. These were not suicides but accidental poisonings.

What Doesn't Appear on the Clock

Below are a few causes of death that I singled out for a special look, either because they had no findings or because of how they compared to other findings (but didn't occur often enough to talk about in the main section of the chapter). For example, exposure to electric current accounts for about the same amount of time on the clock (fourteen seconds) as deaths from skiing or skating accidents (fifteen seconds).

Although many incidents on this table are very infrequent, their appearance here does not mean that your child is necessarily safe from these causes of death. Your child may have a particular susceptibility to electric eels, for example, that is not taken into account here. What this table does show is that across the country over many years, the incidents with ** were so rare that I cannot provide an estimate for the Worry Clock based on the government death statistics.

Incidents That Did Not Make the Worry Clock	
Exposure to electric transmission lines or other electric current	*14 seconds*
Victim of lightning	*4 seconds*
Bitten or struck by dog	**
Bitten or struck by other mammal (e.g., bears)	*4 seconds*
Contact with marine animal (e.g., shark)	**
Contact with venomous snakes and lizards	**
Contact with powered lawnmower	**
Contact with other powered hand tools/machinery	**
Foreign body entering into or through eye or orifice	**

Quiz Time for Ages Ten to Fourteen!

1. How many minutes on the Worry Clock represent youths who died from all gun-related incidents?

2. All the bicycle accidents added to all the pedestrian accidents combined equals approximately what one other category on the clock?

3. True or false: The number-one cause of pedestrian deaths is pedestrians ignoring traffic signals at intersections.

4. What percentage of youths died in cars with more than one other person?

5. True or false: Motorcycle passengers are more likely to die than motorcycle operators.

6. What is the percentage of those who died on bicycles, ATVs, and motorcycles who were not wearing helmets?

7. True or false: The rate of deaths from drowning in natural water (rivers, lakes and streams) is twice that of swimming pools.

8. What are the two main predictors for suicide?

9. True or false: Fireworks are worth one minute of worry.

10. True or false: Failed suicide attempts are a good sign that the youth is not really trying to die.

Answers to Quiz:

1. Adding up all the gun-related deaths:
   Homicide: 5 minutes + Suicide: 2.5 minutes + Guns: 1 minute = 8.5 Minutes

2. Bicycle(two minutes) + Pedestrian (five minutes) = seven minutes
   Either homicide at seven minutes or suicide at eight minutes is about the same.

3. False. The top cause is dashing out mid-block, just like for the toddler stage.

4. Seventy-seven percent were in a car with two or more others.

5. True. Although the deaths were equally divided, we can assume that there were more drivers than passengers (since a driver can be alone, but a passenger cannot). Therefore, the rate of death for passengers was higher—likely significantly higher.

6. The percentage of people who died who were not wearing helmets on:
    Bicycles: 95 percent
    ATVs: 80 percent
    Motorcycles: 50 percent

7. True.

8. Depression and drug/alcohol abuse.

9. No. Although fireworks may be an issue for your particular child and do have many injuries associated with them, they do not even make the clock. The closest similar incident is death by exposure to other flammable materials (e.g., starting a fire with highly flammable materials in the backyard), at about eighteen seconds.

10. False. It's not likely, anyway, given that about one-third of those who do succeed at committing suicide had at least one prior attempt.

Top Ten for Preteens (Ages Ten to Fourteen)

If you aren't sure where to start, here are some ideas. As in all chapters, you know what is best for your child, and these recommendations may not be right for him or her. Talk to your health care providers about what is best for your family.

1. **Know that driving experience matters most.** If you are in one of those states where kids start driving at fourteen, follow the advice in the next section on making sure you teen gets lots of practice with daytime driving first, and limit the number of other teens in the car.
2. **Don't let teens drive with teens, if possible.** If your child is going to be driven by another teen, make sure that teen is following these guidelines, too. Ideally, don't let your child drive with another teen until that teen has been driving for six months or, better, one year.
3. **Seat belt and helmet—ALWAYS.** Seat belts whenever available and helmets on ATVs and bicycles, without fail.

4. **Know that alcohol begins to play a role in judgment with cars and even crossing streets.** Talking to your kids about the data may be one way to help them make better decisions, if only about the timing and surroundings when then drink.

5. **Reflectors are not enough; use many lights and wear protective clothing that provides some level of injury protection.** When riding a bicycle, ATV, motorcycle, or moped—including when riding with a friend—wear all safety gear and clothing with reflective materials.

6. **Talk about why it is important to follow traffic rules.** Especially if your teen assumes that other people will act logically in all situations, make sure she or he understands that traffic rules help set expectations.

7. **If you see signs of depression, get professional help and take all talk of suicide and attempts seriously.** Don't assume that depression is a natural part of teenage years. If your teen is pulling away from you, ask someone at your school that your teen trusts to recommend a professional.

8. **Limit your teen's access to firearms whenever possible.** Access to firearms increases the likelihood that a bad decision will become fatal. Ideally, get all guns out of your house.

9. **Make sure your young teen knows when it is safe to go in the water** at the ocean or in rivers. And ensure she wears a life vest when boating (especially motor boating).

10. **Keep up the supervision.** If you cannot be with your child, try to enforce a buddy system so someone is always there to alert you if something has gone wrong or when situations are risky (e.g., deep holes as cave-in risks).

Conclusion

These ages foreshadow the teen years. Although deaths remain relatively low, the large number of suicides and motor vehicles accidents show what lies ahead.

Teenagers' rate of death is more than those of the three previous age groups combined (all deaths from ages two to fourteen). As always, the percentage of all children who die is small. The pie graph for this age group is a reminder of how many children die for any reason (e.g., cancers, diseases, and accidents); even here, the sliver is barely visible.

Percent of Children Ages 15–19 Who Died
(CDC Mortality Rates, 1999–2007)

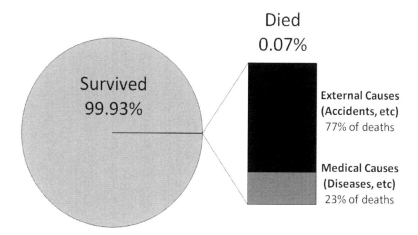

The proportion of deaths that are *accidental* (including suicide and other preventable causes) is higher in teenagers than *ANY* other age group (see the darker part of the bar and compare to the other chapters). Instead of a quarter of all deaths being accidents, now three-quarters are accidents. The remainder of this chapter focuses on the 75 percent of that barely visible slice in the pie that are due to accidents.

As you will see in the next chapter, it is this age group that should account for most of your worry across your child's life, because this is where the most deaths are preventable.

Lessons from the fifteen- to nineteen-year-olds include:
- Teenage years are by far the deadliest for accidents, only rivaled—yet still far surpassing—the rate of the infant year.
- Motorcycle and ATV deaths take up less of the clock only because the other areas grew so much more; these two actually become more deadly (more on this in the next chapter).

- Guns account for 80 percent of homicides and 50 percent of suicides.
- The first six months, extending to the first year, is the deadliest time for a new driver. Getting practice without peers in the car can make a life-or-death difference.

First I review the Worry Clock for Ages Fifteen to Nineteen, which presents the main causes of death, and then I go into each category in more detail and pass along recommendations, primarily from the government, on how to prevent these deaths.

The Worry Clock for Ages Fifteen to Nineteen

The Worry Clock for Ages Fifteen to Nineteen shows that a few key areas explode in the teenage years: motor vehicles, homicide, and suicide. Although transportation accidents still account for about half of the worry minutes, motor vehicle accidents, at twenty-six minutes, now dwarf the other categories. Pedestrian, ATV, and bicycle accidents (which don't even make the clock now) all take a back seat to car accidents, which we would expect as these inexperienced drivers take to the road.

Homicide jumps higher than at any other time, up more than 50 percent to twelve minutes. Suicide increases again, up to eight minutes total. These three categories—car accidents, homicide, and suicide—account for forty-seven minutes, more than three-quarters of your worry.

Making up the remaining thirteen minutes, fire stays significant at four minutes; drowning drops farther to just two minutes; and gun accidents and falls remain at one minute each. Accidental poisoning and breathing-related accidents (e.g., choking) are now less than half a minute each and are lumped into the "other" category.

Reminder: Even during the relatively deadly teen years, the number of children who die is small. The entire Worry Clock for Ages Fifteen to Nineteen is based on three-quarters of that tiny slice of the pie at the beginning of the chapter, about 10,500 children per year, which means that each minute represents about 175 deaths out of the number of children in this age group. The following sections provide more detail on the causes within each of the major components of the Worry Clock and provide recommendations for what to do about them.

As in all chapters, these data and recommendations do not tell you what will happen or prevent something from happening, and may even make things worse. These data are for you to consider and talk about with your health care providers in deciding what is right for your child (now a young adult!).

Worry Clock for Ages Fifteen to Nineteen

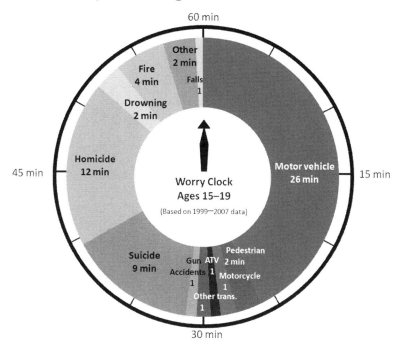

Motor Vehicle Accidents: 26 Minutes

Teen motor vehicle accidents are responsible for nearly half of the Worry Clock for this age group, and about one-quarter of your worry for your child's entire youth. In accidents that involved teens, driver error is by far the most common cause. Over 80 percent of these deaths are due to teen drivers (see the pie graph). One nationally representative study found that teen driver error, as opposed to vehicle or environmental factors, accounted for nearly all of the accidents.[268]

Per mile driven, teen drivers are three to four times more likely than drivers age twenty and older to be in a fatal crash.[269,270] More than half (about 55 to 58 percent)[271] of the teens who die in motor vehicles are the drivers of the vehicles. And of those who are passengers, most are traveling with another teen as the driver (about 60 percent). This is one of the reasons why students are about fifty times more likely to arrive at school alive if they take the bus than if they drive themselves or ride with friends.[272]

Two main factors appear to escalate the fatality rate for teens: 1) lack of driving experience, coupled with 2) increased risk taking and other poor decision-making skills notable for this age group.

Percentage of Teens Who Died in Vehicle Crashes as Drivers or Passengers (2010)

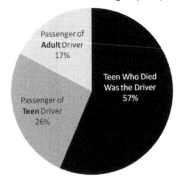

After studying teen crashes, the CDC concluded that "the main cause of teen crashes is driver inexperience."[273] Yes, teens make bad decisions, and so do many adults. The problem is that inexperience can turn bad decisions into catastrophes.

Newly licensed teens are particularly at risk. Most crashes happen during the first year a teen has a license,[274] and crash risk is particularly high during the first months of licensure.[275,276] Teens are more likely than older drivers to underestimate dangerous situations or not be able to recognize hazardous situations.[277]

What types of errors do teens make? A recent study did a thorough analysis and concluded:

> Recognition errors (e.g., inadequate surveillance, distraction) accounted for 46.3 percent of all errors, followed by decision errors (e.g., following too closely, too fast for conditions) (40.1 percent) and performance errors (e.g., loss of control) (8.0 percent). Inadequate surveillance, driving too fast for conditions, and distracted driving together accounted for almost half of all crashes. Aggressive driving behavior, drowsy driving, and physical impairments were less commonly cited as critical reasons. Males and females had similar proportions of broadly classified errors, although females were specifically more likely to make inadequate surveillance errors. [278]

The increase in accidents is due to an element of immaturity in addition to inexperience. When younger novice drivers were compared with older novice drivers, the teens crashed at higher rates, which led the CDC to conclude that these higher crash rates may be due in part to developmental factors such as peer influence, poor perception of risk, and high emotionality.[279]

For a compelling and research-based view of the teenage brain (and many other aspects of development), make sure to read *Nurture Shock*. Bronson and Merryman conclude from the research that some teenagers are simply "wired" to take big risks and have particularly difficult times in the early stages of driving because of the cognitive load:

> "Teenage drivers can score 100% on a paper test of the rules, but when driving, their reaction times are delayed because they have not yet internalized the *grammar* of driving—they have to think about it. This increases the cognitive load, and their ability to maintain attention is stressed to capacity. They are on the verge of making poor decisions. Put a friend in the car and attention systems are easily overloaded—the driver's brain no longer proactively anticipates what could happen, glancing seconds ahead and preloading the rules. Instead, he is left to react, and can't always react accurately, no matter how fast his reflexes are."[280]

Motor Vehicle Point #1: Inexperience is the number-one cause of teen driving accidents.[281] And the first few months carry the highest risk.[282,283]

The good news here is that training and practice are effective countermeasures. As the CDC notes,

> There are proven methods to helping teens become safer drivers. Research suggests that the most comprehensive graduated driver licensing (GDL) programs are associated with reductions of 38 percent and 40 percent in fatal and injury crashes, respectively, among sixteen-year-old drivers…[GDL] systems are designed to delay full licensure while allowing teens to get their initial driving experience under low-risk conditions.[284]

I present more on GDLs in the recommendations section.

In addition to the challenges due to their inexperience, teens are also more likely to create additional dangers by speeding, drinking and driving, texting, not using seat belts, and practicing other risky behaviors, particularly around peers.

Teens have the lowest rate of seat belt use of all the age groups. In 2011, only 54 percent of high school students reported that they always wear seat belts when riding with someone else.[285] In 2010, 56 percent of drivers ages fifteen to twenty who were killed in motor vehicle crashes after drinking and driving were *not* wearing a seat belt.[286] And speed was a factor in 39 percent of fatal teen crashes in 2010.[287]

Using a cell phone and texting while driving are "a national epidemic,"[288] according to some US officials, and teens lead the way. A typical teen sends and receives about a hundred text messages a day, and 58 percent of high school seniors admit to texting while driving.[289] Estimates are that about 10 percent of driver error accidents are due to distractions, including talking on phones and texting.[290]

Given that any distractions appear to affect teens more, it is perhaps not surprising that thirty-nine states ban texting for all age groups, and an additional five states outlaw it for novice teen drivers. A 2012 Associated Press article explained that "authorities are increasingly cracking down. In the last two weeks, teens in Missouri and Massachusetts have been sentenced to jail—one for a year—for fatal accidents involving texting."[291]

Cell phones are also more challenging for teens and younger drivers. "If you put a twenty-year-old driver behind the wheel with a cell phone, their reaction times are the same as a seventy-year-old driver who is not using a cell phone," said University of Utah psychology professor David Strayer, the same researcher whose earlier work found that even hands-free phone use was enough to distract drivers. In fact, drivers who conversed with someone not in the car were less adept at the wheel than drunken drivers with blood alcohol levels exceeding 0.08. In this new work, Strayer's team has found that drivers talking on cell phones were 18 percent slower to react to brake lights.

Perhaps not surprisingly, males in this group are at a significantly increased risk. In 2010, the motor vehicle death rate for male drivers and passengers ages sixteen to nineteen was almost two times that of their female counterparts.[292] The presence of male teenage passengers increases the likelihood of risky driving behavior.[293]

> **Motor Vehicle Point #2:** Teens are more likely to engage in risky behaviors that endanger themselves and others, such as not wearing seat belts, speeding, and texting.

The presence of teen passengers increases the crash risk of unsupervised teen drivers, and this risk increases with the number of teen passengers.[294] Nearly two out of three teen crash deaths that involve sixteen-year-old drivers happen when a new driver has one or more teen passengers.[295] The more kids in the car together, the worse the odds become, which is why some states now limit the numbers of other teens allowed with teen drivers.

The earlier pie graph shows that if we add teens who died driving with teens—one-quarter of those who died—to those who died as drivers, we would find that over 80 percent of teen motor vehicle passenger fatalities are attributable to teen drivers.

> **Motor Vehicle Point #3:** The presence of teen passengers increases the risk of a crash—and the risk goes up with the number of teen passengers. Altogether, teen drivers account for over 80 percent of the teen motor vehicle fatalities.

Take all of the above factors and now add alcohol. Nearly one-quarter (22 percent) of fatal teen crashes in 2010 involved a teen driver who had been drinking.[296] Although young drivers are actually less likely than adults to drive after drinking alcohol, their crash risk is substantially higher when they do. [297] At all levels of blood alcohol concentration (BAC), the risk of involvement in a motor vehicle crash is greater for teens than for older drivers.[298] Drinking while driving is clearly also a factor and likely magnifies the effects of inexperience.

> **Motor Vehicle Point #4:** Although young drivers are actually less likely than adults to drive after drinking alcohol, their crash risk is substantially higher when they do.[299] Teens under any impairment such as alcohol are at greater risk than experienced drivers under those same impairments.[300]

Think your teen won't drive drunk or with another teen who has been drinking? Think twice. In a national survey conducted in 2011, 24 percent of teens—nearly one in four—reported that, within the previous month, they had ridden with a driver who had been drinking alcohol.[301] And 8 percent of these youth reported that they themselves got behind the wheel after drinking at least once in the thirty days prior to the survey. In other words, a high percentage of our children are doing risky things on a regular basis.

Individual states, however, differ significantly on the riskiness reported by their teens. In Utah, just under 14 percent of high school students reported driving with someone who had been drinking, yet in Louisiana, the average was a whopping 32 percent, or almost one-third—and that is just in the last thirty days!

The Youth Risk Behavior Survey, which has a long record of doing a great job of asking kids about their risk taking and documenting it, also produces state estimates. I took three indicators from the survey to explore how these states differ:

1. Percentage of high school students who rode in a car or other vehicle driven by someone who had been drinking alcohol in the thirty days prior to the survey
2. Percentage of high school students who drove a car or other vehicle when they had been drinking alcohol in the thirty days prior to the survey
3. Percentage of high school students who reported that they rarely or never wore a seat belt

In the table below, I present the state-by-state differences. To help see those differences more clearly, I present the *difference from the all-state average*. For example, in Mississippi, North Dakota, and Wyoming, students reported doing these risky behaviors more than in other states, so these three states are marked "higher" in all three columns. Teens in Utah, Virginia, and Alaska, on the other hand, reported that they were consistently less likely to take these risks than children in other states.

	Each State's Percentage-Point Difference from the Average of All States (Unweighted for population; see first row for all-state average)		
	Drove When Drinking Alcohol One or More Times (30 Days)	**Rode with Someone Who Had Been Drinking**	**Rarely Wore Seat Belt**
Average of States	8.0 %	23.1 %	10.4 %
Alabama	HIGHER (+1.9)	AVERAGE (1.3)	HIGHER (+1.7)
Alaska	LOWER (-2.4)	LOWER (-4.5)	LOWER (-1.7)
Arizona	AVERAGE (1.3)	NO DATA	HIGHER (+4.2)
Arkansas	AVERAGE (0.9)	HIGHER (+2.5)	HIGHER (+4.0)
Colorado	LOWER (-2.2)	AVERAGE (-1.3)	NO DATA
Connecticut	AVERAGE (-1.1)	HIGHER (+2.1)	AVERAGE (-1.2)
Delaware	AVERAGE (0.0)	HIGHER (+1.8)	LOWER (-4.7)
Florida	AVERAGE (1.1)	AVERAGE (0.9)	AVERAGE (-1.6)
Georgia	AVERAGE (-1.2)	AVERAGE (1.2)	HIGHER (+2.4)
Hawaii	NO DATA	NO DATA	NO DATA
Idaho	AVERAGE (0.2)	LOWER (-2.3)	LOWER (-2.5)
Illinois	AVERAGE (-0.3)	HIGHER (+2.9)	LOWER (-3.4)
Indiana	LOWER (-2.7)	AVERAGE (-1.4)	LOWER (-1.8)
Iowa	HIGHER (+2.5)	AVERAGE (0.7)	LOWER (-6.0)
Kansas	AVERAGE (0.7)	AVERAGE (0.7)	LOWER (-2.3)
Kentucky	AVERAGE (-1.1)	LOWER (-2.9)	HIGHER (+2.0)
Louisiana	HIGHER (+3.7)	HIGHER (+9.0)	AVERAGE (0.1)
Maine	NO DATA	NO DATA	LOWER (-2.0)

	Drove When Drinking Alcohol One or More Times (30 Days)	Rode with Someone Who Had Been Drinking	Rarely Wore Seat Belt
Maryland	AVERAGE (-0.3)	HIGHER (+2.8)	HIGHER (+1.4)
Massachusetts	AVERAGE (-1.5)	AVERAGE (-0.2)	HIGHER (+3.1)
Michigan	LOWER (-2.0)	AVERAGE (-1.4)	LOWER (-4.5)
Mississippi	HIGHER (+2.0)	HIGHER (+4.2)	HIGHER (+2.2)
Missouri	NO DATA	NO DATA	NO DATA
Montana	HIGHER (+2.6)	HIGHER (+3.0)	AVERAGE (0.8)
Nebraska	AVERAGE (-0.8)	AVERAGE (0.8)	HIGHER (+5.3)
Nevada	NO DATA	NO DATA	NO DATA
New Hampshire	AVERAGE (0.6)	AVERAGE (-0.4)	AVERAGE (0.3)
New Jersey	AVERAGE (-1.6)	AVERAGE (-1.7)	AVERAGE (0.1)
New Mexico	AVERAGE (1.3)	HIGHER (+2.7)	LOWER (-2.4)
New York	LOWER (-2.6)	NO DATA	NO DATA
New York (W/out NY City)	AVERAGE (-1.6)	LOWER (-3.1)	LOWER (-1.9)
North Carolina	AVERAGE (-1.7)	LOWER (-2.1)	LOWER (-2.3)
North Dakota	HIGHER (+3.7)	HIGHER (+2.0)	HIGHER (+3.0)
Ohio	AVERAGE (-0.8)	LOWER (-2.1)	HIGHER (+6.3)
Oklahoma	AVERAGE (-0.8)	LOWER (-3.4)	LOWER (-2.2)
Pennsylvania	NO DATA	NO DATA	NO DATA
Rhode Island	AVERAGE (-1.5)	AVERAGE (-1.2)	AVERAGE (-0.3)
South Carolina	HIGHER (+3.1)	AVERAGE (0.5)	NO DATA
South Dakota	HIGHER (+2.9)	AVERAGE (0.1)	HIGHER (+9.7)
Tennessee	AVERAGE (-0.3)	LOWER (-2.8)	AVERAGE (0.1)
Texas	HIGHER (+2.2)	HIGHER (+9.2)	LOWER (-2.4)
Utah	LOWER (-4.0)	LOWER (-9.6)	LOWER (-3.9)
Vermont	AVERAGE (-0.9)	LOWER (-2.4)	LOWER (-4.0)
Virginia	LOWER (-2.3)	LOWER (-3.1)	LOWER (-3.1)
West Virginia	AVERAGE (-1.3)	LOWER (-4.4)	HIGHER (+3.4)
Wisconsin	AVERAGE (0.7)	AVERAGE (-0.2)	AVERAGE (-0.1)
Wyoming	HIGHER (+3.7)	HIGHER (+2.6)	HIGHER (+5.4)

How to read the chart:

HIGHER = BAD, i.e., more teens reported doing these risky behaviors

LOWER = GOOD, i.e., fewer teens reported doing these risky behaviors

AVERAGE = MIDDLE of the road; about the same amount of teens as compared with the average state

If you want to know the percentage of teens who reported the risky behavior, take the average score at the top of the column and add the score in parentheses. For example, the percentage of teens in Wyoming who reported that they rarely wore a seat belt is 10.4 + 5.4 = 15.8. The percentage of teens in West Virginia who reported the same thing is 10.4 + -0.1 = 10.3.

Note: There is error associated with all estimates. For more on this survey of ninth to twelfth graders, see http://www.cdc.gov/HealthyYouth/yrbs/index.htm

The riskiest states according to these teens? Louisiana, South Dakota, and Wyoming stand out, with Texas, North Dakota, and Mississippi following not far behind.

The least risky states, where fewer teens reported these risky behaviors, were Utah (far ahead of the pack), Alaska, Virginia, Michigan, and Vermont.

> **Motor Vehicle Point #5:** States differ significantly in the reported risk taking of their teens. Is it a surprise that one-third of Louisiana teens report having driven in the last thirty days with a driver who had been drinking? Knowing where your state falls (see table) may help you to predict likely risk taking.

Story Box: Motor Vehicle Accidents, Ages Fifteen to Nineteen

Teens on Way to Beach Drown in Submerged Car

In Kershaw County, South Carolina, on October 28, 2012, authorities found the missing car of two Catawba County youth. The two teen boys were heading from a party to a spontaneous beach trip, accidentally veered off the road, narrowly missed a guardrail, and barreled down an embankment and into the South Carolina River, where they both drowned.[302]

Family of Teens Involved in Fatal Accident Warn Others to Use Seat Belt

In Lacombe, Louisiana, on August 2, 2012, family members of two teens in a fatal accident asked others to remember to wear seat belts. The two cousins were down the road from their grandfather's house when the nineteen-year-old driver tried to pass another car and lost control of the vehicle, which ran into the woods, killing his fifteen-year-old cousin in the passenger seat. Neither was wearing a seat belt. "The boys' family wants other teens to learn from their loss."[303]

Teen Girl Dies after BMW Full of Teens Rolls into Dry Canal

In Nampa, Idaho, on December 15, 2012, one of nine teens crammed into a BMW died when the BMW driver, a twenty-one-year-old, lost control of the car. The fifteen-year-old died from her injuries after the car rolled and landed in a dry canal. Police reported that alcohol was involved in the crash.[304]

Contact Made on Merge; Car Spins, Killing Teen Driver
In Las Vegas, on Saturday, December 8, a teenage driver of a Honda Civic attempted to pass another vehicle. When merging back into the lane, the rear of the teen driver's car made contact with the front of the other vehicle. The car spun out of control and hit a concrete wall. The sixteen-year-old driver died; the sixteen-year-old passenger survived.[305]

Speeding Teen Indicted for Fatal Accident
In Amarillo, Texas, on December 11, 2012, a nineteen-year-old driving a blue Pontiac G6 at high speeds allegedly hit and killed a seventy-seven-year-old driver of a Chevrolet Suburban. [306]

Sixteen-Year-Old Loses Control, Hits Tree
In Valrico, Florida, on January 4, 2013, it was reported that a sixteen-year-old was driving a fifteen-year-old around in his Pontiac Grand Am when he lost control of the car, which ran off the road and hit a tree. The driver was killed; the passenger was unharmed.[307]

Teen Driver and Her Six-Year-Old Sister Die in Crash
In Canyon County, Idaho, on January 3, 2013, a sixteen-year-old driver and her younger sister were turning from a stop sign onto Highway 30 when they were hit by a truck already on the highway. The force of the impact killed both girls.[308]

Boy and Girl Teen Die in Carload of Teens Speeding and Attempting to Pass
In Hillsboro, North Carolina, on the weekend before January 1, 2013, teens were racing each other. Four teens, none of whom was wearing a seat belt, were packed into the front seat of a Ford F-250. The driver was reportedly going over one hundred miles per hour, attempted to pass another car, and lost control of the vehicle, which then hit a tree. Two of the four died immediately, while the other two made it "just barely" and with severe injuries. An on-looking teen who broke down upon seeing the crash reported, "When I took driver's ed, they told us that three to four students in your grade would die from overcorrecting a vehicle, and would just either die on impact or die eventually, and that's what I learned...and it's true."[309]

The CDC points out a few things that they have learned about teen drivers and what parents can do to keep their children safe.

Factor	What Parents Can Do
1. Driver inexperience. *Most crashes happen during the first year a teen has a license.*	Provide at least thirty to fifty hours of supervised driving practice over at least six months. Make sure to practice on a variety of roads, at different times of day, and in varied weather and traffic conditions. This will help your teen gain the skills he or she needs to be safe.
2. Driving with teen passengers. *Crash risk goes up when teens drive with other teens in the car.*	Follow your state's teen driving law for passenger restrictions. If your state doesn't have such a rule, limit the number of teen passengers your child can have to zero or one. Keep this rule for at least the first six months.
3. Nighttime driving. *For all ages, fatal crashes are more likely to occur at night; but the risk is highest for teens.*	Make sure your teen is off the road by nine or ten p.m. for at least the first six months of licensed driving.
4. Not using seat belts. *The simplest way to prevent car crash deaths is to buckle up.*	Require your teen to wear a seat belt on every trip. This simple step can reduce your teen's risk of dying or being badly injured in a crash by about half.
5. Distracted driving. *Distractions increase your teen's risk of being in a crash.*	Don't allow activities that may take your teen's attention away from driving, such as talking on a cell phone, texting, eating, or playing with the radio.
6. Drowsy driving. *Young drivers are at highest risk for drowsy driving, which causes*	Be sure your teen is fully rested before he or she gets behind the wheel.

thousands of crashes every year. Teens are most tired and at risk when driving in the early morning or late at night.	
7. Reckless driving. *Research shows that teens lack the experience, judgment, and maturity to assess risky situations.*	Help your teen avoid the following unsafe behaviors: *Speeding.* Make sure your teen knows to follow the speed limit and adjust speed to road conditions. *Tailgating.* Remind your teen to maintain enough space behind the vehicle ahead to avoid a crash in case of a sudden stop. *Insufficient scanning.* Stress the importance of always knowing the location of other vehicles on the road.
8. Impaired driving. *Even one drink will impair your teen's driving ability and increase the risk of a crash.*	Be a good role model: don't drink and drive, and reinforce this message with your teen.

Note that the CDC states clearly that the research shows that "**traditional driver education is insufficient for reducing the high risk of teen crashes.**" They summarize that "this approach is not effective in reducing the crash risk among newly-licensed teen drivers," and they suggest that "driver education programs may be improved by teaching psychomotor, perceptual, and cognitive skills that are critical for safe driving, and by addressing inexperience, risky behaviors, and other age-related factors that increase the crash risk among young drivers." So don't rely on the driver's education program to address all these concerns.

There are, however, some proven methods to helping teens become safer drivers. Research suggests that the most comprehensive graduated driver licensing (GDL) programs are associated with reductions of up to 38 percent and 40 percent in fatal and injury crashes, respectively, among sixteen-year-old drivers.[310] On average, the programs have reduced teen crashes by 10 to 30 percent.[311]

GDL systems are designed to delay full licensure while allowing teens to get their initial driving experience under low-risk conditions. When parents know their state's GDL laws, they can help enforce these laws and, in effect, help keep their teen drivers safe.

According to the Insurance Institute for Highway Safety, all fifty states and the District of Columbia have a three-stage GDL system (there is no federal law). "Institute research has shown that states with the strongest laws enjoy bigger reductions in teen driver deaths than states with weak laws," the institute reports. "Some states make teens wait a little longer before they get their learner permits and full-privilege licenses. This also saves lives."[312]

The IIHS website shows the laws for your state and what might happen if your state strengthened (or weakened) the laws to align with what they call "five key GDL provisions: permit age, practice driving hours, license age, and night driving and passenger restrictions." For example, according to their data, California could reduce fatal accidents by one-quarter (25 percent) if it just instituted best-practice laws (for example, increasing the license age from sixteen to seventeen reduces fatalities by 13 percent). Mississippi could halve their rate. The calculator is located on the institute's website, http://www.iihs.org/laws/gdl_calculator.aspx.

The CDC provides a number of recommendations for parents:
- **Spend AT LEAST thirty to fifty hours of supervised driving practice** over at least six months. Teens should practice on a variety of roads, at different times of day, and in varied weather and traffic conditions. Remember, most crashes happen during the first year a teen has a license.
- **Follow your state's teen driving law for passenger restrictions, or limit the number of teen passengers to zero or one** for at least the first six months. Teens are very sensitive to measures that may cause them to lose their driving privileges.
- **Make sure your teen is off the road by nine or ten p.m.** for at least the first six months of licensed driving. For all ages, fatal crashes are more likely to occur at night, but the risk is highest for teens.
- **Always, always wear seat belts.** The simplest way to prevent crash deaths is to buckle up. Parents should require their teen to wear a seat belt on every trip. This simple step can reduce their teen's risk of dying or being badly injured in a crash by about half. Parents should set a good example and always buckle up, too.
- **Prohibit cell phone use, texting, and other distracting behaviors while driving**, for parents and teens alike.
- **Treat drowsy driving seriously.** Young drivers are at highest risk for drowsy driving, which causes thousands of crashes every year. Parents should ensure their teen is fully rested before he or she gets behind the wheel.

- **Stress the importance of avoiding unsafe behaviors, such as speeding and tailgating.** Research shows that teens lack the experience, judgment, and maturity to assess risky situations.
- **Avoid even one drink before driving.** Even one drink will impair a teen's driving ability and increase the risk of a crash.
- **Make safety the first consideration in buying a car for the teen to drive.** Teens are more likely than older drivers to drive either smaller or older cars, especially when they own the car. While it may be tempting to choose a first car for a teen based on price or style, parents should consider a car's safety features first and foremost.

Pedestrian Accidents – 2 Minutes

Although compared to motor vehicle accidents pedestrian accidents are a relatively small portion of your worry time, deaths due to these accidents have actually doubled from the early teen years. This is possibly because the teen Worry Clock represents four and a half times the number of deaths in early teen years.

In fact, the numbers of pedestrian deaths, while diminishing for other age groups, are on the rise for teens. And it does not appear to be due to a likely culprit: alcohol consumption. Alcohol is known to play a significant role in pedestrian accidents; about one-quarter (27 percent) of teen (sixteen- to twenty-year-olds) pedestrian fatalities in 2010 involved alcohol. However, that rate is down from 33 percent in 2001.[313]

Safe Kids USA blames the rise in fatalities on an increase in the use (and misuse) of portable electronic communication devices. In the last five years, injuries among sixteen- to nineteen-year-olds increased 25 percent over the previous five years. According to Safekids.org, fourteen- to nineteen-year-olds account for 50 percent of child pedestrian injuries. "We suspect one cause of this disturbing trend is distraction, since the increase in teen injuries seems to correlate with the prevalence of cell phone use, both among walkers and drivers," said Safe Kids' CEO Kate Carr.

New research from the University of Washington[314] also showed that pedestrians who text are four times less likely to look before crossing the street, cross at designated areas, or obey traffic lights. And it is not just a small percentage of us doing it. More than one-third of pedestrians were found doing some distracting activity while crossing the street, including listening to music (11.2 percent), text messaging (7.3 percent), and using a handheld phone (6.2 percent). Those using smartphones "crossed more slowly, and were less likely to look around before stepping out into the street." In addition, they "crossed against the light more than undistracted pedestrians."[315]

The pedestrian safety suggestions from the National Highway Traffic Safety Administration and Safe Kids include:

- Drivers:
    - Remember that you are required to yield the right-of-way to pedestrians crossing streets in marked or unmarked crosswalks in most situations. Be especially careful at intersections where the failure to yield right-of-way often occurs when drivers are turning onto another street and a pedestrian is in their path.
    - Slow down and be especially alert in residential neighborhoods and school zones, before and after school hours.
    - Know that most walkers are injured mid-block, not at intersections.
- Pedestrians:
    - Don't rely on signals or assume cars will do the right thing.
    - Always stop and look left, right, and left again before crossing.
    - When possible, cross the street at a designated crosswalk.
    - Remove headphones when crossing the street.
    - If you need to use your phone, stop walking.
    - Distraction among drivers is at an all-time high today, so try to make eye contact with the driver before you step into the road.
    - If a parked vehicle is blocking the view of the street, stop at the edge line of the vehicle and look around it before entering the street.

- o Increase visibility at night by carrying a flashlight when walking and by wearing retro-reflective clothing that helps to highlight body movements.
- o Walk on a sidewalk, where it is much safer. If you must walk in the street, walk facing traffic.

And, yes, in case you were wondering, there are about four times as many pedestrian fatalities on Halloween as on any other day of the year.[317] It is the "deadliest day of the year," according to State Farm.[318] The greatest number of fatalities was for children age twelve to fifteen (about one-third), and young drivers accounted for about one-third of the accidents. With the link to alcohol, consider how to:

- Ensure teens have reflective or lighted jackets or costumes.
- Keep inexperienced teen drivers off the road on this day.

ATV, Motorcycle, and Other Transportation – 3 Minutes

ATV, motorcycle, and other transportation accidents follow the same pattern as pedestrian accidents; although they are relatively less important, they actually account for more deaths than in early teen years. For example, ATV deaths are 50 percent higher in number. Again, most of this is attributable to the mix of alcohol and other risk-taking behaviors, such as not wearing helmets. The recommendations are similar, too. Try to create good habits as early as possible so that wearing helmets, for example, is an automatic process.

Story Box: Other Transportation Accidents, Ages Fifteen to Nineteen

Teen Killed by Boat Propeller
On June 20, 2012, in Aransas Pass, Texas, a sixteen-year-old out with family friends on a powerboat trip was accidentally thrown out the front of the boat and was hit and killed by the propeller as the boat quickly traveled over her.[319]

For the first time, suicide takes a place on the Worry Clock. We switch from worrying about external accidents, from falling trees and swerving cars, to the internal concerns of our children and their own desire to harm themselves.

Suicide isn't just a problem, it is a *common* problem. One in twelve high school students reported *attempting* suicide just in the preceding year. Even more (one in six) seriously considered it but did not act.[320] Of course, these are the ones who lived to report it.

And there are many who do not live to report their attempts. *The number of* *completed suicides in this age group is* *greater than all* *the accidental deaths of the four-* *to nine-year-old age group.*

Suicide Point #1: Serious suicidal thoughts are common for teens, and a significant number commit suicide. One in six teens reported seriously thinking about suicide in the last year. [321] The number of successful suicide attempts in this age group is equal to more than all the accidental deaths of the four-to-nine age group.

We'll talk more about the relative importance of suicide in the across-age chapter. For now, let's look at how teens commit suicide and then who is at most risk.

Firearms are the number-one choice of teens committing suicide; just over half (54 percent) of all male suicides were by rifles, handguns, and the like, and nearly one-third (29 percent) of female suicides. In fact, suicide is the most common cause of firearm-related death in the United States for all ages.[322] Hanging and related forms of strangulation accounted for almost an additional 40 percent. So the vast majority of suicides (almost 90 percent) were done by one of these two methods. Drugs—prescription and illegal—accounted for an additional 5 percent. Suicide by jumping from a high place or in front of a moving object such as a train accounted for another 4 percent. Other suicide methods included using poisonous gases (e.g., carbon monoxide) and intentionally crashing a motor vehicle. Exposure to alcohol, unlike other drugs, was not a method that accounted for a measurable number of deaths (i.e., there were too few to produce a reliable estimate).

Method of Suicide	% of All Suicides	Worry Clock Estimate
Firearm (e.g., rifle, handgun)	50%	4 min. *30 seconds*
Hanging, strangulation, and suffocation	37%	3 min *20 seconds*
Drugs (e.g., sedatives, narcotics)	5%	*30 seconds*
Jumping from a high place or in front of a moving object	4%	*20 seconds*
Other	4%	*20 seconds*
Total	100%	9 minutes

Males are most at risk. Nearly five times as many males as females ages fifteen to nineteen died by suicide.[323] This is not because males are more likely to be depressed; females actually had two times as many suicide attempts.[324] The gender difference according to experts is due to the fact that males are more likely to use guns for their suicide attempt, and guns are 90 percent effective. In other words, if suicide is attempted with a firearm, it is successful nine times out of ten.[325]

Suicide Point #2: Attempting suicide with a gun is 90 percent effective, which is why males, who prefer guns, are more likely to die from an attempt and why it is important to limit access to firearms.

Teens who commit suicide are likely to have certain risk factors, listed below. Yes, many of these factors fall into the "duh" category, such as a previous suicide attempt, but I tried to include details that may be a bit more informative. Obviously, having these risk factors doesn't mean the teen will commit suicide, and not having them doesn't mean he won't.

Based on a summary by the American Academy of Pediatrics, a child is at risk for suicide if he has:

- **Mental health problems.** "More than 90 percent of adolescent suicide victims met criteria for a psychiatric disorder before their death." These psychiatric disorders include depression, bipolar disorder, substance abuse or dependence, psychosis, posttraumatic stress disorder, panic attacks, and a history of aggression, impulsivity, or severe anger.

- **A previous suicide attempt.** "Most suicide attempts are expressions of extreme distress, not harmless bids for attention,"[326] writes the National Institute for Mental Health. Estimates are that about 20 percent of successful suicides (all ages) were preceded by an unsuccessful attempt.[327]

- **Presence of firearms in the home.** Yup, the simple presence of firearms in the home, regardless of whether they are kept unloaded or stored locked up, are associated with a higher risk for adolescent suicide. Guns transform what would have been a hospital statistic into a coroner's report. In fact, the AAP makes its summary of the research clear: "In states where there are more guns, more people commit suicide. Studies have shown that the risk of suicide is four to ten times higher in homes with guns than in those without. If the gun is a handgun or is stored loaded or unlocked, the risk of suicide is even higher."[328] The academy concludes, "Parents must be warned about the lethality of firearms in the home and be advised strongly to remove them from the premises." Got a firearm in the house? Consider asking someone else whose kids are grown to keep the guns for you for a few years.

- **Gay or bisexual orientation.** Youth with gay or bisexual orientation are two to three times more likely to attempt suicide,[329] [330] and this is one of the reasons why good antibullying initiatives include a component to address the needs of these children.

- **Family mental health problems.** A family history of suicide or suicide attempts and parental mental health problems have also been found to be consistent risk factors.

- **A history of physical or sexual abuse**. Keep in mind that you may not know about this history. The CDC estimates that nearly one in five women has been raped in their lifetime (and of these women, about 40 percent of them experienced this before age eighteen), and one in seventy-one men has been raped in their lifetime (and of these, about 30 percent experienced this before the age of ten).[331]

- **Social isolation,** which may include an impaired parent-child relationship, living outside of the home (homeless or in a correctional facility or group home), and/or not attending work or school.

- **Experienced bullying as the victim or the perpetrator.** The link between those involved in bullying, both the victim and perpetrator, and suicide is fairly well documented, which is why many schools have now rolled out antibullying campaigns.[332] Bullying does not mean that suicide is inevitable, but it is a red flag for bringing help and resources to both sides of the bullying equation.

Suicides generally, not just for teens, are likely to have immediate precursors other than mental health conditions, including intoxication (associated with around a third to a half of suicide attempts)[333], a crisis of some kind during the preceding or impending two weeks (about 30 percent, all ages), or intimate partner problems (also 30 percent).[334] Less common but still frequently noted (10–20 percent of the incidents) were physical health problems and job and financial problems.[335]

Telling people is more often *not* a part of what people do when contemplating suicide. More than 70 percent of people (all ages) don't tell friends or family in advance that they are planning to commit suicide (29 percent disclosed their intent). [336]

There are some things parents can do. Below is an initial list, put together from a number of sources (see endnotes). There are many, many other, perhaps far better suggestions available online. So if this might, could, potentially, maybe, even remotely possibly be an issue for your teen, please follow these links, explore more sites, and most of all talk to your child's health care provider or mental health professional—as well as your child!

- **Know the signs.** If the teen talks about hurting or killing himself and talks or writes about death, dying, and suicide, seek help for him. If a youth shows any of the following behaviors or symptoms, he may be in a crisis:[337]
  - Feelings of **hopelessness**
  - **Anxiety**, agitation, trouble sleeping, or sleeping all the time
  - Expressions of having no reason for living; no sense of **purpose** in life
  - Feelings of being **trapped**, like there's no way out
  - Increase **alcohol and/or drug use**
  - **Withdrawal** from friends, family, and community
  - Rage, uncontrolled **anger**, expressions of wanting or seeking revenge
  - **Reckless** behavior or more risky activities, seemingly without thinking
  - Dramatic **mood changes**
  - **Giving away** prized possessions

If he shows these signs, says the American Association of Suicidology, "an evaluation by a mental health professional is essential to rule out the possibility of suicide and/or to initiate appropriate treatment." [338]

- **Get professional help.** There is mounting evidence that available treatments for depression and suicide-related disorders do actually work. In fact, researchers who divided the country into 588 two-digit zip-code zones found a significant ($P < .001$) 0.23-per-100,000 annual decrease in adolescent suicide with every 1 percent increase in antidepressant prescription.[339] Other studies have shown significant clinical improvement in 71 percent of adolescents with major depression, resulting from a combination of antidepressant medication and cognitive behavioral therapy."[340]

- **If you cannot go straight to a psychiatrist or other mental health professional, ask your pediatrician or another medical professional your child trusts to do an assessment.** According to the AAP, "The best way to assess for suicidal ideation is by directly asking or screening via self-report. Self-administered scales can be useful for screening, because adolescents may disclose information about suicidality on self-report that they deny in person." Although they warn that these surveys are oversensitive, they also conclude that "adolescents who endorse suicidality on a scale should always be assessed clinically."

- **Get guns and ammunition out of the house.** The AAP suggests that pediatricians ask the parents of children demonstrating the risk factors to remove firearms and ammunition from the home.

- **Secure or remove supplies of potentially lethal medications.**

- **Reinforce positive relationships and connections to family and community.** Connections to others appear to be protective, so keeping children connected to their loved ones and others and their community may help.[341]

Story Box: Suicide, Ages Fifteen to Nineteen

Popular Teen Posts Picture of Gun in Last Call for Help

In Houston, Texas, on February 1, 2012, a popular seventeen-year-old girl, who wrote, "I might not struggle financially but I struggle emotionally and mentally," posted a picture of the gun she acquired. Friends mistakenly "liked" the post, not realizing that the teen would only moments later use the gun to shoot herself in the head.[342]

Fifteen-Year-Old Commits Suicide after Ongoing Bullying
In Morristown, New Jersey, on March 28, 2012, a well-liked kid who loved bowling took his own life (means undisclosed). Prosecutors looked into reports of bullying and later prosecuted the bullies. Mourners stated that bad parenting is responsible for bullies.[343]

Tormented Fifteen-Year-Old Jumps to Death in Front of Train and Peers
In Staten Island, New York, on October 25, 2012, a teenager was allegedly driven to her death when a sexual encounter she had with football players at the school was made public and said to have been recorded. The teen, although smiling, tweeted, "I cant, im done, I give up" (sic). She killed herself by jumping in the path of a train in front of many of her classmates.[344]

Homicide – 12 Minutes

Homicide, now worth almost a quarter of one's worry, has some similar issues to suicide. First and foremost is the prevalence of firearms. Firearms were the instrument of death in 83 percent of homicide cases, whereas knives and other sharp objects made up less than 10 percent (see table). Again, firearms are likely to be effective first time around; researchers estimate gun lethality at a minimum of twice that of a knife attack.[345] Young adults and adolescents are disproportionately victimized by firearm-related homicide. [346]

Method of Homicide	% of All Homicides	Worry Clock Estimate
Firearm (e.g., rifle, handgun)	83%	10 minutes
Sharp object (e.g., knives)	8%	1 minute
Hanging, strangulation, and suffocation	2%	*15 seconds*
Other	7%	1 minute
Total	100%	12.25 minutes

There is no question that the violence proportionately affects young black men. For example, although our country was made up of 16 percent of black youth ages fifteen to seventeen in 2009,[347] that group comprised 56 percent of homicide victims. In terms of raw numbers from 1999 to 2007, blacks also had a greater number of deaths compared with whites, despite their proportion in the population.

The FBI's supplementary homicide reports[348] tell us a little about the perpetrators and victims. Perpetrators are almost always males (96 percent in my analysis). The majority of homicides are within race: more than 80 percent of whites were killed by other whites, and 92 percent of blacks were killed by other blacks (see table). Around 15–20 percent of the time, there was more than one perpetrator.

	Perpetrator same race		Perpetrator different race		Totals
Victim Race	#	%	#	%	#
White	1,654	84%	322	16%	1,976
Black	2,093	92%	177	8%	2,270
Amer. Indian/ Alaskan Native	17	52%	16	48%	33
Asian/Native Hawaiian/PI	53	60%	36	40%	89
Total	3,817	87%	551	13%	4,368

The victim is more likely to be male, but roughly one in five is a female (for white victims, this percentage is slightly higher, meaning a greater percentage of white females are killed). Females are slightly more likely to have the perpetrator as a family member or acquaintance. The relationship between the victim and perpetrator also appears to vary by age. In cases when a family member was the perpetrator, nearly half were between the ages of twenty-five and forty-nine, whereas in cases when an acquaintance or stranger committed the crime, these killers were more likely to be peers (see table).

Age of Perpetrator by Relationship with Victim, 1999–2007[349]

	12–17	18–24	25–49	50+	Un-known	Total
Family	21%	21%	48%	11%	0%	100%
Acquaintance	31%	51%	14%	1%	3%	100%
Stranger	22%	49%	18%	2%	10%	100%
Unknown	6%	14%	7%	1%	71%	100%

Will your child be around guns? Likely, yes. Household gun ownership ranges from roughly 10 to 80 percent, with most local areas clustering around the mean ownership level of 43 percent.[350] As a National Academies of Sciences report on this topic notes, "For every one thousand people in the United States in 1999 there were nearly 926 firearms, 336 of which were handguns."[351]

Teens also report many behaviors associated with escalating violence.[352] Nearly one in ten teenage boys (9 percent) and 1 percent of teen girls reported that they had carried a gun in the last thirty days. On school property, about the same percentage of males, one in ten, and one in twenty females reported being threatened by or injured with a weapon on school property in the preceding thirty days. And 6 percent of students had *not* gone to school on at least one day during the thirty days because they felt they would be unsafe at school or on their way to or from school.

Story Box: Homicide, Ages Fifteen to Nineteen

Eighteen-Year-Old Dies near University, Car Stolen
In San Antonio, Texas, on January 15, 2013, an eighteen-year-old was heard yelling that his car was being stolen. It was around eleven p.m. on a Tuesday night, near the University of Texas at San Antonio campus. When police arrived, they found the teen dead of multiple gunshot wounds.[353]

Sixteen-Year-Old Found Shot to Death While Baby-Sitting Seven-Year-Old Brother
In Kearny, New Jersey, on January 17, 2013, a "nice" and "quiet" sixteen-year-old was shot in the head in her family's apartment. Police are

investigating what happened, including whether an earlier street fight that day, which involved some of her family members, may have been related.[354]

Teen Killed at Night Club
In Tuscaloosa, Alabama, at two a.m. on December 30, police were called to investigate the shooting of an eighteen-year-old boy. The boy was shot in his back and died at the local hospital.[355]

Drowning: 2 Minutes

When we get to the teenage years, we see a clear shift to drowning occurring in natural water. Half or more of these deaths occur in places like lakes, rivers, quarries, and oceans. Less than 10 percent occur in swimming pools during teen years.

This is almost exclusively a problem for young men, not women. Their rate of drowning in natural water in this age group, for example, is nearly twenty times that for young women of the same age.[356] This time of young men's lives, with the early twenties, represents the greatest risk for drowning in natural water.[357]

The CDC provide some suggestions for why males are most at risk, and these align with many of the issues raised earlier about teens' mistakes in judgment in deadly combination with alcohol use. "Among adolescents and adults, alcohol use is involved in up to 70 percent of deaths associated with water recreation, almost a quarter of [emergency room] visits for drowning, and about one in five reported boating deaths. Alcohol influences balance, coordination, and judgment, and its effects are heightened by sun exposure and heat."[358]

Safety tips based on those recommended by the CDC[359] not previously mentioned that may have particular importance for this age group:

- **Use buddy systems and lifeguards.** "Regardless of your age, always swim with a buddy. And select swimming sites that have lifeguards whenever possible."
- **Heed warning flags.** Know the meaning of and obey beach warning flags (see inset), which may vary from one beach to another.
- **Know the terrain.** Be aware of and avoid drop-offs and hidden obstacles in natural water sites. Always enter water feet-first.
- **Avoid rip currents; if caught in a rip tide, swim parallel.** Watch for dangerous waves and signs of rip currents (e.g., water that is discolored and choppy, foamy, or filled with debris and moving in a

channel away from shore). If you are caught in a rip current, swim parallel to shore; once free of the current, swim toward shore. The United States Lifesaving Association estimates that more than a hundred people die on our nation's beaches each year due to rip currents.

- **Use life jackets.** Most (72 percent) boating deaths that occurred in 2010 were caused by drowning, with 88 percent of victims not wearing life jackets. Twenty-nine percent of deaths occurred on boats that were anchored, docked, moored, or drifting. Use US Coast Guard--approved life jackets when boating.

- **Avoid alcohol.** Avoid drinking alcohol before or during swimming, boating, or water skiing. When boating, safety risks from alcohol use are increased for boat operators and passengers. Do not drink alcohol while supervising children.

Beach Flags[360]

Ever wanted to know what those flags on the lifeguard stands meant? Here you go, thanks to the International Life Saving Federation.

Yellow – Medium hazard. Moderate surf and/or currents are present. Weak swimmers are discouraged.

Red – High hazard. Rough conditions such as strong surf and/or currents are present. All swimmers are discouraged.

Double red – Water is closed.

Purple – Marine pests, such as jellyfish, stingrays, sea snakes, or other marine life which can cause minor injuries are present. This flag is not intended to indicate the presence of sharks. In this latter case, the red flag or double red flag may be hoisted.

Red/yellow (halved red over yellow) – The area is protected by lifeguards; swimming is permitted in front of the area where the flag is flown, and that the area is under the supervision of a qualified person.

Quartered (black/white) – These flags indicate a designated area or zone along a beach or waterfront that is used by those with surfboards and other nonpowered watercraft.

Yellow flag with central black ball – Surfboards and other nonpowered watercraft are prohibited.

Orange windsock – This cone-shaped device is used to indicate the direction of offshore winds and to show that it is unsafe for inflatable objects to be used in the water.

The risk for fires remains in teenage years and the lessons are very similar to those presented in the toddler chapter.

What is different that is related to fire in the household is that teens are the ones likely to start those fires. **More than half (53 percent) of** *all* **arrests for arsons (intentional fires) are someone under eighteen years of age,**[361] and children are the most likely victims (85 percent).[362]

Fire setting is still reported to most likely occur in the child's bedroom and to be started with matches and lighters. [363]

The US Fire Administration divides juvenile fire setters into three groups: The first, "curiosity fire setters," consists of children under the age of eight who generally start fires accidentally or out of curiosity. The second group, "intentional fire setters," includes children between eight and twelve years of age who, although sometimes motivated by curiosity, are more often driven by underlying psychosocial conflict. Finally, the third group, "crisis fire setters," consists of adolescents between thirteen and eighteen years of age who tend to have a long history of undetected fire play and fire-starting behavior and are often motivated by psychosocial conflict or intentional criminal behavior.

The different motivations affect the choice of setting. Gang-related or vandalism fires are often started in abandoned buildings. An older juvenile responding to family crisis who feels alienated and angry may choose his home or school for the fire.

Children who have demonstrated fire setting should be evaluated by a mental health professional, even if you don't think there is an issue. The US Fire Administration notes that "early detection and intervention improve the likelihood of preventing future fire setting."[364]

Story Box: Fire, Ages Fifteen to Nineteen

Trapped in Second Floor Room, Teen Dies Week after House Fire
In Marrero, Louisiana, on January 15, 2013, a fifteen-year-old girl died from her injuries resulting from a house fire the week before. Five other children and the parents were rescued from the house, but the teen was trapped in a second story bedroom in the home.[365]

Other: 2 Minutes

Although it's difficult to learn much from most of the "other" category (e.g., death due to an "unspecified factor," when the doctor was not able to determine the cause), this section highlights a few additional areas. Teens getting struck by or striking objects accounted for thirteen seconds, and less than 10 percent of these were cited as specifically resulting from sports' equipment. Deaths due to firearms discharged by police or similar authorities authorized to carry those firearms accounted for another twelve seconds. Electric current deaths, about one-third of which are from transmission lines, add eleven seconds. See table for more.

Categories of death falling into "Other"	Percent in "Other"	Time on Worry Clock
Exposure to unspecified factor	27%	*32 seconds*
Struck by projected or falling object, or striking object (e.g., sports equipment)	10%	*13 seconds*
Legal intervention (e.g., police) involving firearm discharge	10%	*12 seconds*
Electric current	9%	*11 seconds*
Medical or surgical procedures	7%	*8 seconds*
Exposure to excessive heat or cold	6%	*7 seconds*
Agricultural and other machinery	6%	*7 seconds*
Miscellaneous other categories (too many to list)	26%	*31 seconds*
Total	**100%**	***120 seconds***

Guns: 1 Minute

This category includes all the gun deaths that don't fall into the homicide or suicide categories. An accidental discharge of a gun while cleaning it or when a teen accidentally shoots a friend would be included here. Most of the gun types are not classified, but of those that are, 40 percent are handguns. The earlier suggestions about gun storage and safety apply.

Falls: 1 Minute

The falls that are big enough to kill a teen are, according to the data, falls out of buildings and between building levels. Again, these accidents may be in part due to the alcohol use tied to risk taking at this age. I found no research to specifically address teens' risk of falling.

What Doesn't Appear on the Clock

Below are a few causes of death that I singled out for a special look, either because they had no findings or because of how they compared to other findings (but didn't occur frequently enough to talk about in the main section of the chapter). For example, teens are too large, presumably, to be killed by a dog, other mammals could be lethal.

Although many incidents on this table are very rare, their appearance does not mean that your child is necessarily safe for these causes of death. Your child may have a particular susceptibility to heat, for example, that is not taken into account here. What this table does show is that across the country over many years, these incidents with ** were so rare that I cannot provide an estimate for the Worry Clock.

Exposure to excessive natural heat	*3 seconds*
Exposure to excessive natural cold	*4 seconds*
Victim of lightning	*2 seconds*
Victim of avalanche, landslide, and other earth movements	*1 second*
Victim of cataclysmic storm	*2 seconds*
Victim of flood	**
Striking against or struck by other objects	*2 seconds*
Striking against or struck by sports equipment	*1 second*
Caught, crushed, jammed, or pinched in or between objects	*1 second*
Contact with lifting and transmission devices, not elsewhere classified	*2 seconds*
Contact with sharp glass	*1 second*
Contact with knife, sword, or dagger	**
Contact with powered lawnmower	**
Contact with other powered hand tools and household machinery	**
Exposure to electric transmission lines	*3 seconds*
Exposure to other specified electric current	*3 seconds*
Exposure to unspecified electric current	*5 seconds*

Exposure to excessive cold of manmade origin	**
Exposure to high and low air pressure and changes in air pressure	**
Bitten or struck by other mammals (e.g., bears)	*1 second*
Bitten or struck by dogs	**
Contact with venomous snakes and lizards	**
Contact with hornets, wasps, and bees	**
Discharge of firework	**

Some of these causes of death likely interact with causes covered in this chapter. For example, exposure to heat/cold and electric current may be related to excessive alcohol consumption.

Quiz Time for Ages Fifteen to Nineteen!
Here's a chance to test your ability to keep all these statistics in your head. After the quiz, I propose a top ten list of action steps to give you some idea of where to start.

1. What is the number-one cause (major category) of death for ages fifteen to nineteen?

2. Name three categories of accidents in which are boys significantly more likely than girls to die.

3. In what percentage of teen motor vehicle deaths was the teen him- or herself driving or another teen?

4. Which was more likely, fire or drowning deaths, and by roughly how much?

5. Of the unlikely causes of death, which was more likely: dying by being bitten or struck by a mammal other than a dog, or dying from fireworks?

6. If you add up all the kids who die from gun-related deaths, how many minutes would you have on the Worry Clock?

7. True or false: Teens drive after drinking *less* frequently than do adults.

8. What may be one reason teen pedestrian deaths are on a steep rise?

9. True or false: Teens are likely to warn friends or family before committing suicide.

10. What is the national percentage of teens who reported driving with someone who had been drinking? Which state had the highest average, and what was that average?

Answers to Quiz:

1. Motor vehicle accidents.

2. Any three of the following: motor vehicle accidents, homicide, suicide, and drowning.

3. Eighty-three percent. Almost all the accidents in this age group result from teen drivers.

4. Fire, twice as likely. Fire is an ever-present worry; get the fire alarms up and active.

5. Fireworks.

6. Fifteen minutes, thirty seconds. More than one-quarter of your worry at this age is children dying from guns.

7. False. Teens actually do this risky behavior less often than adults, but they are far worse drivers when they do.

8. Portable electronic devices and focusing on those instead of on the surrounding traffic.

9. False. More than 70 percent do not.

10. Nationally, 23 percent of teens reported that in the last thirty days they had driven with someone who had been drinking. Texas and Louisiana topped the state list, with nearly one-third (32 percent) of their teens reporting this behavior.

Top Ten for Teens

You made it through all the data, now where to begin? If you feel overwhelmed and don't know where to start, here are some suggestions based on the most frequent causes of death in the past data. As you are keenly aware, doing these things doesn't guarantee a safe child, but they give you a place to start.

Top ten suggestions for increasing safety for ages fifteen to nineteen:

1. **Spend AT LEAST thirty to fifty hours of supervised driving practice** over at least six months. One drivers' education course is not enough. Teens should practice on a variety of roads, at different times of day, and in varied weather and traffic conditions. Remember, most crashes happen during the first year a teen has a license.

2. **Follow your state's teen driving law for passenger restrictions, or limit the number of teen passengers to zero or one** for at least the first six months. Teens are very sensitive to measures that may cause them to lose their driving privileges.

3. **Make sure your teen is off the road by nine or ten p.m.** for at least the first six months of licensed driving. For all ages, fatal crashes are more likely to occur at night, but the risk is highest for teens.

4. **Set standards** for safety practices as early as possible so they become habits. Most important are wearing seat belts and putting handheld devices down when in the car and crossing streets on foot. Motorcyclists, bicyclists, and ATV riders should always wear a helmet.

5. **Make safety the first consideration in buying a car for your teen.** Teens are more likely than older drivers to drive either smaller or older cars, especially when they own the car. While it may be tempting to choose a first car for a teen based on price or style, parents should consider a car's safety features first and foremost.

6. **Watch for the signs of psychological stress, particularly around events the teen perceives as crises, and get professional help if you see those signs.** There is mounting evidence that currently available treatments for depression and suicide-related disorders work.

7. **If you cannot go straight to a psychiatrist or other mental health professional, ask your pediatrician or other medical professional whom your child trusts to do an assessment.** According to the American Academy of Pediatrics, the best way to assess for suicidal ideation is by asking teens directly.

149

8. **Get guns and ammunition out of the house.** The AAP suggests that pediatricians ask the parents of children demonstrating risk factors for suicide to remove firearms and ammunition from the home. Keeping the weapons locked up is a step better, but even having a locked-up gun in the house is shown to have an effect on suicide completion. I am reminded of a friend telling me that as a teen, he busted into his father's gun safe by trying every potential combination on the padlock. He had a lot of free time as a teen, but then many teens do.

9. **Talk to your teens** about where the big risks are, research that shows where teen brains are likely to have challenges (e.g., assessing risk), and strategies for addressing those challenges when you are not there to help them.

10. **Reinforce positive relationships and connections to family and community.** Connections to others appear to be protective, so keeping children connected to their loved ones and others and their community may help.[366]

Conclusion

The proportion of accidental deaths is higher in teenagers than in all other age groups. Teenagers' rate of death is more than the three previous age groups combined (ages two to fourteen). The three main culprits are motor vehicle accidents, homicides, and suicides, with alcohol and guns playing significant supporting roles in each.

In this chapter we put all the data together.[367] Throughout the book we focused on only one age group at a time and looked at the relative dangers within that age group. I took this approach because as a parent I wanted to know what I should focus on *now*, given my children's ages. But I also want to know what matters most *across* my children's lives. I might take a very different approach as a parent if I knew that, say, all the accidents happened in the first few years of life and then it was relatively clear sailing. Alternatively, what if deadly accidents in the teenage years swamped all the other age groups?

As you will soon see, some of the age groups do matter a lot more than others. But first let's remind ourselves that, looking at all age groups, loss of a child is rare, accounting for less than one-tenth of 1 percent (see barely visible pie slice).

Percent of Children Ages Birth to 19 Who Died
(CDC Mortality Rates, 1999–2007)

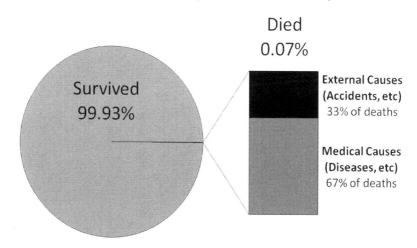

You will see how infant and teenage years are the two points of greatest importance in securing children's safety. You will also see how the major causes of death change across children's lives. Fires, for example, pose more of a risk to toddlers and teens than to other age groups.

The Worry Clock for All Age Groups

The Worry Clock across all age groups is pictured below. The motor vehicle accidents category, a perpetually large chunk of the Worry Clock, overall accounts for over one-quarter of your worry, or seventeen minutes on the all-ages clock. Pedestrian accidents contribute another three minutes, and motorcycles and ATVs each add one minute. Other transportation accidents, including bicycles, add the final transportation minute, totaling twenty-three minutes—approaching half—of the worry for your child's well-being from birth to nineteen.

It seems unbelievable in our great nation, and yet there it is: homicide is the second major cause of death for our children after transportation accidents. Homicide is worth just over ten minutes of your worry. Gun accidents (not due to suicide and without malicious intent, see more about this later in the chapter) add another minute.

Suffocation, strangulation and related threats to breathing primarily driven by infant suffocation deaths comes in next at ten minutes.

Suicide contributes five minutes to the clock, about half the amount of homicide.

Drowning adds four minutes, and fire adds another three. And with "other," poisoning, and falls, they compose the final quarter and complete the clock.

Reminder: The number of children who die is small. The entire Worry Clock for Birth to Age Nineteen is based on one-third of that tiny slice of the pie at the beginning of the chapter and is an average of about seventeen thousand children per year (a rate of just over twenty out of one hundred thousand), which means each minute represents about 290 deaths. The data and recommendations presented throughout this chapter do not tell you what will happen or prevent something from happening, but are here to help you think through the issues.

An added caveat here: This clock is different than previous clocks. Because there are large differences in the sizes of the age populations making up this Worry Clock, this clock is based on rates of death (numbers of deaths by numbers in the population). Previous Worry Clocks were based on the percentages of deaths (number of deaths of one type over the total number of deaths). The graphs throughout the chapter are based on rates.[368]

Worry Clock Birth to Age Nineteen

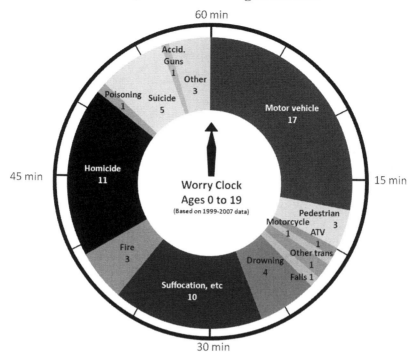

In the following sections we look at the breakdowns and how the age groups contribute to the clock. For example, while fire is a fairly consistently present danger, motor vehicle accidents grow disproportionately over the age groups.

Just like in the previous chapters, we will review each of these causes in more detail in the following sections, but we'll do this in a slightly different way. We need to look at the *rates* of death, instead of the worry clock minutes. So, I'm going to throw a different type of chart at you, but if you've made it this far, you'll be fine.

Now that you have gotten used to looking at the Worry Clocks, we want to begin to compare the clocks. Comparing circles is harder than comparing lines, so we are going to turn the clocks into bars.

Bar charts are just the Worry Clocks cut and laid out vertically; the data in them and how you read them are the same. Let's go back to the fictitious Worry Clock from the introduction.

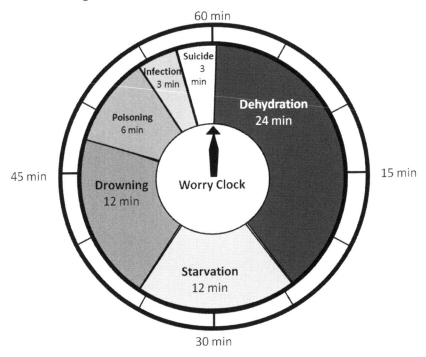

Worry Clock Example
for Being Marooned on a Deserted Island (Data Not Real)

Remember that this is a made-up Worry Clock for what you might die from if you were trapped on a deserted island.

Now, if I wanted to turn this into a bar chart, I would cut the circle and lay it out like this:

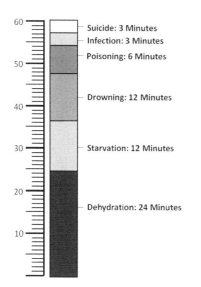

Suicide: 3 Minutes
Infection: 3 Minutes
Poisoning: 6 Minutes

Drowning: 12 Minutes

Starvation: 12 Minutes

Dehydration: 24 Minutes

This is the Worry Clock— same numbers, same information— laid out in a different way, in a stacked bar chart.

Notice that dehydration still accounts for twenty-four minutes, starvation for twelve minutes, and so on.

To compare all of the Worry Clocks we have covered so far, we would lay them out right next to each other, as in the graph below.

Worry Clocks for All Age Groups Compared

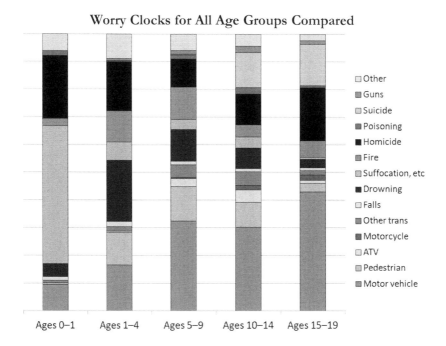

Other
Guns
Suicide
Poisoning
Homicide
Fire
Suffocation, etc
Drowning
Falls
Other trans
Motorcycle
ATV
Pedestrian
Motor vehicle

Ages 0–1   Ages 1–4   Ages 5–9   Ages 10–14   Ages 15–19

You can see by comparing these Worry Clocks that motor vehicle accidents, the first block on the bottom of each bar, increase disproportionately as children age. That is, motor vehicles accidents account for a greater percentage of your worry the older your child gets.

I know the rest of the graph is hard to read, so ignore it for now; I've got just one more leap for you to take: What if you wanted to also know how many more kids died at each age? That is, is one age group more likely to die than other age groups? In that case the bars would be different heights, and the height of the bar would tell you the relative number of children who died. To understand what I mean, it may help to look at the data; see the new chart, next.

Worry Clocks from All Age Groups Compared *and* Showing Rates of Death

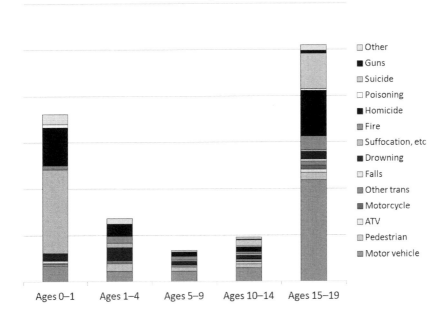

For those who care, the y-axis (height of the bars) on the graphs shows the crude rates per one hundred thousand in the population, so we can compare across age groups without worrying about differing numbers in the base population (e.g., a population "bubble" of teens).

For those who don't care, ignore the axis and just look at the differences between the bars. Know that you can compare the amount or section within one bar to a section in another bar and conclude that in these data, more kids died from the causes represented by the larger bar.

What probably immediately leapt out at you is how high the teen bar is, then the infant bar. Conversely, you may have noticed how relatively small the toddler, young child, and preteen bars are.

Here's the same information on a Worry Clock. See the Worry Clock Based on Rates of Death by Age Group for Ages Birth to Nineteen. Notice that if you added up the minutes for ages one to fourteen, you would get fifteen minutes, more than ten minutes less than just for teen years *and* less than for the infant year.

In fact, three-quarters of your worry goes to just two age groups: infants and teenagers. Teens alone make up over twenty-five minutes, or nearly half your worry. The other three age groups, from ages one to fourteen, make up only fifteen minutes of worry combined.

Worry Clock Based on *Rates* of Death by Age Group for Ages Birth to Nineteen[369]

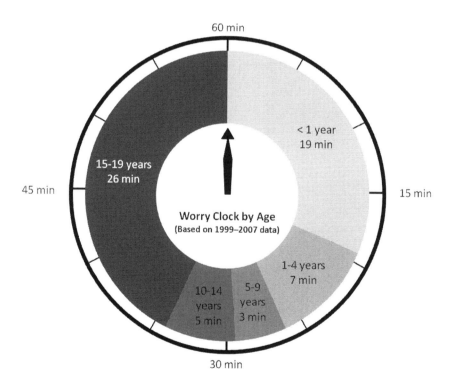

If I can show the information in a Worry Clock, why am I using the bar charts? Why is it so important to introduce this new graph? The new graph will compare the relative numbers of deaths in each age group. Right now, for example, you know that motor vehicle accidents are a top cause of death in each age group, but you do not know that teen car accidents total more than all the other ages combined. If you go back and look at the bar chart, you will see that the first section in each bar, the rate of motor vehicle deaths, is highest in the teen years and totals more than all the other age groups combined.

I will use the bar charts throughout the rest of this chapter to point out how the different ages contribute to the overall Worry Clock. For example, you will see that for breathing issues, the infant year contributes the vast majority of deaths.

If you are still not comfortable with the bar charts, don't worry about it. I will spell out what I am trying to show in the bar graphs.

Motor Vehicle (17 Minutes) and Other Transportation (6 Minutes) Accidents

Motor vehicle deaths, while fairly consistent across age groups below teens, shoot up in the teen years, as may be seen on the bar chart below (see black section, the bottom chunk, of each bar). When children are riding with experienced adult drivers, the rates remain constant, up through age fourteen. Yet as soon as the teens themselves or their peers represent a larger percentage of the drivers, the rate of death increases by tenfold. The teen years account for higher rates of motor vehicle deaths than all other ages combined. There is good evidence that this is due to their (or their peer driver's) inexperience driving (see teen chapter).

Pedestrian accidents (the darkened sections just above the black sections) are also high in teen years and show about the same rate of death as in the toddler years. Halloween night, at least in an analysis of data from the mid 1970s to the mid 1990s, showed a fourfold increase in pedestrian deaths.[370]

Across all ages (including adults), alcohol involvement—either for the driver or for the pedestrian—is a factor in half (47 percent) of the traffic crashes that resulted in pedestrian fatalities. Of the pedestrians involved, 33 percent had a blood alcohol concentration (BAC) of .08 grams per deciliter (g/dL) or higher.[371]

Motor Vehicle and Other Transportation Rates of Death by Age

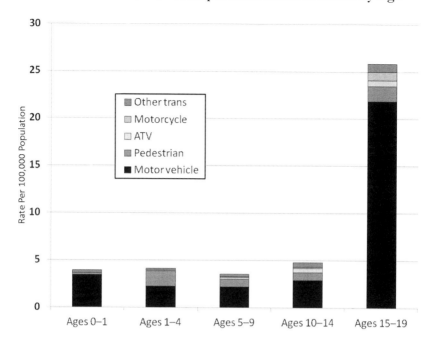

Deaths due to ATV and motorcycle accidents (gray sections) steadily increase over the years. ATVs have higher rates of death until the teenage years, when motorcycles leap ahead to a 50 percent higher rate than ATVs.

Bicycles (not shown) don't even make it onto the chart, but they are the major contributor to the "other transportation" category. Bicycle death rates peak in the early teen years, presumably because teens switch to alternative transportation such as motorcycles.

Homicide (11 Minutes)

Homicide's enormous presence is due primarily to infant and teen homicide rates. The toddler contribution is likely the remnant of the infant issues related to excessive crying and a caregiver's unchecked anger. There is a difference in the method of death, too, with guns playing a much more significant role in teenage years, a point I return to at the end of the chapter with a look specifically at the role of firearms.

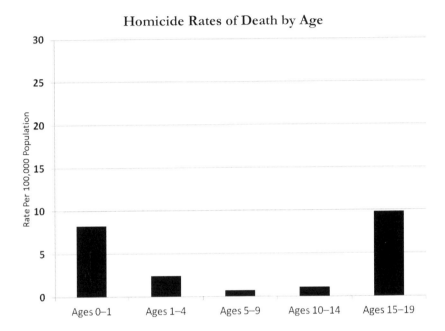

Homicide Rates of Death by Age

Suffocation and Breathing-Related Deaths (10 Minutes)

Nearly all of the deaths attributed to threats to breathing, such as suffocation while sleeping or choking on food, happen during the infant year. As you can see from the bar chart at the beginning of the chapter, these deaths alone are greater than all the accidental deaths *from all causes* in each of the next three age groups.

Breathing-Related Rates of Death by Age

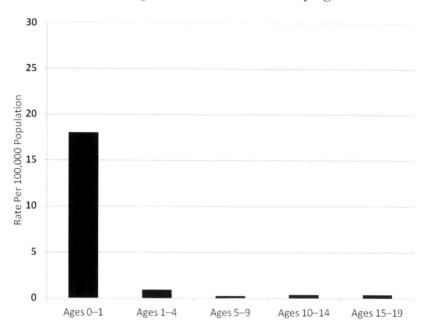

Suicide (5 Minutes)

Suicide is the fourth leading cause of death across all age groups. These deaths appear as a major category for the first time in the early teen years, and rates jump by six times that in teenage years. As noted earlier, the method of choice also changes from hanging to guns, which may relate to the higher rates in the teen years. More teens committed suicide than children ages five to nine died in total from all accidents.

Suicide Rates of Death by Age

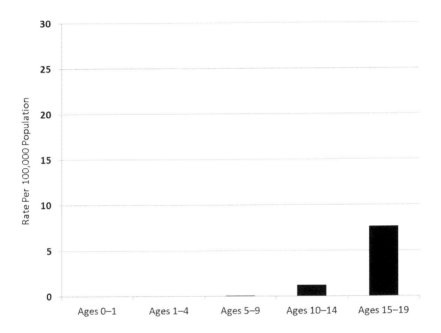

Drowning (4 Minutes)

Drowning is somewhat constant across the ages, but there are a few ages when it is notably higher. Toddlers have just shy of twice the rate of any other group. They are followed by infants and teens (the latter incidents likely involving alcohol) at about half the rate of toddlers.

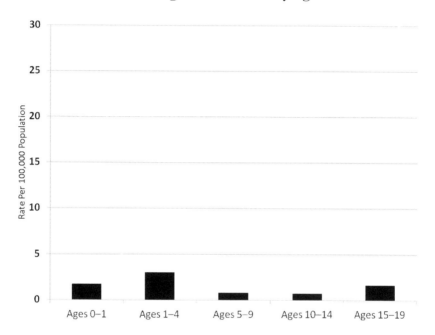

Drowning Rates of Death by Age

Fire (3 Minutes)

Fires had something I had not noticed in the earlier analyses: teens have a much higher rate than other ages. I didn't notice because this higher rate is masked by the even greater increases in the other causes of death. Yet fire deaths in the teen years almost equals all the other ages fire-deaths combined. I wasn't able to find any additional data on this statistic. It could be that teens are more likely to be around other teens who set fires, or that drugs or alcohol or simply sound sleeping impair their ability to escape from fires.

Fire-Related Rates of Death by Age

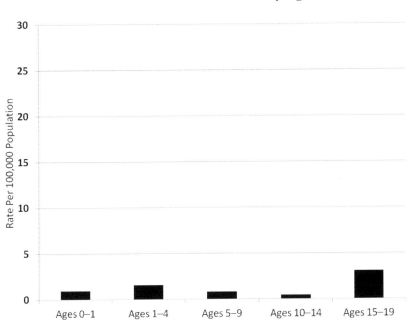

Falls (1 Minute)

Teens and infants have the highest rates of death from falls (not shown) and are about equally divided. Toddlers contribute about half their rate.

Poisoning (1 Minute)

Infants have the highest rates of poisoning (not shown), with teens not far behind, and early teens also contributing at the rate of about equal to that of infants.

Guns (1 Minute or 8 Minutes?)

Accidental gun deaths, in which no one meant to pull the trigger and hurt himself or someone else, contribute one minute to the total Worry Clock. The rate is highest for teens and second highest for early teens, who contribute about one-third of what teens do for these accidental gun deaths. And accidental firearm deaths appear on the first worry clock starting at age five.

As the National Research Council of the National Academies of Sciences pointed out some time ago—and will hopefully update soon—guns play a role in a lot more deaths than this one minute would suggest, and some of these deaths may in fact be attributable to the gun itself. In other words, what might have ended as a recoverable mistake due to all-too-common poor teenage judgment (and lack of risk assessment) instead ends with a deadly error.

For the first time in this book, I will add together all deaths by guns. Just how many cases involve firearms? Across our children's lives, about **one out of every eight deaths** is from a gun.[372] If we separated out the gun deaths, eight minutes on the Worry Clock reflect gun violence. As many know, the United States has the highest rate of firearm-related deaths (including homicide, suicide, and unintentional deaths) among industrialized countries.[373] I knew guns would appear on the Worry Clocks somewhere, but I admit I was surprised by their prominence.

The vast majority of these deaths are in the teenage years. In fact, if we looked at gun violence just **in the teen years, we would see that one in four teen deaths is by a gun**.

I know some will criticize my separation of the data in this way, but in researching for this book I have become convinced that (a) teenage judgment is diminished in significant ways and (b) that judgment becomes lethal both in a car and with a gun.

Gun-Related Rates of Death by Age

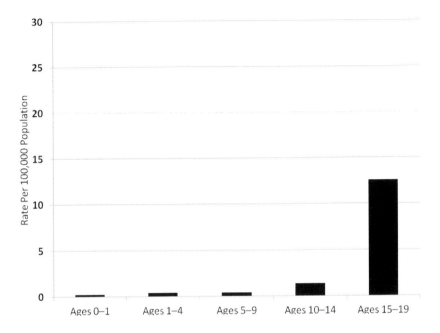

For driving, I recommend increased training. For guns? I'm not convinced. In driving, it is the lack of driving experience that *causes* the accident, and increased skill even with the poor judgment could avert an accident. Evaluations of graduated driver licensing programs provide evidence that this is true. A teen may still make a bad call and text while driving, but with more practice, that mistake is *less likely* to be fatal.

With guns, the reverse may be true. Training with a gun may only *increase* the fluidity and accuracy of shooting and therefore the likelihood that the split second or momentary poor choice of judgment, to some degree perhaps inevitable with teenagers, will be fatal. Further, and perhaps more convincingly, the simple access to guns in the home, as cited earlier, has been shown to increase suicide risk.

Top Ten for Childhood (All Ages 0–19)

You made it through all the data, now where to begin? If you feel overwhelmed and don't know where to start, here are some suggestions based on the most frequent causes of death in the past data. In this chapter, I am extrapolating from the data in previous chapters. You should consider whether the strategies listed here are right for you and your child. Although these strategies generally come from reliable, primarily government sources, they may not be right for your child. As you are keenly aware, doing these things doesn't guarantee a safe child, but they give you a place to start.

Top ten suggestions for increasing safety for birth to nineteen:

1. **Spend AT LEAST thirty to fifty hours of supervised driving practice** over at least six months, and limit the number of teen passengers to zero or one for at least the first six months. Teens are very sensitive to measures that may cause them to lose their driving privileges.

2. **Always wear seat belt (or helmet) and get your child in the habit** of wearing one while they are young so that they form the habit. Model good driving behavior.

3. **Keep guns and ammunition out of your house—and out of the hands of teenagers.** Once you get the guns out of your home, consider actively supporting some of the gun-restriction legislation. Or come up with and get funded better ways to prevent the deaths of one out of eight of our children from guns.

4. **Do not hesitate to get professional, psychological help for your child if she seems depressed or stressed—or if she plays with fire.** Why wait? If your child seems skeptical, ask someone she trusts to recommend someone. There is mounting evidence that currently available treatments for depression and suicide-related disorders work.

5. **Always put infants to sleep on their backs in a crib or bassinet that conforms to CPSC and ASTM International standards and do room sharing without bed sharing or co-sleeping.** No pillows, no blankets, no people.

6. **Give your child swimming lessons as soon as possible and be mindful of any bodies of water near houses you visit.** One source estimated that participation in formal swimming lessons could reduce the risk of drowning by 88 percent among children ages one to four years.[374] Remember that toddlers were most often last seen in the house and not expected to be out near a pool. Bring a door alarm if needed.

7. **Talk about the statistics on pedestrian deaths with older teens and hold tightly to your toddler's hand whenever around cars.** Developing automatic habits early will help to prepare teens, as well as informing them of the statistics and having them develop strategies to address higher risk taking. Toddlers, who have never darted before, might dart into the street for no apparent reason.

8. **Get the right fire equipment now,** including *working* photoelectric *and* ionization detectors and escape rope ladders for rooms that need them. Your home probably has ionization detectors but may not have photoelectric ones, which detect a more common type of fire. Check and make sure that you have both types in good working order. In your children's rooms, you may want to also have the detectors that allow for your voice to be recorded, giving escape instructions to the child.

9. **Talk to your teen about strategies to slow down in making decisions, and talk to older adults they trust.** Homicide, suicide, fire, drowning, all may have elements of poor judgment of teen years and strategies to build the capacity to avoid snap judgments may help.

10. **Spend more time building an even closer relationship with your child now.** By the time you need your relationship to be strong, it may be too late to start building the necessary trust. You are your child's best protective factor.

Conclusion

For those who would like a one-table summary of this book, see below. It shows each ages worry clock and the size of the font is proportional to the time on the worry clock. The exact minutes are in the parentheses. Notice that motor vehicles are pretty consistent and get more important as the child ages. Suffocation, a huge issue for infants, basically goes away after the first year.

Nearly fifty percent of your worry over your child's entire childhood (birth through nineteen) boils down to just two factors: cars and guns. In the case of cars, states have made great strides recently in focusing on building the experience of the newest drivers in safe ways (e.g., without other teens in the car, during the day first). Take those requirements seriously; they are based on good data and show results—they save lives.

In the case of guns, states like New York are also making strides by trying new policies to address our gun violence epidemic. I hear others suggesting all kinds of strategies, some more based on research than others, and I applaud action. Even if I do not agree with a strategy, I am willing to try it and let the results, the data, speak for me. Data may be complicated and misrepresented often, but most scientists when looking at the same data tend to agree on what the data say. Listen for it; you will hear it. Whatever your politics, agree that in this case something needs to be done; worrying without action is not enough.

Ages 0 – 1	Ages 2 – 4	Ages 5 – 9	Ages 10 – 14	Ages 15 – 19	All Ages 0-19
Motor vehicle (6)	Motor vehicle (10)	Motor vehicle (20)	Motor vehicle (18)	Motor vehicle (26)	Motor vehicle (17)
Homicide (14)	Homicide (11)	Homicide (6)	Homicide (7)	Homicide (12)	Homicide (11)
			Suicide (8)	Suicide (9)	Suicide (5)
Drowning (3)	Drowning (13)	Drowning (7)	Drowning (4)	Drowning (2)	Drowning (4)
Fire (2)	Fire (7)	Fire (7)	Fire (3)	Fire (4)	Fire (3)
	Pedestrian (7)	Pedestrian (7)	Pedestrian (5)	Pedestrian (2)	Pedestrian (3)
Suffocation (27) & Choking (3)	Suffocation (1) & Choking (3)	Suffocation (1) & Choking (3)	Suffocation & Choking (2)		Suffocation & Choking (10)
		ATV (2)	ATV (3)	ATV (1)	ATV (1)
		Bicycle (2)	Bicycle (2)	Motorcycle (1)	Motorcycle (1)
	Other trans (1)	Other trans (1)	Other trans (1)	Other trans (1)	Other trans (1)
Falls (1)	Falls (1)	Falls (1)	Falls (1)	Falls (1)	Falls (1)
Poisoning (1)	Poisoning (1)	Poisoning (1)	Poisoning (1)		Poisoning (1)
Medical complications (1)					
		Accid gun discharge (1)	Accid gun discharge (1)	Accid gun discharge (1)	Accid gun discharge (1)

Arguably, this chapter should not be in this book. The type of child abduction that probably leaps to mind—kidnapping by a stranger—is rare and does not even appear on the earlier Worry Clocks.

So why this chapter? Because in survey after survey, child abduction ranks at the top of parents' concerns for their children.[375] Thus, this chapter takes the reverse approach. Instead of the data leading us to a worry, our worry is examined in the context of the data. This chapter is a conscious exception to our data-driven approach because, for so many parents, movie-of-the-week kidnapping, stereotypical abduction, is the number-one fear we have for our children.

But let's all agree that this fear is irrational. Estimates[376]—albeit rough estimates because the numbers are so low—are that one in six hundred thousand children is abducted by a stranger annually. Children are one thousand times more likely to be abducted by their own mom, dad, or close relative, often for reasons far from that child's well-being,[377] a point I return to later.

Point #1: Do I need to say it? The horrific, stereotypical kidnappings are rare: less than one in six hundred thousand annually. Children are more than one thousand times more likely to be abducted by their own parent or family member.

Despite the comparisons, some of you might say, "Less than one in a million? That is more than I thought! After all, it is much more likely than winning the lottery, which is easily one in a few million!"[378] The astute reader will point out that stereotypical abduction is also still fifteen times more likely than a child's being hit by lightning. And that's true, but I don't spend a lot of time advocating avoiding metal objects and open fields in thunderstorms, either. So bring on the data.

In this chapter I begin by taking a look at what happens when children go missing, to put these stereotypical kidnappings into context. Then I go into depth about stereotypical kidnappings: the victims, the perpetrators, the situations, and the outcomes. For example, research suggests that stereotypical abductions are most likely to happen:

- About the age you start thinking you've made it past this worry (young teens).

- Right near your house (within three blocks, but often in the front yard).
- By someone younger than you might think (almost 60 percent of abductors are under twenty-nine and many are in their late teens).

The rest of this chapter examines these data more closely, if not to contribute in some small way to the eradication of this type of abduction, then at least to focus the discussion more on the available data and perhaps to spur better data collection, particularly in the area of attempted abductions.

Warning: Even if you have gotten this far in reading about horrible things that could happen to your child, this chapter takes it to a whole new level. As in other chapters, I highlight some points in bold. If you want to skip the detail and drama of this chapter, just read the bold remarks.

Caveat: The numbers here are so small that these estimates and data are universally questionable. I exclude data that seem to grossly mislead, but drawing the line is challenging. I present these data to say that this is the best I could find, but I welcome researchers and the government furthering the discussion by bringing better data to bear.

Abduction: Putting It into the Context of When a Child Goes Missing

If we look at just "caretaker missing" kids—that is, when mom, dad, or other caregiver noticed that the kid was missing and reported the missing child either actively (by calling police) or passively (on a later survey)[379]—here's what the Worry Clock for these missing kids would look like.

Worry Clock: When a Child Goes Missing
(Based on data from 1999)

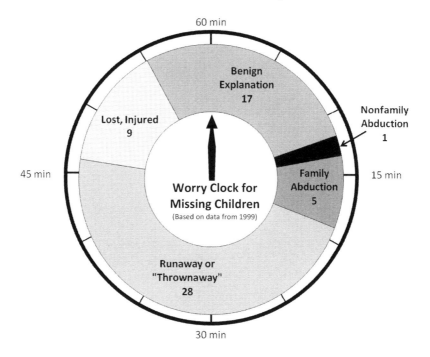

The Worry Clock above shows the worry allocation for kids who have already gone missing based on some of the most thorough national estimates of missing kids. Mom, Dad, or caretaker noticed the child was missing and, in many cases, they called police. However, in some cases, as with "thrownaways,"[380] children kicked out of the house with no place to go, caretakers may not have informed the police, and we base these estimates on later interviews with those caretakers.

Almost half, twenty-eight minutes of worry, go to runaways or thrownaways. So if you are worried about your child going missing, half of your worry by the data would be focused on preventing your child from running away. Seventeen minutes, or just over one-quarter, are missing children who later turn up with no ill effects, the "benign" group. Another nine minutes goes to children who were injured or similarly unable to get home (e.g., broke an arm and ended up in the hospital instead of home). Family abduction adds five minutes. Often Mom or Dad, about to undergo a custody battle, takes a child away from the ex-partner, more for revenge than protection or love.[381] The final minute on the clock are the nonfamily abductions, which is where most of the fear is focused, so let's look closely at this one minute.

The nonfamily abduction minute on the Worry Clock includes two types of abduction:

- **General nonfamily abduction** (hereafter referred to just as "nonfamily abductions") occurs when a nonfamily perpetrator takes a child by the use of physical force or threat of bodily harm or detains a child for at least one hour in an isolated place by the use of physical force or threat of bodily harm without lawful authority or parental permission; or when a child who is younger than fifteen years old or mentally incompetent, is, without lawful authority or parental permission, taken or detained by or voluntarily accompanies a nonfamily perpetrator who conceals the child's whereabouts, demands ransom, or expresses the intention to keep the child permanently. This could be a fourteen-year-old girl sneaking out to be with her nineteen-year-old boyfriend who lies about where she is, or it could be a middle-aged neighbor who detains and molests an eleven-year-old. *Both* fit into this category.

- **Stereotypical kidnappings** are when a stranger or slight acquaintance abducts a child and detains him overnight, transports the child at least fifty miles, holds the child for ransom with intent to keep him permanently, or kills the child. These kidnappings are by definition a stranger or slight acquaintance, and these are the stories that seem to fill the news.

In short, the difference between these is severity. Cases move from nonfamily abduction to a stereotypical kidnapping when the child is detained longer, transported farther, or killed. Nonfamily abductions, such as a fifteen-year-old who gets detained and sexually assaulted in a school bathroom, are significantly more common. A neighbor's assaulting your four-year-old child and then releasing her also fits into the nonfamily abduction category. These abductions account for almost all (59.9 of all 60 seconds) of the nonfamily worry.

The stereotypical kidnappings are the more serious and abound with stories that make the national news: a child is taken by a stranger who then kills the child. But these are rare. Stereotypical abductions are statistically worthy of about *three-tenths of a second* on the Worry Clock—and remember, this Worry Clock is for *all* children who go missing for *any* reason.

In *both* of these cases, general nonfamily and stereotypical abductions, the child is likely to return alive. Shocking? In more than 99 percent of general nonfamily abduction cases, the children are returned alive.[382] In stereotypical abductions, statistics suggest that *more than half (57 percent) are returned alive.*[383] Further, 90 percent of the episodes are over within twenty-four hours. Timing is everything; more on this later.

Point #2: Even in the nightmare situation of a stereotypical kidnapping, significantly more than half (57 percent) of children returned alive.

For every ten thousand reports of a missing child, less than one ends in a murder.[384] We would all agree that there should not even be one, so let's dig deeper into the data. For the rest of this chapter, I will focus on the stereotypical kidnappings. Remember these are so small—three-tenths of a second—that I didn't even separate them from the nonfamily abductions category because then they would not have appeared on the clock. These incidents, despite their infrequency, loom large in parental fears, however, so we are only looking at this small, small number of cases.

Stereotypical Kidnappings

Remember, these are the more serious cases, by definition those by a stranger or acquaintance, where about 40 percent of children end up murdered. Roughly one in six hundred thousand kids have been abducted under this category, and one in 1.5 million ended up killed. First we will look at the victims, then perpetrators, and then where and how the abduction happens.

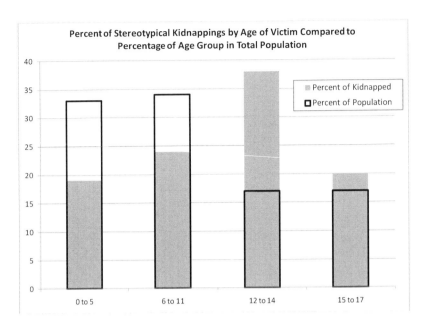

Percent of Stereotypical Kidnappings by Age of Victim Compared to Percentage of Age Group in Total Population

Victims

The typical victim of abduction and murder is a white (75 percent) girl (74 percent) about twelve years old (average age was between eleven and twelve) from a middle-class (35 percent) or blue-collar (36 percent) family living in a single-family residence (71 percent) with a good family situation (50 percent) and considered a low-risk (84 percent), average kid.[385] That get your attention? That is the case with those who are murdered, but the statistics on who is actually abducted are, not surprisingly, not very different.

Let's take a closer at the ages of the stereotypically abducted kids. Check out the solid bars in the graph on this page. Those bars show the percentages of victims at various ages. The twelve- to fourteen-year-olds have the highest percentage (highest solid bar); more than one-third of abductions occur in this age group alone.

Now look at the outlined empty boxes and ignore the solid bars. These boxes show the percentage of each age group in the population. About one-third of the population is age birth to five, another third is six to eleven, and the last third is the two teenage groups. We might expect that the blue bars would align with these boxes; if there are more six- to eleven-year-olds around, then more of them would be targets of abduction. But that is not what we see. For the younger ages, there are fewer abductions relative to the number of children. For the older teens, there are only slightly more abductions. However, look at the younger teens from twelve to fourteen years old: this group has twice as many abductions as one might expect based on their numbers in the population.

Point #3: Don't think of kidnappings as about kids under ten; twelve- to fourteen-year-olds show the highest rates of stereotypical abduction and two times the rate one would expect based on their numbers in the population.

Boys are not immune to stereotypical abduction. While girls are still disproportionately represented, almost one-third (31 percent) of the kidnapping victims were boys. For many kidnappers, this is a crime of opportunity not necessarily dependent on child gender.

Whites and blacks were also disproportionately represented. Eighty percent of the victims were white (though only 65 percent of the population) and 20 percent were black (15 percent of the population).

For those who are concerned about infant abduction, there are disproportionately low rates and estimates are that fewer than twenty occur annually. One study[386] that looked at infant abduction over ten years (1983–1992) found that the abductors were usually women, disproportionately black (43 percent), and abducted male and female infants at about the same rate. Three-quarters of the infants were recovered within five days.

We'll look at where these kids are abducted after we examine who the abductors are.

Perpetrators
The perpetrators were likely to be men (estimates ranged from 86 to 99 percent), but about *half* of the time they had partners in their crime. Let me repeat that: almost half (48 percent) of the children abducted were abducted by more than one person. Further, more than 20 percent of perpetrators were teenagers (between thirteen and nineteen years old). The research on child molesters suggests that most molest for the first time during their teenage years.[387] Fifty-seven percent of perpetrators were less than thirty years old. A study of over eight hundred child abduction–murders found that the oldest murderer was sixty-one and the youngest was nine. The median age of those who killed was about twenty-eight.[388] The image of the older, lone man does not hold up to statistics. Think more about the younger guy down the street.

Seventy-five percent of the murderers lived with someone. That's right: they had wives, girlfriends, kids, or roommates. Only one in three lived with his parents. Given that 20 percent are teens, this suggests that an additional 13 percent are older and living with their parents. Only 17 percent lived alone.

Point #4: The idea of the lone, middle-age perpetrator is not accurate. One in five perpetrators is a teenager, and there's a fifty-fifty chance he has a buddy working with him.

Let's take a closer look at what data we have on perpetrators. I couldn't find much data on these abductors generally, but did find data a detailed study of abductors who had killed.[389] Of those who killed, most (70 percent) were white and half were unemployed (48 percent). Of those who were employed, half of them (26 percent of the total) worked in construction; this is probably because construction work often involves moving a lot (45 percent moved three or more times in the last five years). Almost two-thirds had prior arrests for violent crimes, with slightly more than half of those prior crimes committed already against children. *One in ten murderers had already killed or attempted to kill another child.*[390]

Combine these prior arrests data with knowing that sex offenders have been found four times more likely to be rearrested compared to non–sex offenders[391] and it is easy to understand why Megan's Law came to be— and why it is important for you to check out your state's registry of sex offenders. **Megan's Law** is actually a series of bills that passed the New Jersey Assembly in 1994 and were named after seven-year-old Megan Kanka, who was raped and murdered by a sex offender who had been previously convicted of sex crimes and lived across the street from Kanka together with four other sex offenders. Congress quickly followed with its own version, the Wetterling Act, which requires states to form registries of offenders convicted of sexually violent offenses or offenses against children, and to establish more rigorous registration requirements for sex offenders. To search for registered sex offenders near you, you can search by zip code at the Dru Sjodin National Sex Offender Public Website, http://www.nsopw.gov/Core/Portal.aspx. You will likely get more information by going to your state's page, however. A quick search on Google for "sex offender registry" and your state's name should get you there. Map out both the offender's home and work addresses, and the likely route in between. When I typed one of our local offender's work addresses into Google Maps, I found out that the unassuming address where he was listed as working was actually a popular gym near our home—a gym with child care services.

> **Point #5:** Perpetrators are four times more likely to reoffend, and 10 percent of murderers had a prior record of murder or attempted murder of a child.

Having said that, I'd be remiss if I didn't point out that studies[392] have not found a significant difference in prevention of new offenses resulting from the registries. It is unclear why no effect was found (e.g., did people not use the registries). Overall, rates of abduction in the places studied went down, so the changes may be masked or there may be an overall discouragement because of the registries.

As far as a profile for molesters generally, a study[393] of over four thousand individuals who admitted to molesting a child found that:

- Only 10 percent molested children that they did not know.
- Sixty-eight percent molested children in their own family (nieces and nephews, children they parent, grandchildren, and siblings as teenagers).
- More than 40 percent began molesting before the age of fifteen and the majority by the age of twenty.
- More than 70 percent of those who molested boys claimed to be heterosexual in their adult preference.
- Of those who molested girls, 21 percent also molested boys, and of those who molested boys, 53 percent also molested girls.
- Sixty percent had other paraphilia, including voyeurism and exhibitionism.

An earlier study of sex offenders concluded that the typical sexual offender against children is male, begins molesting by age fifteen, engages in a variety of deviant behavior, and molests an average of 117 youngsters, most of whom do not report the incidents.[394]

Note again the consistent early onset: most molesters begin molesting before the age of twenty, and the molestation likely begins within the family. This suggests that it is a big mistake to excuse an older sibling's molesting a younger one as "experimenting," especially since early treatment of pedophilia may mean that it is curable.[395]

Baby-sitters, by the way, account for approximately 4 percent of crimes committed against children less than six years old—a rate below that of complete strangers.[396]

Where and How the Abduction Occurs

Where is the abduction occurring? About one in every six stereotypical abductions (16 percent) happens in the child's **own home or yard**. Given that the age of victims is often eleven or twelve, the idea that their own front yard is not safe may be quite disturbing. Two out of five (40 percent) are in streets or cars. Parks or wooded areas are the next most common.

> **Point #6:** One in six abductions occurs in or immediately around the home. Even more occur on the streets nearby.

Unlike murderers in general, child abduction murderers were "much less likely to select certain types of victims based on personal characteristics" (e.g., blond hair). Only 10 percent selected victims for those reasons. Forty percent of murderers selected their victim purely because the opportunity presented itself. In another 13 percent of cases, murderers were targeting a specific individual, and in 14 percent they had an existing relationship that let them create an opportunity. [397]

The statistics vary on whether the child knows the abductor. For stereotypical abductions, one study reported that 30 percent of kids knew their abductor (were acquaintances).[398] The study that looked at those who abducted and then murdered shows they were strangers only about 44 percent of the time and friends or acquaintances about 42 percent. In other words, roughly the same number was known to the child as was unknown. As a child ages, the likelihood of the abductor being a stranger appears to increase. [399]

One area to think about is also online solicitation. While the abductor-murderer study found that 5 percent of the perpetrators met their victim intentionally (rather than just happening upon the kid), the online world may be changing things. According to the National Center for Missing & Exploited Children, one in seven kids is solicited for sex online; one in thirty-three kids receives aggressive online solicitations to meet in person; one in three kids receives unsolicited sexual content online; and 34 percent of kids online indicate they communicate with people they don't know.[400]

To gain control of the child, about half of murderers used a direct physical assault, and 10 percent employed deception. They also tended to use the same modus operandi (e.g., what they said, what weapons they used) in each situation. If you know of an attempted abduction where the perpetrator said that his dog was in the car and needed help, then you know he might use that same story again. [401]

NCMEC analyzed more than 4,200 *attempted* abductions for the five-year period from February 2005 and March 2010 and found that the five most common lures included offering a child a ride, offering the child candy or sweets, showing the child an animal or asking for help finding a lost animal, offering the child money, and asking the child for directions.

NCMEC also reported that:
- Thirty-eight percent of attempted abductions occur while a child is walking alone to or from school, riding the school bus, or riding a bicycle.
- Thirty-seven percent of attempted abductions occur between the hours of two p.m. through seven p.m. on a weekday.
- Forty-three percent of attempted abductions involve children between the ages of ten and fourteen.
- Seventy-two percent of attempted abduction victims are female.
- Sixty-eight percent of attempted abductions involve the suspect driving a vehicle.

These numbers are consistent with the data about successful abductions: mostly female victims with a significant percentage between ten and fourteen years of age, approached outside, involving cars.

There is also evidence that being with peers is not enough. Some research suggested that the majority of attempted abductions occurred when the child was with friends.[402] Adding to that the finding that about half of the time a weapon is used in stereotypical kidnappings,[403] it may be the case that two perpetrators (since half the time they have partners) who have a gun approach kids on bicycles and drag one of the kids into a car. Just this past July, in Baltimore, a typical scenario was reported in the *Baltimore Sun* (July 12, 2011): "A light green, newer model Ford Taurus with two people inside stopped near Darrick and his friends....One of the people inside the car got out, grabbed Brown and threw him into the trunk before the vehicle sped away...."[404]

Police want (or should want) you to call them even if you are unsure whether your kid is missing. Why? Because if bad things are to happen, they happen fast. If previous statistics predict future rates, then for those 40 percent of children who will be murdered, almost half will be murdered in the first hour (47 percent), three-quarters within the first two hours (76 percent), and almost nine out of ten (89 percent) in the first twenty-four hours.[405] The sooner the parents call, the better.

What to Do

So, after all this horrific detail, where is the hope? In your kids. A critical finding of the NCMEC study was that "children were their own best protectors." Among nearly 3,500 cases of attempted abduction, 31 percent of children yelled, kicked, or pulled away and 53 percent walked or ran away. "The child should do whatever is necessary to stay out of the car, because once the child is in that car, it dramatically reduces the chances of escape," NCMEC Director Ernie Allen said. Only 16 percent received help from an adult.

> **Point #7:** Children were their own best protectors and successfully avoided abductions by yelling, kicking, pulling, and walking or running away.

NCMEC emphasizes that parents also "need to understand that most of those who abduct children are not 'strangers.'" Research shows that of the fifty-eight thousand nonfamily abductions each year, 63 percent involved a friend, long-term acquaintance, neighbor, caretaker, baby-sitter, or person of authority, and only 37 percent involved a stranger. (Note that these are *all* nonfamily abductions, not just stereotypical kidnappings.) NCMEC also noted that while the number of strangers is not insignificant, it remains far smaller than other offenders who have easy and legitimate access to children. Further, teaching "stranger danger" may not be an effective strategy. As pointed out on the HBO special *How to Raise a Street-Smart Child* (1987), most children didn't know how to define "stranger." Here are two examples of kids defining a stranger cited on that show: "A stranger sometimes wears a hat...sometimes a black or brown jacket and is a guy with a beard...some hair and a mustache and some glasses" and "I think a stranger is like...a punk rocker that drinks beer all day and sits around in a vacant lot."[406] If children know the person at all, which is true in the majority of cases, they won't consider the person a stranger.

Specific tips from NCMEC are below. Ernie Allen, the president and CEO of NCMEC, also made three great points in a separate paper, "Keeping Children Safe: Rhetoric and Reality":[407] our current teachings may go directly against encouraging our kids to fight back. Here are the three lessons he asks all of us to rethink:

- **"Don't take candy *from strangers*."** Chances are good the abductor won't be a stranger and may even be pretty skilled at convincing your kid he isn't a stranger. Stranger or not, tell kids not to get into anyone else's car. In cases of emergencies, I have heard of parents who have code words with their kids. The kids know that if the person picking them up is not who they expected, they should ask for the code word.

- **"Don't be a tattletale."** As we all learned in Bronson and Merryman's *Nurture Shock*, discouraging children from tattling means that we encourage our children to lie to us. But we want kids to let us know when someone is doing bad things.
- **"You're just a kid. Be respectful to adults; they know what they're doing."** For some kids, questioning an adult, let alone trying to physically assault one, is way too far a leap and certainly not one that would happen in seconds.

How do you teach these things? Honestly, I am just not sure. If you have ideas, post them to the worryclock.com website.

Ten Important Back-to-School Safety Tips
from the National Center for Missing and Exploited Children

1. Teach your children to always **TAKE A FRIEND** with them when walking or biking, and stay with a group while standing at the bus stop. Make sure they know which bus to ride.
2. Walk the route to and from school with your children, pointing out landmarks and safe places to go if they're being followed or need help. Teach your children they should **NEVER TAKE SHORTCUTS** and always stay in well-lit areas.
3. It is not safe for young children to walk to and from school, even in a group. Parents should always provide supervision for young children to help ensure their safe arrival to and from school. If your children wait for a bus, wait with them or make arrangements for supervision at the bus stop.
4. Teach your children that if anyone bothers them or makes them feel scared or uncomfortable, they should trust their feelings and immediately get away from that person. Teach them it is OK not to be polite and **IT IS OK TO SAY NO.**
5. Teach your children that if anyone tries to take them somewhere, they should **RESIST** by kicking and screaming, try to run away, and DRAW **ATTENTION** by kicking and screaming, "This person is trying to take me away" or "This person is not my father/mother."
6. Teach your children **NOT TO ACCEPT A RIDE** from anyone unless you have said it is OK in that instance. If anyone follows them in a vehicle, they should turn around, go in the other direction, and run to a trusted adult for help.

7. Teach your children that grownups should **NOT ASK CHILDREN FOR DIRECTIONS**, they should ask other adults.
8. Teach your children to **NEVER ACCEPT MONEY OR GIFTS** from anyone unless you have told them it is OK in each instance.
9. Make sure the school has current and accurate emergency contact information on file for your children and confirm names of those authorized to pick them up.
10. Always know where your children will be. Teach your children to always **CHECK FIRST** before changing their plans before or after school. Teach your children to never leave school with anyone unless they **CHECK FIRST** with you or another trusted adult, even if someone tells them it is an emergency.

More information and other tip sheets are available from NCMEC at www.missingkids.com.

Returning to the beginning of the chapter and the When a Child Goes Missing Worry Clock, your time might be better spent working on your marriage and your relationship with your kids, since family abduction (five minutes) and runaway/thrownaway kids (twenty-eight minutes) combined should account for most of the worry. Let's say you gave yourself an hour every year to worry about your child going missing. Since you've read this chapter, which probably took about five minutes, you've expended your worry time on stereotypical abduction for the next *one thousand years.* You've done your job; it's time to move on.

Natalia Pane, M.A., M.B.A, combined her love of data and research with her love of being a mom. She is currently the Vice President for Research Operations at Child Trends, an organization devoted to using research to improve the lives and well-being of children and youth.

For fifteen years, Natalia worked with leaders within the U.S. Departments of Education and Health and Human Services on federal data collection, analysis, and use to improve programs and policies. She served as the Executive Director of the National Assessment for Educational Progress Education Statistics Services Center and trained thousands of people on how to use data better to achieve their missions. Now she uses that statistical knowledge and looks at it from a whole new perspective—a mom who wants to continuously become a better mom.

She wrote this book to start a discussion about how we can use data more to answer questions that matter to parents. She readily admits that she doesn't have all the answers; this book is just a beginning. If you have better research, better data, better research-based suggestions on what to do, she wants to hear from you: Natalia@worryclock.com.

[1] Actually, this is the percentage who died from 1999 to 2007, which is the time frame we are using to estimate how many children die of a particular cause. See the "A word about the data" box for more. Children, based on the age ranges used by the government, go up to age nineteen.

[2] Thirty-three percent of the causes of death for ages birth to nineteen fall into the CDC's "external causes" category, discussed in more detail in the later chapters.

[3] This statistic is for children ages one to four and reports that the number who died from exposure to electrical current (i.e., what all those outlet covers are designed to prevent) was 0.02 per 100,000.

[4] Department of Defense, *US Army Survival Manual FM21-76* (Dorset Press, 1998). See *Wikipedia* for a summary of the ideas: http://en.wikipedia.org/wiki/Survival_skills#cite_note-14.

[5] Yes, there is an in-between category of incidents such as diseases, which may be the subject of a later book.

[6] The CDC considers Sudden Infant Death Syndrome, the leading cause of death for infants, as a medical condition and therefore *not* an external cause of death, or what I am labeling accidents. If we included SIDS in our analysis, since the prevention of SIDS follows many of the same guidelines for prevention of other types of suffocation, that additional category would add 8 percent, bringing the percentage of deaths addressed in this chapter to 13 percent of the total infant deaths.

[7] If I were to include SIDS on the Worry Clock, this category would account for a whopping forty-five minutes. But it should also be noted that the number of deaths that Worry Clock represents would have *more than doubled*. Either way, safe sleeping trumps everything else by far in this first year of your baby's life.

[8] CDC definition, as posted on http://www.cdc.gov/sids/index.htm.

[9] American Academy of Pediatrics, Task Force on Sudden Infant Death Syndrome, Policy Statement: "SIDS and Other Sleep-Related Infant Deaths: Expansion of Recommendations for a Safe Infant Sleeping Environment" (October 17, 2011), doi:10.1542/peds.2011-2284, http://pediatrics.aappublications.org/content/early/2011/10/12/peds.2011-2284.

[10] Dorothy A. Drago and Andrew L. Dannenberg, "Infant Mechanical Suffocation Deaths in the United States, 1980–1997," *Pediatrics* 103, no. 5 (1999): e59.

[11] The eight minutes classified as "other" were mostly undetermined and likely belong in the suffocation in bed category, but there was not enough evidence at the time of classification to put them there.

[12] Drago and Dannenberg, "Infant Mechanical Suffocation Deaths."

[13] See Consumer Product Safety Commission, e.g., http://www.cpsc.gov/Newsroom/News-Releases/1995/CPSC-Warns-Consumers-That-Used-Cribs-Can-Be-Deadly/.

[14] F. W. Jeffrey, "Public Health. Death from Plastic Film," *Can Med Assoc J.* 81 (1959): 687–688. Cited in Drago and Dannenberg, "Infant Mechanical Suffocation Deaths."

[15] Drago and Dannenberg, "Infant Mechanical Suffocation Deaths."

[16] American Academy of Pediatrics, Task Force on Sudden Infant Death Syndrome, "SIDS and Other Sleep-Related Infant Deaths: Expansion of Recommendations for a Safe Infant Sleeping Environment," *Pediatrics* 128, no. 5 (November 1, 2011): 1030–1039, accessed February 2013, http://pediatrics.aappublications.org/content/128/5/1030.full.

[17] Consumer Product Safety Commission, http://www.cpsc.gov/onsafety/2011/02/baby-monitor-cords-have-strangled-children/.

[18] Why do I make note of well-educated moms? Because in many cases, the mother's level of education is a predictive (and protective) factor, as many of you already know. In putting these notes in the analyses, my point is that education does not make one immune to childhood dangers.

[19] Although this is proportionately lower than the population in this group, since about 30 percent of women have sixteen-plus years of education, the point here is that this still happens to these moms.

[20] Matt Campbell, "Police: Infant Likely Suffocated on Couch," WZZM13, 2012, http://WZZM13.com.

[21] Kirk Brown, "Honea Path Infant Dies While Sleeping in Mother's Bed," *Anderson Independent Mail*, 2012, http://Independentmail.com.

[22] "Cops: Infant Likely Fell out of Bed, Suffocated," *Herald-News*, February 27, 2012.

[23] Bernard O'Donnell, "Macon Infant Dies after Smothering in Crib," 13WMAZ, May 4, 2012, http://13WMAZ.com.

[24] Erin Murphy, "Baby Dies Sleeping on Grandmother's Chest, Warning for Parents," WISH-TV, 2012.

[25] "Waterford Baby Dies While Sleeping in Same Bed as Mother," *Modesto Bee*, June 26, 2012.

[26] Consumer Product Safety Commission, "Incidents from 2007–2011" (July–August 2012), http://www.cpsc.gov/library/neiss.html.

[27] These include the National Institute of Child Health and Human Development at the National Institutes of Health, the Maternal and Child Health Bureau of the Health Resources and Services Administration, the US Centers for Disease Control and Prevention, and the US Food and Drug Administration.

[28] AAP policy statement, "SIDS and Other Sleep-Related Infant Deaths."

[29] Centers for Disease Control and Prevention, "Variation in Homicide Risk during Infancy—United States, 1989–1998," *Morbidity and Mortality Weekly Report* 51 (2002): 187–189.

[30] Ibid.

[31] Ibid.

[32] Ibid.

[33] Ibid.

[34] Ronald G. Barr, "What Is All That Crying About?," *Bulletin of the Centre of Excellence for Early Childhood Development* 6, no. 2 (September 2007).

[35] Ibid.

[36] Ibid.

[37] Estimates of the percentage of homicides resulting from shaken baby syndrome and similar abuse were difficult to obtain. Some studies, including Tenney-Soeiro & Wilson (2004) and Keenan, Runyan et al. (2003), would suggest that over 75 percent of the homicides fall into this category, but taking out guns, poisoning, and other clearly unrelated homicides as coded in the CDC data would cap the number at about 75 percent.

[38] Definition taken from the Centers for Disease Control and Prevention, "Preventing Shaken Baby Syndrome: A Guide for Health Departments and Community-Based Organizations," *Heads Up* series (n.d.), downloaded August 19, 2012, http://www.cdc.gov/concussion/pdf/preventing_sbs_508-a.pdf.

[39] Robert M. Reece, "What Does the Recent Literature Tell Us about Shaken Baby Syndrome?," *Never Shake a Baby Arizona*, downloaded September 1, 2012, http://www.nsbaz.org/index.php?option=com_content&view=article&id=73:what-does-science-tell-us-about-abusive-head-injuries-in-infants-and-young-children&catid=7:sbs-research&Itemid=45

[40] Barr, "What Is All That Crying About?"

[41] R. G. Barr, R. B. Trent, and J. Cross, "Age-Related Incidence Curve of Hospitalized Shaken Baby Syndrome Cases: Convergent Evidence for Crying as a Trigger to Shaking," *Child Abuse & Neglect* 30 (2006): 7–16.

[42] S. P. Starling, S. Patel, B. L. Burke, A. P. Sirotnak, S. Stronks, and P. Rosquist, "Analysis of Perpetrator Admissions to Inflicted Traumatic Brain Injury in Children," *Arch Pediatr Adolesc Med.* 158, no. 5 (2004): 454–458. These numbers include cases where abuse was admitted and cases where it was not admitted but was suspected based on the physical evidence.

[43] Ronald G. Barr, "What Is All That Crying About?"

[44] US Bureau of Labor Statistics, "Hours Spent on Childcare by Mothers and Fathers, 2003–07" (December 9, 2009), http://www.bls.gov/opub/ted/2009/ted_20091209.htm.

[45] H. T. Keenan, D. K. Runyan, S. W. Marshall, M. Nocera, D. F. Merten, and S. H. Sinal, "A Population-Based Study of Inflicted Traumatic Brain Injury in Young Children," *JAMA* 290, no. 5 (2003): 621–626.

[46] American Academy of Pediatrics Committee on Child Abuse and Neglect, "Shaken Baby Syndrome: Rotational Cranial Injuries—Technical Report," *Pediatrics* 108, no. 1 (2001): 206–210.

[47] Keenan, Runyan et al., "A Population-Based Study of Inflicted Traumatic Brain Injury in Young Children."

[48] Ibid.

[49] National Center on Shaken Baby Syndrome, "Frequently Asked Questions," http://www.dontshake.org/sbs.php?topNavID=3&subNavID=21&navID=21.

[50] I found this statistic on Medline as well as a number of other places, but could not find an original study to support the claim. MedlinePlus, "Shaken Baby Syndrome," accessed August 17, 2012.

[51] National Center on Shaken Baby Syndrome, "Frequently Asked Questions," http://www.dontshake.org/sbs.php?topNavID=3&subNavID=21&navID=21.

[52] Centers for Disease Control and Prevention, "A Journalist's Guide to Shaken Baby Syndrome," accessed September 1, 2012, http://www.cdc.gov/concussion/pdf/sbs_media_guide_508_optimized-a.pdf.

[53] For example, the rates of death were about one to two in every one hundred thousand births for college-educated mothers (calculated using CDC WONDER linked birth-death records 1992–2005;

ran August 19, 2012).

54 National Center for Shaken Baby Syndrome, "Frustration of Caring for a Crying Infant Compounded with Stresses Created during an Economic Recession Makes Prevention Program Developed by the NCSBS More Important Than Ever," http://dontshake.org/sbs.php?topNavID=3&subNavID=30&subnav_1=157&navID=701.

55 S. P. Starling, S. Patel et al., "Analysis of Perpetrator Admissions to Inflicted Traumatic Brain Injury in Children."

56 Medline Plus, "Shaken Baby Syndrome," downloaded September 1, 2012, http://www.nlm.nih.gov/medlineplus/ency/article/000004.htm.

57 S. P. Starling, S. Patel S et al., "Analysis of Perpetrator Admissions to Inflicted Traumatic Brain Injury in Children."

58 Centers for Disease Control and Prevention, "A Journalist's Guide to Shaken Baby Syndrome," accessed September 1, 2012, http://www.cdc.gov/concussion/pdf/sbs_media_guide_508_optimized-a.pdf.

59 Dan Metcalf, "Draper Boy Dies after Being Shaken by Father," ABC4 Salt Lake City, August 27, 2012, http://www.abc4.com/content/news/slc/story/Police-Draper-baby-dies-after-being-shaken-by/ZLK4teTgxUark4myRnPHpQ.cspx.

60 Leanne Gendreau and Amanda Raus, "Infant's Death May Be Shaken Baby Syndrome," NBC Connecticut, 2011, accessed September 1, 2012, http://www.nbcconnecticut.com/news/local/5-Month-Old-Boy-Killed-in-Ansonia-Police-123909104.html.

61 Nick Malawskey, "Family of Ten-Month-Old Killed in Babysitter's Care: 'Justice Was Served,'" *The Patriot News*, April 18, 2012, http://www.pennlive.com/midstate/index.ssf/2012/04/family_of_10-month-old_killed.html.

62 Centers for Disease Control and Prevention, "Child Passenger Safety Fact Sheet" (n.d.), accessed May 2013, http://www.cdc.gov/motorvehiclesafety/child_passenger_safety/cps-factsheet.html.

63 National Highway Traffic Safety Administration, "Misuse of Child Restraints" (January 2004), DOT HS 809 671.

64 Centers for Disease Control and Prevention, "Motor Vehicle Safety Fact Sheet," accessed September 2, 2012, http://www.cdc.gov/motorvehiclesafety/child_passenger_safety/cps-factsheet.html.

65 Ibid.

66 R. A. Shults, "Child Passenger Deaths Involving Drinking Drivers—United States, 1997−2002," *Morbidity and Mortality Weekly Report* 53, no. 4 (2004):77–9. Published erratum appears in *Morbidity and Mortality Weekly Report*.

67 Centers for Disease Control and Prevention, "Motor Vehicle Safety Fact Sheet."

68 US Consumer Product Safety Commission, "CPSC Warns Consumers of Suffocation Danger," Washington, DC (n.d.), pub. 5087 012012, http://www.cpsc.gov/CPSCPUB/PUBS/5087.pdf.

69 Washington State, "Choking/Suffocation Prevention" (n.d.), http://www1.dshs.wa.gov/pdf/ca/choking.pdf.

70 Ibid.

71 Consumer Product Safety Commission, "CPSC Decides Choking Issues" (March 22, 1990), http://www.cpsc.gov/CPSCPUB/PREREL/prhtml90/90055.html.

72 MedlinePlus, "Gastroesophageal Reflux in Infants," accessed August 19, 2012, http://www.nlm.nih.gov/medlineplus/ency/article/001134.htm.

73 For example, see D. G. Johnson, S. G. Jolley, J. J. Herbst, and L. J. Cordell, "Surgical Selection of Infants with Gastroesophageal Reflux," *J Pediatr Surg.* 16, no. 4, suppl. 1 (August 1981): 587–594.

74 MedlinePlus, "Gastroesophageal Reflux in Infants."

75 Jessica King, "One-Year-Old Dies, Officials Say He Choked on a Penny," ImperfectParent.com (October 4, 2011), http://www.imperfectparent.com/topics/2011/10/04/one-year-old-dies-from-choking-on-penny/.

76 Washington State, "Choking/Suffocation Prevention" (n.d.), http://www1.dshs.wa.gov/pdf/ca/choking.pdf; Department of Health, New York State, "Choking Prevention for Children," http://www.health.ny.gov/prevention/injury_prevention/choking_prevention_for_children.htm.

77 Washington State, "Choking/Suffocation Prevention."

78 KTAR Newsroom, "Infant Drowns after Being Left in Tub Unattended" (December 20, 2012), http://ktar.com/22/1597040/Infant-drowns-after-being-left-in-tub-unattended.

79 D. L. Chadwick, G. Bertocci, E. Castillo et al., "Annual Risk of Death Resulting from Short Falls among Young Children: Less Than 1 in 1 million," *Pediatrics* 121, no. 6 (2008): 1213–1224.

[80] Ibid.

[81] S. Monson, E. Henry, D. Lambert, N. Schmutz, and R. Christensen, "In-Hospital Falls of Newborn Infants: Data from a Multihospital Health Care System," *Pediatrics* 122, no. 2 (August 1, 2008): e277–e280, doi:10.1542/peds.2007-3811.

[82] D. L. Chadwick, G. Bertocci, E. Castillo et al., "Annual Risk of Death Resulting from Short Falls among Young Children."

[83] Ibid.

[84] M. D. Smith, J. D. Burrington, and A. D. Woolf, "Injuries in Children Sustained in Free Falls: An Analysis of Sixty-Six Cases," *J Trauma* 15, no. 11 (1975): 987–991; J. L. Meller and D. W. Shermeta, "Falls in Urban Children: A Problem Revisited," *Am J Dis Child*, 141, no. 12 (1987): 1271–1275.

[85] It is also likely true that people are more likely to call poison control for a younger child, so the number of cases is simply inflated for this age group.

[86] A. Bronstein, D. Spyker, L. Cantilena, J. Green, B. Rumack, and R. Dart, *2010 Annual Report of the American Association of Poison Control Centers' National Poison Data System (NPDS), 28th Annual Report*, downloaded October 2012, http://www.poison.org/stats/2010%20NPDS%20Annual%20Report.pdf.

[87] American Association of Poison Control Centers, "Tips for Caregivers," accessed October 2012, http://www.aapcc.org/dnn/PoisoningPrevention/TipsforBabysittersorotherCaregivers.aspx.

[88] Centers for Disease Control and Prevention, "Unintentional Drowning Fact Sheet," http://www.cdc.gov/homeandrecreationalsafety/water-safety/waterinjuries-factsheet.html.

[89] Consumer Product Safety Commission, "CPSC Safety Barrier Guidelines for Home Pools," http://www.cpsc.gov/cpscpub/pubs/pool.pdf.

[90] Centers for Disease Control and Prevention, "Unintentional Drowning Fact Sheet."

[91] Consumer Product Safety Commission, "Safety Barrier Guidelines for Home Pools," http://www.cpsc.gov/cpscpub/pubs/pool.pdf.

[92] Centers for Disease Control and Prevention, "Unintentional Drowning Fact Sheet."

[93] About 1.9 to 1.1 per 100,000.

[94] See http://www.cdc.gov/Features/dsDrowningRisks/.

[95] C. M. Branche and S. Stewart, eds., *Lifeguard Effectiveness: A Report of the Working Group* (Atlanta: Centers for Disease Control and Prevention, National Center for Injury Prevention and Control, 2001).

[96] http://www.cpsc.gov/cpscpub/prerel/prhtml02/02169.html.

[97] Ibid.

[98] Mario Vittone and Francesco Pia, "It Doesn't Look Like They're Drowning," http://www.uscg.mil/hq/cg5/cg534/On%20Scene/OSFall06.pdf.

[99] Associated Press, "Rhode Island Child Drowns in Attleboro Swimming Pool," *Herald News*, 2011, http://www.heraldnews.com/news/x1860267086/Rhode-Island-child-drowns-in-Attleboro-swimming-pool.

[100] Darran Simon, "Toddler Drowns in South Jersey Lake," *Philadelphia Inquirer*, 2011, http://articles.philly.com/2011-08-02/news/29842513_1_toddler-child-abduction-response-team-aunt.

[101] Amy Powell, "Twenty-Month-Old Girl Drowns in Fontana Hot Tub," *Inland Empire News*, 2011, http://abclocal.go.com/kabc/story?section=news/local/inland_empire&id=8256182.

[102] "Big Island Toddler Dies in Plastic Tank," *Hawaii News Now*, February 22, 2013, http://www.hawaiinewsnow.com/story/21311748/toddler-drowns-in.

[103] Centers for Disease Control and Prevention, "Unintentional Drowning Fact Sheet."

[104] The CDC data are not particularly helpful in understanding the deaths by assault (homicide). I turned to the Bureau of Justice Statistics for these data, but it reports higher rates. I assume that the percentages (or composition) of the assault categories remain consistent across the two collections.

[105] In over one-third of the cases, we don't know who killed the child, so for our purposes, I am assuming that the numbers we have are an accurate reflection of those we are missing—i.e., an equal percentage of that group were the moms and dads, but they got away with it.

[106] Bureau of Justice Statistics, "Homicide Trends in the United States 1980–2008" (November 2011), NCJ 236018, http://bjs.ojp.usdoj.gov/content/pub/pdf/htus8008.pdf. (Note that the BJS cites higher rates of homicide than I found in the CDC data set, which may be due to differences in classifications.)

[107] Ibid.

[108] "Affton Mother Charged with Murder in Beating Death of Her Toddler Son," FOX 2 St. Louis, 2011, http://www.fox2now.com/news/ktvi-missing-affton-mo-toddler-police-search-

111511,0,5340800.story.

[109] Associated Press and NBC 10, "Baby-Sitter Charged in Death of Philly-Area Child," NBC10 Philadelphia, 2011, http://www.nbcphiladelphia.com/news/local/Baby-Sitter-Charged-in-Death-of-Philly-Area-Child-136485583.html.

[110] Accidents in which cars hit children in their driveways on the house side of the sidewalk are considered nontraffic accidents, while those that occur on or after the sidewalk line are considered traffic accidents. While I appreciate this distinction for federal data collections, I do not believe it is helpful for prevention, which is why I separated all these data into the pedestrian section.

[111] CDC data.

[112] National Highway Traffic Safety Administration, US Department of Transportation, "Traffic Safety Facts: 2008 Data" (2008): 1, DOT HS 811 162, http://www-nrd.nhtsa.dot.gov/Pubs/811162.pdf.

[113] See http://www.fhwa.dot.gov/publications/publicroads/01novdec/brakes.cfm for a summary.

[114] Whether a car seat or other restraint was used was missing in over half the cases, so I only looked at the proportion for those where data were available.

[115] National Highway Traffic Safety Administration, US Department of Transportation, "Traffic Safety Facts: 2008 Data," 3.

[116] This estimate is likely conservative, since one might imagine many parents who insist that children are belted when they are not.

[117] National Highway Traffic Safety Administration, US Department of Transportation, "Traffic Safety Facts: 2008 Data," 3.

[118] Centers for Disease Control and Prevention, "Motor Vehicle Safety," PowerPoint presentation, http://www.cdc.gov/WinnableBattles/MotorVehicleInjury/.

[119] My analyses showed that about 20 percent of the fatalities were ejections, and others have found this number to be about one-third, e.g., National Highway Traffic Safety Administration, US Department of Transportation, "Traffic Safety Facts: 2008 Data."

[120] National Highway Traffic Safety Administration, US Department of Transportation, "Traffic Safety Facts 2009: Alcohol-Impaired Driving," Washington, DC (2010), cited January 25, 2011, http://www-nrd.nhtsa.dot.gov/Pubs/811385.pdf.

[121] Ibid.

[122] Insurance Institute for Highway Safety, http://www.iihs.org/research/qanda/speed_limits.html.

[123] Ibid.

[124] National Highway Traffic Safety Administration, "Distracted Driving, 2009" (2010), http://www.distraction.gov/research/PDF-Files/Distracted-Driving-2009.pdf.

[125] Jason M. Watson and David L. Strayer, "Supertaskers: Profiles in Extraordinary Multitasking Ability," *Psychonomic Bulletin & Review* 17, no. 4 (2010): 479–485, doi:10.3758/PBR.17.4.479.

[126] Yes, you matter. For example, see this document that gives statistics on parent-child seat belt use: http://www.nhtsa.gov/DOT/NHTSA/Traffic%20Injury%20Control/Articles/Associated%20Files/810654.pdf.

[127] Centers for Disease Control and Prevention, "Motor Vehicle Safety," PowerPoint presentation.

[128] American Automobile Association, "AAA Foundation Tips to Being a Heads-Up Driver," http://www.aaafoundation.org/multimedia/headsuptips.cfm.

[129] Ibid.

[130] Ibid.

[131] Data here are from the Not-in-Traffic Surveillance System (NiTS) 2007: "Noncrash Fatalities by Incident Type," NVSS 2003–2004.

[132] http://www.nhtsa.gov/safety/hyperthermia, downloaded January 2012.

[133] Ibid.

[134] Sonja Butler and Amber Rollins, "Keeping Your Children Safe," *The Safety Report* (May 23, 2011), http://thesafetyreport.com/2011/05/keeping-your-children-safe/.

[135] Ibid.

[136] Ibid.

[137] http://www-nrd.nhtsa.dot.gov/pubs/811085.pdf.

[138] http://www.preventioncouncil4youth.org/health/unattend_child.pdf.

[139] "Five-Year-Old Boy Dies after Car Crash on I-83," WJZ Baltimore, December 28, 2011, http://baltimore.cbslocal.com/2011/12/28/2-children-seriously-injured-in-car-crash-on-695/.

[140] Bruce Tomaso, "Toddler Dies from Injuries Sustained When He Was Ejected from Car; Police Say He May Not Have Been Properly Secured," *Dallas News*, March 23, 2011, http://www.dallasnews.com/news/community-news/dallas/headlines/20110323-toddler-dies-from-injuries-sustained-when-he-was-ejected-from-car-police-say-he-may-not-have-been-properly-

secured.ece.

[141] Martin Weil, "Northern Virginia Child Dies; Was Found in Van," *Washington Post*, June 17, 2011, http://www.washingtonpost.com/local/missing-child-found-dead-in-van/2011/06/17/AGKvqVZH_story.html.

[142] Data downloaded January 2012 from the online Fatality Analysis Reporting System. Only 2010 was used because variables changed from the previous year. Analyses are therefore not as reliable as those based on multiple years of data. See http://www-fars.nhtsa.dot.gov/QueryTool/QuerySection/SelectOptions.aspx .

[143] Not-in-Traffic Surveillance System (NiTS) 2007, "Nontraffic Crashes Analyses for Fatalities Ages 1–4."

[144] Ibid.

[145] Ibid.

[146] National Highway Traffic Safety Administration, US Department of Transportation, "Fatalities and Injuries in Motor Vehicle Backing Crashes: Report to Congress" (November 2008), DOT HS 811 144.

[147] Ibid.

[148] Consumer Reports, "The Danger of Blind Zones: The Area behind Your Vehicle Can Be a Killing Zone," http://www.consumerreports.org/cro/cars/car-safety/car-safety-reviews/mind-that-blind-spot-1005/overview/index.htm.

[149] Ibid.

[150] Butler and Rollins, "Keeping Your Children Safe."

[151] Charly Arnolt, "Family Witnesses Toddler Hit and Killed While Crossing the Street," FOX59 WXIN, September 13, 2011, http://www.fox59.com/news/wxin-family-witnesses-toddler-hit-and-killed-while-crossing-the-street-20110913,0,4275073.story.

[152] KOMO-TV, "Toddler, Fourteen Months, Killed in Backover Accident in Kent," seattlepi.com, March 22, 2011, http://www.seattlepi.com/local/article/Toddler-14-months-killed-in-backover-accident-1306584.php#ixzz1kg8ibkYa.

[153] US Department of Homeland Security, US Fire Administration National Fire Data Center, "Fire Risk to Children in 2007," *Topical Fire Report Series* 11, issue 9 (February 2011), www.usfa.dhs.gov/statistics/.

[154] I could not find data that gave me the causes by age group, so these data are for all children, even though we know that half are under five.

[155] US Fire Administration, accessed January 2010, http://www.usfa.fema.gov/citizens/home_fire_prev/candle.shtm, based on National Fire Protection Association "Candle Fires" (2007).

[156] National Fire Protection Association, "For Consumers," downloaded January 2012, http://www.nfpa.org/categoryList.asp?categoryID=244&URL=Safety%20Information/Safety%20tips%20&%20fact%20sheets.

[157] Ibid.

[158] Ibid.

[159] Ibid.

[160] Federal Emergency Management Agency, "Learn about Fire: The Nature of Fire," downloaded January 2012, http://www.usfa.fema.gov/citizens/about_fire.shtm.

[161] "Man Died Trying to Save Granddaughter in Connecticut Fire: Fireplace Ashes Caused Christmas Morning Blaze That Killed Five," MSNBC.com, December 28, 2011, http://www.msnbc.msn.com/id/45787994/ns/us_news-life/t/man-died-trying-save-granddaughter-conn-fire/.

[162] Stephanie Scurlock, "Toddler Dies in Memphis House Fire; Mother Rescues Four Others," WREG-TV Memphis, January 30, 2011, http://www.wreg.com/news/wreg-toddler-house-fire-story,0,4481997.story.

[163] Consumer Reports, "CO and Smoke Alarm Buying Guide" (January 2011), accessed January 2012, http://www.consumerreports.org/cro/co-and-smoke-alarms/buying-guide.htm.

[164] William Dennehy, "Ionization Detectors DO NOT WORK," personal review on Amazon.com (August 22, 2010), accessed January 2012, http://www.amazon.com/First-Alert-SA720CN-Photoelectric-Sensor/dp/B000PFNCHI.

[165] http://www.ready.gov/fires.

[166] Robert Altkorn, Xiao Chen, Scott Milkovich, Daniel Stool, Gene Rider, C. Martin Bailey, Angela Haas, Keith H. Riding, Seth M. Pransky, and James S. Reilly, "Fatal and Non-Fatal Food Injuries among Children (Aged 0–14 Years)," *International Journal of Pediatric Otorhinolaryngology* 72, issue 7 (July 2008): 1041–1046, ISSN 0165-5876, 10.1016/j.ijporl.2008.03.010,

http://www.sciencedirect.com/science/article/pii/S0165587608001298.

[167] http://well.blogs.nytimes.com/2010/05/31/for-very-young-peril-lurks-in-lithium-cell-batteries/.

[168] Ibid.

[169] Consumer Product Safety Commission, "Memorandum on Portable Youth Bed Rail Entrapments and Hangings" (June 7, 2000), accessed January 2012, http://www.cpsc.gov/library/bedrail00.pdf; see also appendix of cases here: http://www.cpsc.gov/LIBRARY/Bedrails2.pdf.

[170] Andrew Martin, "Concern Grows over Window Blind Safety," *New York Times*, April 20, 2011, http://www.nytimes.com/2011/04/21/business/21blinds.html?pagewanted=all.

[171] http://www.cpsc.gov/LIBRARY/co09.pdf.

[172] While many of these numbers are too low to reliably compare, these two estimates are not too low.

[173] Jeffrey J. Sacks, Leslie Sinclair, and Julie Gilchrist, "Vet Med Today Special Report: Breeds of Dogs Involved in Fatal Human Attacks in the United States between 1979 and 1998," *JAVMA* 217, no. 6 (September 15, 2000), downloaded October, 2012, http://www.cdc.gov/HomeandRecreationalSafety/images/dogbreeds-a.pdf.

[174] You might be thinking that toilets are safer now because everyone locks them, but at least one survey suggests that probably is far from the case. One-third of adults surveyed could not name any safety action taken in their homes (the survey included homes without children, so it is likely higher for families). See "Safe Haven—A Look at the Nation's Knowledge and Use of Home Safety Products and Practices," http://www.homesafetycouncil.org.

[175] Centers for Disease Control and Prevention, "Unintentional Drowning Fact Sheet."

[176] Fatality Analysis Reporting System data from 2008 and 2009, downloaded October 2012.

[177] Analysis of Fatality Analysis Reporting System data from 2009, downloaded October 2012, http://www-fars.dot.gov/.

[178] About 82 percent of the nation wears seat belts, according to the CDC. The percentage of fatal accidents in which children in this age group were not wearing restraints varies. See CDC for other examples.

[179] R. A. Shults, "Child Passenger Deaths involving Drinking Drivers," 77–79.

[180] Robert Davis and Anthony DeBarros, "Older, Dangerous Drivers a Growing Problem," *USA Today*, May 2, 2007, accessed October 2012, http://usatoday30.usatoday.com/news/nation/2007-05-02-older-drivers-usat1a_N.htm.

[181] Eric Stevick, "Death Hits Close to Home," *Everett Herald*, 2012, updated November 4, 2012.

[182] "Five-Year-Old Dies after Northeast-Side Collision with VIA Bus," KENS5.com, November 2, 2012.

[183] CNN Wire staff, "Packed SUV Flips, Killing Five Children on Way to Texas Water Park," CNN, August 22, 2012.

[184] Associated Press, "Authorities ID Five-Year-Olds Killed in DUI Crash in Otay Lakes," CBS8 San Diego, August 6, 2012, http://www.cbs8.com/story/19201551/2-children-pulled-from-submerged-car.

[185] Ryan Hutchins, "Father, Six-Year-Old Son Killed in Car Crash on Middletown Border," *Star-Ledger*, September 30, 2012.

[186] Victor Martinez, "Montana Vista Crash Kills Five: Three Children among Dead in Two-Car Collision; Man Arrested," *El Paso Times*, July 23, 2012.

[187] Bianca Cain Jonson, "Child Killed, Two Injured in Peach Orchard Road Crash," *Augusta Chronicle*, October 29, 2012.

[188] Centers for Disease Control and Prevention, "Motor Vehicle Safety Fact Sheet."

[189] National Highway Traffic Safety Administration, "Right-of-Way" (October 2012), downloaded from: http://www.nhtsa.gov/Driving+Safety/Bicycles/RightOfWay.

[190] See, for example, the state of Virginia's page citing roundabouts as having been shown to reduce fatal and injury crashes as much as 75 percent (http://www.vdot.virginia.gov/info/faq-roundabouts.asp), or Arizona's page citing a fatal accident reduction of up to 90 percent (http://www.vdot.virginia.gov/info/faq-roundabouts.asp).

[191] "Five-Year-Old Killed in ATV Accident," KPVI News 6, October 16, 2012, accessed November 2012.

[192] Pedestrian and Bicycle Information Center, accessed October 2012, http://www.bicyclinginfo.org/facts/crash-facts.cfm.

[193] Estimate comes from the Pedestrian and Bicycle Information Center, http://www.bicyclinginfo.org/facts/crash-facts.cfm, accessed October 2012.

[194] National Center for Statistics and Analysis, National Highway Traffic Safety Administration, "Bicycle Helmet Use Laws" (2008), DOT HS 810 886W, http://www.nhtsa.gov/DOT/NHTSA/Communication%20&%20Consumer%20Information/Articl

es/Associated%20Files/810886.pdf.

[195] Ibid.

[196] National Highway Traffic Safety Administration, "My Choice…Their Ride," Washington, DC (n.d.), http://www.trafficsafetymarketing.gov/staticfiles/tsm/PDF/schoolbus_safety2.pdf.

[197] Fatality Analysis Reporting System data from 2008 and 2009, downloaded October 2012.

[198] Ibid.

[199] Ibid.

[200] National Center for Statistics and Analysis, National Highway Traffic Safety Administration, "Traffic Safety Facts: 2007 Data" (2008), http://www-nrd.nhtsa.dot.gov/Pubs/810987.pdf.

[201] Alyson McCarthy, "Child Hit, Killed by Garbage Truck," KLAS-TV 8 News Now Las Vegas, 2012.

[202] American Academy of Pediatrics, accessed October 2012, http://www2.aap.org/family/ttipsfor.htm.

[203] Granted, kids do a lot more walking than bicycling, so it shouldn't be surprising that pedestrian numbers are significantly higher.

[204] Fatality Analysis Reporting System data from 2008 and 2009, downloaded October 2012.

[205] Penny Eims, "Texas Boy Killed While Trying to Save a Puppy," Examiner.com, October 31, 2012.

[206] Rick Couri, "Police ID Seven-Year-Old Boy Killed on His Way to School," KRMG.com, October 31, 2012, accessed November 2012.

[207] National Highway Traffic Safety Administration, "Prevent Pedestrian Crashes: Parents and Caregivers of Elementary School Children" (revised October 2008), DOT HS 811 027.

[208] T. Redmon, D. Gelinne, L. Walton, and J. Miller, Federal Highway Administration, "Spotlight on Pedestrian Safety," *Public Roads* 75, no. 4 (January/February 2012), http://www.fhwa.dot.gov/publications/publicroads/12janfeb/03.cfm.

[209] National Highway Traffic Safety Administration, "Traffic Safety Facts: 2010 Data" (August 2012), DOT HS 811 625, http://www-nrd.nhtsa.dot.gov/Pubs/811625.pdf.

[210] Transportation for America, "Dangerous by Design" (2011), http://t4america.org/resources/dangerousbydesign2011/states/worst-metros/. Data taken from the 2010 census but not verified.

[211] "Neighbor Pulls Four from Fatal Fire," Fox News Tampa, October 30, 2012.

[212] Alexis Shaw, "Georgia Fire Engulfs Home, Takes Lives of Woman, Four Children," WSB-TV/ABC News, April 27, 2013, http://abcnews.go.com/US/ga-house-fire-kills-woman-children-years/story?id=19056921#.UbZxQPmyCSo.

[213] "Five-Year-Old Drowns in Pool at Dearborn Hyatt Hotel," CBS Detroit, October 6, 2012.

[214] "Florida Keys Boy, Six, Drowns in Canal," WSVN Miami, October 12, 2012, http://www.wsvn.com.

[215] Chris Dolmetsch, "Nanny Charged with Murder in Manhattan Child Killings," *Bloomberg BusinessWeek*, November 4, 2012.

[216] "Knoxville Man Charged in the Death of His Girlfriend's Five-Year-Old Son," Wate.com, Knoxville, TN, November 8, 2012.

[217] L. A. Fingerhut and M. Warner, *Injury Chartbook, Health, United States, 1996–1997* (Hyattsville, MD: National Center for Health Statistics, 1997).

[218] G. B. Eber, J. L. Annest, J. A. Mercy, and G. W. Ryan, "Nonfatal and Fatal Firearm-Related Injuries among Children Aged Fourteen Years and Younger: United States, 1993–2000," *Pediatrics* 113, no. 6 (June 2004): 1686–1692.

[219] S. Tavernise and Gebeloff, "Share of Homes with Guns Shows Four-Decade Decline," *New York Times*, March 9, 2013, http://www.nytimes.com/2013/03/10/us/rate-of-gun-ownership-is-down-survey-shows.html?pagewanted=all&_r=0.

[220] Based on guidance from www.savetheguns.com.

[221] See the Centers for Disease Control and Prevention's *Morbidity and Mortality Weekly Report* January 1996, http://www.cdc.gov/mmwr/preview/mmwrhtml/00039929.htm.

[222] N. B. Hampson and D. M. Norkool, "Carbon Monoxide Poisoning in Children Riding in the Back of Pickup Trucks," *JAMA* 26, no. 4 (1992): 538–40, doi:10.1001/jama.1992.03480040086036.

[223] See Centers for Disease Control and Prevention, "Summary of Carbon Monoxide Dangers in Boating," http://www.cdc.gov/niosh/topics/coboating/.

[224] National Highway Traffic Safety Administration, "Teen Seat Belt Use" (n.d.), accessed June 2013, http://www.nhtsa.gov/Driving+Safety/Teen+Drivers/Teen+Drivers+Education/Teen+Drivers+-+Seat+Belt+Use.

[225] National Highway Traffic Safety Administration, "Traffic Safety Facts, 2011: Motorcycles" (May 2013), http://www-nrd.nhtsa.dot.gov/Pubs/811765.pdf.

[226] Separate analysis of Fatality Analysis Reporting System data for 2010 and 2008.

[227] National Highway Traffic Safety Administration, "Traffic Safety Facts, 2008: Motorcycle Helmet Use Laws," Washington, DC (2008).

[228] Centers for Disease Control and Prevention, "Motorcycle Safety" (n.d.), accessed February 2013, http://www.cdc.gov/features/motorcyclesafety/.

[229] "Community Mourns Loss of Twelve-Year-Old Sammy Reagan Killed in I-275 Pileup," ABC9 Cincinnati, WCPO.com, January 22, 2013, http://www.wcpo.com/dpp/news/region_north_cincinnati/mason/Community-mourns-loss-of-12-year-old-Sammy-Reagan-killed-in-I-275-pileup.

[230] "Eleven-Year-Old Killed in Crash," WMTV Madison, NBC15.com, October 22, 2012, http://www.nbc15.com/home/headlines/11-Year-Old-Killed-In-Crash-175801671.html.

[231] Kristie Reeter, "Thirteen-Year-Old Killed in Crash," ABC17News Missouri, July 30, 2011, http://www.abc17news.com/news.php?id=3160.

[232] "Classmates Remember Twelve-Year-Old Crash Victim," Fox 8 Cleveland, January 25, 2013, http://fox8.com/2013/01/25/boy-12-killed-in-accident-before-school/.

[233] "Eleven-Year-Old Daly City Boy Killed in Crash IDed," KGO-TV San Francisco, 2012, http://abclocal.go.com/kgo/story?section=news/local/peninsula&id=8933891.

[234] Deanna Boyd, "Boy, Eleven, Dies from Injuries in Motorcycle Wreck," *Star Telegram*, February 13, 2013, http://www.star-telegram.com/2013/02/13/4618642/boy-12-dies-from-injuries-in-motorcycle.html.

[235] The data in this section are based on an analysis of the Fatality Analysis Reporting System data for 2010 and 2011 for ten- to fourteen-year-olds, pedestrian fatalities, downloaded January 2013.

[236] Ibid.

[237] Aaron Feis, "Twelve-Year-Old Girl Struck and Killed by Car in LES," *New York Post*, January 13, 2012.

[238] "Fourteen-Year-Old Struck, Killed by Car on I-10," KHOU Houston, July 29, 2012, KHOU.com.

[239] Based on the CDC data and the denominator is the sum of drivers + passengers, i.e., where position was specified.

[240] Based on a separate analysis of Fatality Analysis Reporting System 2009 and 2010 data, accessed February 2013.

[241] Kathleen Conti, "Dirt Bike Driver Questioned on Fatal Crash," *Boston Globe*, December 10, 2012, http://www.bostonglobe.com/metro/2012/12/10/plymouth-north-student-killed-atv-crash-sunday-dirt-bike-driver-being-questioned/icgoN7UsLavFPZCIM0yfWM/story.html.

[242] The data in this section are based on an analysis of the Fatality Analysis Reporting System data for 2010, 2011 for ten- to fourteen-year-olds, pedestrian fatalities, downloaded January 2013.

[243] "Bicycle Lighting," *Wikipedia* (n.d.), accessed April 21, 2013, http://en.wikipedia.org/wiki/Bicycle_lighting.

[244] Katy Moeller, "After Ten-Year-Old Is Killed on Bicycle, Neighbors Grieve Boy's Death," *Idaho Statesman*, July 6, 2012.

[245] R. N. Anderson, National Center for Health Statistics, "Deaths: Leading Causes for 2000," *National Vital Statistics Reports* 50, no. 16 (2002).

[246] E. R. Galaif, S. Sussman, M. D. Newcomb, and T. F. Locke, "Suicidality, Depression, and Alcohol Use among Adolescents: A Review of Empirical Findings," *International Journal of Adolescent Medicine and Health* 19, no. 1 (2007): 27–35, PMC free article.

[247] M. S. Gould, T. Greenberg, D. W. Velting, and D. Shaffer, "Youth Suicide Risk and Preventive Interventions: A Review of the Past Ten Years," *Journal of the American Academy of Child and Adolescent Psychiatry* 42, no. 4 (2003): 386–405.

[248] Youth Risk Behavior Surveillance System, accessed February 2013, http://apps.nccd.cdc.gov/youthonline/App/Default.aspx?SID=HS.

[249] Galaif, Sussman et al., "Suicidality, Depression, and Alcohol Use among Adolescents."

[250] National Institute of Mental Health, *Transformative Neurodevelopmental Research in Mental Illness: Report of the National Advisory Mental Health Council's Workgroup* (2007).

[251] Office of Adolescent Health, Mental Health, accessed September, 2013, http://www.hhs.gov/ash/oah/adolescent-health-topics/mental-health/

[252] D. A. Brent, "Risk Factors for Adolescent Suicide and Suicidal Behavior: Mental and Substance Abuse Disorders, Family Environmental Factors, and Life Stress," *Suicide Life Threat Behav.* 25 (1995):52–63, PubMed.

[253] National Institute of Mental Health, *Transformative Neurodevelopmental Research in Mental Illness*.

[254] Galaif, Sussman et al., *Suicidality, Depression, and Alcohol Use among Adolescents*.

[255] E. Y. Deykin, J. C. Levy, and V. Wells, "Adolescent Depression, Alcohol, and Drug Abuse," *Am J*

Public Health 77 (1987): 178–182, PMC free article.

[256] National Institute of Mental Health, *Transformative Neurodevelopmental Research in Mental Illness.*

[257] Ibid.

[258] Ibid.

[259] US Coast Guard (2013). Boating Under the Influence Initiatives, accessed June, 2013 http://www.uscgboating.org/safety/boating_under_the_influence_initiatives.aspx

[260] Pickens, Kim (undated). The Other 20% -- When Wearing a Life Jacket Is Not Enough. Accessed at http://www.usps.org/education/files/other_20_handout.pdf and validated using data from the U.S. Coast Guard 2012 report, http://www.uscgboating.org/assets/1/workflow_staging/Page/705.PDF

[261] Pickens, Kim (undated). The Other 20% -- When Wearing a Life Jacket Is Not Enough. Accessed at http://www.usps.org/education/files/other_20_handout.pdf and validated using data from the U.S. Coast Guard 2012 report, http://www.uscgboating.org/assets/1/workflow_staging/Page/705.PDF

[262] Jennifer Medina, "Girl, Twelve, Drowns at Beach on Class Trip to Long Island," *New York Times,* June 22, 2010, http://www.nytimes.com/2010/06/23/nyregion/23drown.html?_r=0.

[263] Renee Kiriluk-Hill, "Eleven-Year-Old Dies of Injuries from Holland Township Home Fire," *Hunterdon Democrat*/NJ.com, February 14, 2013, http://www.nj.com/hunterdon-county-democrat/index.ssf/2013/02/11-year-old_charlie_runge_dies.html.

[264] Curtis Rush, "Oshawa Boy Dies in Prank That Went Horribly Wrong," theSpec.com, 2012, http://www.thespec.com/news/ontario/article/830166--oshawa-boy-dies-in-prank-that-went-horribly-wrong.

[265] Lisa Rathke, "Ski Injuries Decline, but Number of Fatalities Holds Steady," Associated Press, December 13, 2010, http://www.mnn.com/health/fitness-well-being/stories/ski-injuries-decline-but-number-of-fatalities-hold-steady.

[266] National Conference of State Legislatures, http://www.ncsl.org/issues-research/env-res/carbon-monoxide-detectors-state-statutes.aspx.

[267] Darshak Sanghavi, "The Blizzard's Biggest Killer—And How to Prevent It Next Time," WBUR, February 2013, http://cognoscenti.wbur.org/2013/02/15/carbon-monoxide-darshak-sanghavi.

[268] A. E. Curry, J. Hafetz, M. J. Kallan, F. K. Winston, and D. R. Durbin, "Prevalence of Teen Driver Errors Leading to Serious Motor Vehicle Crashes," *Accident Analysis and Prevention,* April 11, 2011.

[269] Insurance Institute for Highway Safety, "Fatality Facts: Teenagers 2010" (Arlington: 2012, cited September 28, 2012, http://www.iihs.org/research/fatality.aspx?topicName=Teenagers&year=2010.

[270] Centers for Disease Control and Prevention, "Parents Are the Key to Safe Teen Drivers" (n.d.), accessed November 2012, http://www.cdc.gov/parentsarethekey/.

[271] Insurance Institute for Highway Safety, "Fatality Facts 2010: Teenagers" (n.d.), accessed November 2012, http://www.iihs.org/research/fatality.aspx?topicName=Teenagers&year=2010. This statement is also based on a separate analysis I did of Fatality Analysis Reporting System data, completed November 2012.

[272] National Highway Traffic Safety Administration, "My Choice…Their Ride" (n.d.).

[273] Centers for Disease Control and Prevention, "Parents Are the Key to Safe Teen Drivers" (n.d.), accessed November 2012, http://www.cdc.gov/parentsarethekey/.

[274] Centers for Disease Control and Prevention, "Eight Danger Zones," accessed December 2012, http://www.cdc.gov/ParentsAreTheKey/danger/index.html.

[275] D. R. Mayhew, H. M. Simpson, and A. Pak, "Changes in Collision Rates among Novice Drivers during the First Months of Driving," *Accident Analysis and Prevention* 35 (2003): 683–691.

[276] A. T. McCartt, V. I. Shabanova, and W. A. Leaf, "Driving Experiences, Crashes, and Teenage Beginning Drivers," *Accident Analysis and Prevention* 35 (2003): 311–320.

[277] B. A. Jonah and N. E. Dawson, "Youth and Risk: Age Differences in Risky Driving, Risk Perception, and Risk Utility," *Alcohol, Drugs and Driving* 3 (1987): 13–29.

[278] A. E. Curry et al., "Prevalence of Teen Driver Errors Leading to Serious Motor Vehicle Crashes."

[279] Centers for Disease Control and Prevention, Research Update, accessed January 2012, http://www.cdc.gov/MotorVehicleSafety/teen_drivers/GDL/youngdrivers.html.

[280] P. Bronson and A. Merryman, *NurtureShock: New Thinking About Children*, January 5, 2011, Twelve, New York

[281] Centers for Disease Control and Prevention, "Parents Are the Key to Safe Teen Drivers" (n.d.).

[282] Mayhew et al., "Changes in Collision Rates among Novice Drivers during the First Months of Driving."

283 McCartt et al., "Driving Experiences, Crashes, and Teenage Beginning Drivers."

284 Centers for Disease Control and Prevention, National Center for Injury Prevention and Control, Web-Based Injury Statistics Query and Reporting System (WISQARS) (2010), cited October 18, 2010, http://www.cdc.gov/ncipc/wisqars.

285 Centers for Disease Control and Prevention, National Center for HIV/AIDS, Viral Hepatitis, STD, and TB Prevention, Division of Adolescent and School Health, "Youth Risk Behavior Surveillance System 2011 YRBS Data User's Guide" (online: 2012).

286 National Highway Traffic Safety Administration, US Department of Transportation, "Traffic Safety Facts 2010: Young Drivers" (Washington, DC: May 2012).

287 National Highway Traffic Safety Administration, US Department of Transportation, "Traffic Safety Facts 2010: Speeding" (Washington, DC: August 2012).

288 Michael Stobbe, "Teen Texting and Driving: More Than Half Admit to Doing It," Associated Press, June 8, 2012, accessed January 2013 from *Christian Science Monitor*, http://www.csmonitor.com/The-Culture/Family/2012/0608/Teen-texting-and-driving-More-than-half-admit-to-doing-it.

289 Ibid.

290 National Highway Traffic Safety Administration, US Department of Transportation, "Teen Distracted Driver Data 2010" (2012), http://www-nrd.nhtsa.dot.gov/Pubs/811649.pdf.

291 Stobbe, "Teen Texting and Driving."

292 Centers for Disease Control and Prevention, National Center for Injury Prevention and Control, Web-Based Injury Statistics Query and Reporting System (WISQARS) (2012), www.cdc.gov/ncipc/wisqars.

293 B. Simons-Morton, N. Lerner, J. Singer, "The Observed Effects of Teenage Passengers on the Risky Driving Behavior of Teenage Drivers," *Accident Analysis and Prevention* 37, no. 6 (2005): 973–982.

294 L. Chen, S. P. Baker, E. R. Braver, and G. Li, "Carrying Passengers as a Risk Factor for Crashes Fatal to Sixteen- and Seventeen-Year-Old Drivers," *JAMA* 283, no. 12 (2000): 1578–1582, http://jama.jamanetwork.com/article.aspx?articleid=192524.

295 Centers for Disease Control and Prevention, "Parents Are the Key to Safe Teen Drivers."

296 National Highway Traffic Safety Administration, US Department of Transportation, "Traffic Safety Facts 2010: Young Drivers" (Washington, DC: May 2012).

297 Insurance Institute for Highway Safety, "Fatality Facts 2010: Teenagers" (n.d.), accessed November 2012, http://www.iihs.org/research/fatality.aspx?topicName=Teenagers&year=2010. This statement is also based on a separate analysis I did of Fatality Analysis Reporting System data, completed November 2012.

298 R. B. Voas, P. Torres, E. Romano, and J. H. Lacey, "Alcohol-Related Risk of Driver Fatalities: An Update Using 2007 Data," *J Stud Alcohol Drugs* 73, no. 3 (May 2012): 341–350.

299 Insurance Institute for Highway Safety, "Fatality Facts 2010: Teenagers" (n.d.), accessed November 2012, http://www.iihs.org/research/fatality.aspx?topicName=Teenagers&year=2010. This statement is also based on a separate analysis I did of Fatality Analysis Reporting System data, completed November 2012.

300 Voas et al., "Alcohol-Related Risk of Driver Fatalities."

301 Centers for Disease Control and Prevention, "Youth Risk Behavior Surveillance—United States, 2011," *Morbidity and Mortality Weekly Report* 61, no. 4 (2012).

302 Sharon Smith, "Spokesperson: Missing Catawba Co. Teens Drowned in SC River," Fox Carolina, October 28, 2012, accessed January 2013.

303 Ashley Rodrigue, "Family of Teens Involved in Fatal Accident Warn Others to Use Seat Belt," WWLTV.com, August 2, 2012, accessed January 2013.

304 "Fifteen-Year-Old Killed, Seven Others Injured in Alcohol-Related Crash," KBOI TV, December 15, 2012, accessed January 2013, KBOI2.com.

305 William D'Urso, "Sixteen-Year-Old Driver Killed in Weekend Crash," *Las Vegas Sun*, December 9, 2012.

306 Brandon Carpenter, "Racing Teen Indicted for Fatal Crash," KVII-TV, December 11, 2012, accessed January 2013, ConnectAmarillo.com.

307 Taylor Katz, "Bloomingdale High School Student, Zach McCarthy, Was Killed Wednesday in Car Crash," WTSP 10 News, January 4, 2013, WTSP.com.

308 "Seventeen-Year-Old Girl, Six-Year-Old Sister Identified in Fatal Canyon County Car Crash," *Idaho Statesman*, January 3, 2013, accessed January 2013.

309 "Two NC Teens Were Killed during 100 mph Racing Crash, Teen Boy Charged, Troopers Say,"

WNCN/WBTW, January 1, 2013, accessed January 2013, WBTW.com.

[310] S. P. Baker, L. Chen, and G. Li, *Nationwide Review of Graduated Driver Licensing* (Washington DC: AAA Foundation for Traffic Safety, 2007), http://www.aaafoundation.org/pdf/NationwideReviewOfGDL.pdf.

[311] Insurance Institute for Highway Safety, "Young Driver Licensing Systems in the US" (2013), accessed January 2013, http://www.iihs.org/laws/graduatedlicenseintro.aspx.

[312] Ibid.

[313] US Department of Transportation, "Traffic Safety Facts 2010 Data: Pedestrians," Washington DC (August 2012), accessed January 2013, http://www-nrd.nhtsa.dot.gov/Pubs/811625.pdf.

[314] L. Thompson, F. Rivara, R. Ayyagari, and B. Ebel, "Impact of Social and Technological Distraction on Pedestrian Crossing Behaviour: An Observational Study," *Injury Prevention* (December 13, 2012).

[315] National Institutes of Health, "Texting While Walking May Be as Dangerous as Texting While Driving," HealthDay News, December 13, 2012, accessed January 2013, http://www.nlm.nih.gov/medlineplus/news/fullstory_132184.html

[316] Carmen Irish, "Lockwood Teen Dies from Injuries Suffered in Pedestrian-Vehicle Collision," *Billings Gazette*, January 5, 2013, http://billingsgazette.com/news/local/lockwood-teen-dies-from-injuries-suffered-in-pedestrian-vehicle-collision/article_d33448e6-5562-57d3-bbc3-892045d75961.html#ixzz2HFaYnEow.

[317] Centers for Disease Control and Prevention, "Childhood Pedestrian Deaths during Halloween" (1997), http://www.cdc.gov/mmwr/preview/mmwrhtml/00049687.htm.

[318] PRNewswire, "Halloween Is 'Deadliest Day' of the Year for Child Pedestrian Fatalities," State Farm, October 23, 2012, accessed January 2013, http://www.multivu.com/mnr/56790-state-farm-halloween-pedestrian-child-safety.

[319] "Teen Dies in Aransas Pass Boating Accident," NBC 6 News Corpus Christi, July 20, 2012, KRIStv.com.

[320] Centers for Disease Control and Prevention, "Suicide Prevention" (n.d.), accessed January 2013, http://www.cdc.gov/violenceprevention/pub/youth_suicide.html.

[321] Ibid.

[322] National Center for Health Statistics, 2003; see Table 3-3 in the National Academies of Sciences report "Firearms and Violence: A Critical Review" (2004), available at http://www.nap.edu/openbook.php?record_id=10881&page=60#p2000ba499960060001.

[323] Centers for Disease Control and Prevention, National Center for Injury Prevention and Control, Web-Based Injury Statistics Query and Reporting System (WISQARS) (2010), www.cdc.gov/ncipc/wisqars.

[324] Centers for Disease Control and Prevention, *Morbidity and Mortality Weekly Report, MMWR Surveill Summ.* 53, no. 2 (2004): 1–96, www.cdc.gov/mmwr/PDF/SS/SS5302.pdf.

[325] American Academy of Pediatrics, "Suicide and Suicide Attempts in Adolescents," *Pediatrics* 105, no. 4 (April 1, 2000): 871–874.

[326] http://www.nimh.nih.gov/health/publications/suicide-in-the-us-statistics-and-prevention/index.shtml.

[327] Debra L. Karch, Joseph Logan, and Nimesh Patel, "Surveillance for Violent Deaths—National Violent Death Reporting System, Sixteen States, 2008," *Morbidity and Mortality Weekly Report* 60 (SS10) (August 26, 2011): 1–54.

[328] http://www.healthychildren.org/English/health-issues/conditions/emotional-problems/Pages/Teen-Suicide-and-Guns.aspx?nfstatus=401&nftoken=00000000-0000-0000-0000-000000000000&nfstatusdescription=ERROR%3a+No+local+token.

[329] S. French, M. Story, M. D. Resnick, and R. Blum, "The Relationship between Suicide Risk and Sexual Orientation: Results of a Population-Based Study," *Am J Public Health* 88 (1998): 57–60m. In: *Pediatrics* 120, no. 3 (September 1, 2007): 669–676, doi:10.1542/peds.2007-1908.

[330] Centers for Disease Control and Prevention, "Lesbian, Gay, Bisexual, and Transgender Health" (n.d.), accessed January 2013, http://www.cdc.gov/lgbthealth/youth.htm.

[331] Centers for Disease Control and Prevention, The National Intimate Partner and Sexual Violence Survey (NISVS), accessed January 2013, http://www.cdc.gov/violenceprevention/nisvs/index.html.

[332] See, for example, Y. S. Kim and B. Leventhal,"Bullying and Suicide. A Review," *International Journal of Adolescent Health* 20, no. 2 (April–June 2008): 133–54; A. Brunstein Klomek, A. Sourander, and M. Goiuld, "The Association of Suicide and Bullying in Childhood to Young Adulthood: A Review of Cross-Sectional and Longitudinal Research Findings," *Canadian Journal of Psychiatry* 55, no. 5 (May 2010): 282–88; and C. Winsper, T. Lereva, M. Zanarini, and D. Wolke, "Involvement in Bullying and Suicide-Related Behavior at Eleven Years: A Prospective Birth Cohort Study," *Journal of Academic*

Childhood Adolescent Psychiatry 51, no. 3 (March 2012): 271–282e3.

[333] Centers for Disease Control and Prevention, "Suicide: Facts at a Glance, 2012," http://www.cdc.gov/ViolencePrevention/pdf/Suicide_DataSheet_2012-a.pdf.

[334] Karch et al., "Surveillance for Violent Deaths."

[335] Ibid.

[336] Ibid.

[337] American Association of Suicidology, "Suicide Warning Signs" (n.d.), accessed January 2013, http://www.suicidology.org/web/guest/stats-and-tools/suicide-warning-signs.

[338] Ibid.

[339] American Academy of Pediatrics, "Suicide and Suicide Attempts in Adolescents," *Pediatrics* 120, no. 3 (September 1, 2007): 669–76.

[340] Ibid.

[341] http://www.cdc.gov/ViolencePrevention/pdf/Suicide_Strategic_Direction_Full_Version-a.pdf.

[342] Tiffany Craig, "Houston Teen Kills Herself after Posting Online about Gun, Suicide," ABC/KVUE.com, February 1, 2012.

[343] "Morristown Teen's Apparent Suicide Being Investigated as Possible Bullying Case, Officials Say," *Star Ledger*, March 31, 2012.

[344] B. Chapman, J. Kemp, C. Siemaszko, and J. Tasch, "Tormented Fifteen-Year-Old Felicia Garcia Jumped to Death in Front of Train after Bullying over Sex with Football Players," *New York Daily News*, October 25, 2012.

[345] Jeffrey Roth, "Firearms and Violence, Research in Brief," *NCJ* 145533 (December 1994), https://www.ncjrs.gov/pdffiles1/Digitization/145533NCJRS.pdf.

[346] Committee on Law and Justice, National Research Council, "Three Patterns of Firearm-Related Violence," *Firearms and Violence: A Critical Review* (Washington, DC: The National Academies Press, 2004).

[347] US Census tables, http://www.census.gov/compendia/statab/cats/population/estimates_and_projections_by_age_sex_raceethnicity.html.

[348] C. Puzzanchera, G. Chamberlin, and W. Kang, "Easy Access to the FBI's Supplementary Homicide Reports: 1980–2010" (2012), http://www.ojjdp.gov/ojstatbb/ezashr/. Data were for 1999–2007 to keep consistent with the CDC data presented.

[349] Ibid.

[350] Committee on Law and Justice, National Research Council, "Three Patterns of Firearm-Related Violence."

[351] Ibid.

[352] Centers for Disease Control and Prevention, "Youth Risk Behavior Surveillance—United States, 2011," *Morbidity and Mortality Weekly Report* 61 (2012), http://www.cdc.gov/mmwr/pdf/ss/ss6104.pdf.

[353] J. Quintanilla, "Eighteen-Year-Old Shot to Death near UTSA," WOAI News4, January 16, 2013, http://www.woai.com/mostpopular/story/18-year-old-shot-to-death-near-UTSA/JNvT7q0dUEWgr4_M4_SMMA.cspx.

[354] "Sixteen-Year-Old Girl Found Shot to Death in Kearny Home," CBS New York, January 18, 2013, http://newyork.cbslocal.com/2013/01/18/16-year-old-girl-found-shot-to-death-in-kearny-home/.

[355] Kelvin Reynolds, "Teen Killed in Tuscaloosa Club Shooting," Fox AL, December 30, 2012, http://www.myfoxal.com/story/20476714/teen-killed-in-tuscaloosa-club-shooting.

[356] Centers for Disease Control and Prevention, "Drowning Risks in Natural Waters" (n.d.), accessed January 2013, http://www.cdc.gov/Features/dsDrowningRisks/.

[357] Ibid.

[358] Centers for Disease Control and Prevention, "Unintentional Drowning: Get the Facts" (n.d.), accessed January 2013, http://www.cdc.gov/Features/dsDrowningRisks/.

[359] Ibid.

[360] *http://c.ymcdn.com/sites/www.usla.org/resource/resmgr/lifeguard_library/flagwarningstandardsilsfinal.pdf*

[361] US Fire Administration, *Topical Fire Research Series* 1, issue 6 (December 2001), http://www.usfa.fema.gov/downloads/pdf/tfrs/v1i6.pdf

[362] Office of Juvenile Justice and Delinquency Prevention, *Juvenile Justice Bulletin* (May 2005), https://www.ncjrs.gov/pdffiles1/ojjdp/207606.pdf.

[363] US Fire Administration, *Topical Fire Research Series* 1.

[364] U.S. Fire Administration, *Special Report: Arson and Juveniles: Responding to the Violence*, USFA-TR-095 (January, 1998).

[365] "Fifteen-Year-Old Girl Dies after Marrero House Fire; Five Siblings, Mother and Father Rescued,"

WWLTV, January 15, 2013, accessed January 2013, http://www.wwltv.com/news/15-year-old-girl-dies-after-Marrero-house-fire-five-siblings-mother--father-rescued-187040811.html.
[366] http://www.cdc.gov/ViolencePrevention/pdf/Suicide_Strategic_Direction_Full_Version-a.pdf.
[367] For those interested in the actual numbers underlying the estimates of death for each age group, here they are in one table (CDC Mortality Data 1999–2007).

	Numbers of Deaths	Population	% Who Died	Numbers of External (or Accidental) Deaths	% of Deaths That Were External
Age Up to 1	253640	36243470	0.70%	13111	5%
Ages 1 to 4	44033	142332392	0.03%	19388	44%
Ages 5 to 9	26907	179720009	0.01%	12155	45%
Ages 10 to 14	35032	186897294	0.02%	17851	51%
Ages 15 to 19	122750	185992933	0.07%	94790	77%
ALL Ages	482362	731186098	0.07%	157295	33%

[368] Why are rates important now when they were not earlier? Writing this book from the perspective of a mom, I estimated that the differential loadings of ages within the age groups, as defined by the CDC for their clustering, was likely not going to meaningfully impact the overall lessons and did not merit the additional complexity for the readers. Across all the age groups, however, there are sizable and meaningful differences in the populations (population bubbles) making the examination of crude rates of death (per 100,000 in the population) more meaningful.
[369] There are a few different ways I could have computed these estimates, and I hope to hear some discussion and improvements. After much debate, I decided to take the rates of deaths, per the bar graph just shown. So, the numbers are adjusted for base population from the 1999-2007 data, but not reweighted for their approximate proportion in the current population. I also did not do any kind of survival analysis (multiplying the probabilities of making it through successive ages).
[370] Centers for disease Control, Childhood Pedestrian Deaths During Halloween, MMWR Weekly, October 24, 1997, 46(42); 987-990. http://www.cdc.gov/mmwr/preview/mmwrhtml/00049687.htm
[371] National Traffic Highway Safety Administration, US Department of Transportation, "Traffic Safety Facts 2011" (2011), DOT HS 811 625, http://www-nrd.nhtsa.dot.gov/Pubs/811625.pdf.
[372] If we were just looking at the actual data from 1999-2007, not using rates, one in six deaths (about 17 percent) children from birth to nineteen was attributable to a gun.
[373] Fingerhut and Warner, *Injury Chartbook*.
[374] Centers for Disease Control and Prevention, "Unintentional Drowning Fact Sheet."
[375] Ernest Allen, "Keeping Children Safe: Rhetoric and Reality," *Juvenile Justice Journal* V, no. 1 (May 1998).
[376] Data in this chapter come from the National Incidence Studies of Missing, Abducted, Runaway, and Thrownaway Children (NISMART) (https://www.ncjrs.gov/pdffiles1/ojjdp/196467.pdf) unless otherwise noted.
[377] Ernest Allen, "The Kid Is with a Parent, How Bad Can It Be?," *The Crisis of Family Abductions* (1998).
[378] Check out Discover's Webmath.com to calculate your odds given the specifics of the lottery: http://www.webmath.com/lottery.html.
[379] These data come from NISMART and include caretakers who called the police as well as those who reported in an interview or other form that they knew their child had been missing at some point.
[380] Obviously, in those cases the caretaker may not have reported this to the police. These data include information from surveys and interviews of caretakers instead of only police reports.
[381] Ernest Allen, "The Kid Is with a Parent, How Bad Can It Be?"
[382] NISMART, 2002. Since the killing of a child by a stranger or acquaintance automatically pushes the case into stereotypical abduction, only those killers who are close to the family remain in this category, which is extremely small.
[383] NISMART, 2002.

384 Finklehor, Hotaling, and Sedlak, 1992.

385 Brown, Keppel, Weis, and Skeen, 2006.

386 http://www.missingkids.com/en_US/publications/NC66.pdf An Analysis of Infant Abduction.

387 Able and Harlow, "Child Molestation Prevention Study" (2002),
http://www.childmolestationprevention.org/pdfs/study.pdf.

388 Brown, Keppel, Weis, and Skeen, 2006.

389 Brown, Keppel, Weis, and Skeen, *Investigative Case Management for Missing Children Homicides: Report II* (2006).

390 Ibid.

391 Matthew R. Durose, Patrick A. Langan, and Erica L. Schmitt (2003),
http://bjs.ojp.usdoj.gov/index.cfm?ty=pbdetail&iid=1136.

392 See study of New Jersey laws, for example,
https://www.ncjrs.gov/pdffiles1/nij/grants/225370.pdf.

393 Able and Harlow, *Child Molestation Prevention Study* (2002),
http://www.childmolestationprevention.org/pdfs/study.pdf

394 G. Abel. "Use of pornography and erotica by sex offenders." (1985) Paper presented to the United States Attorney General's Commission on Pornography, Houston, TX.

395 Child Molestation Research and Prevention Institute,
http://www.childmolestationprevention.org/pages/focus_on_the_cause.html.

396 Finkelhor and Ormrod, "Crimes against Children by Babysitters," *Juvenile Justice Bulletin* (Office of Juvenile Justice and Delinquency Prevention, September 2001).

397 Brown, Keppel, Weis, and Skeen, 2006, p. 30

398 NISMART 2002, *Nonfamily Abductions.*

399 Brown, Keppel, Weis, and Skeen, 2006.

400 National Center for Missing and Endangered Children, "Online Victimization of Youth: Five Years Later,"
http://www.missingkids.com/missingkids/servlet/ResourceServlet?LanguageCountry=en_US&PageId=2530.

401 Brown, Keppel, Weis, and Skeen, 2006.

402 Gallagher, Bradford, and Pease, "Attempted and Completed Incidents of Stranger-Perpetrated Child Sexual Abuse and Abduction," Centre for Applied Childhood Studies, Harold Wilson Building, University of Huddersfield, Queensgate, Huddersfield HD1 3DH, United Kingdom, 32, no. 5: 517–28 (May 2008), e-pub May 29, 2008.

403 NISMART 2002, *Nonfamily Abductions.*

404http://weblogs.baltimoresun.com/news/crime/blog/2011/07/woman_recounts_finding_abducte.html.

405 Brown, Keppel, Weis, and Skeen, 2006.

406 As cited in Ernie Allen's statement: http://www.ojjdp.gov/jjjournal/jjjournal598/safe.html.

407 http://www.ojjdp.gov/jjjournal/jjjournal598/safe.html.

Made in the USA
San Bernardino, CA
01 November 2013